Praise for the
Jam Today
Series

"Delightful . . . written by a woman who values food, family and friends."
—**Shelf Awareness**

"Davies's creative joy in food and the world around her is infectious."
—**Bookslut**

"*Jam Today*, whose title is culled from a line in one of Lewis Carroll's *Alice in Wonderland* books, isn't so much a cookbook as it is ruminations on food preparation and living right." —**Cascadia Weekly**

"Tod Davies takes a physicist's approach to social change . . . like the minds behind a particle accelerator, her primary goal is to cause collisions."
—**Portland Mercury**

"Just my kind of book . . . In addition to some great meals made to satisfy desires, needs, whims or simply to make use of what's at hand, *Jam Today* is a complete pleasure to read." —**Deborah Madison**, author of
The New Vegetarian Cooking for Everyone

"The spirit of M.F.K. Fisher surely hovers over this book, amused and beguiled by a cook whose prose has the same artful composure, and whose cooking possesses a similar innate sense of style."
—**John Thorne**, author of *Serious Pig: An American Cook in Search of His Roots* and *Mouth Wide Open: A Cook and His Appetite*

"These days we understand that exercise is its own reward. The effects of exercise make you want to exercise again. Cooking, when it's done regularly and so loses the 'performance' aspect, has the same kind of multiplier effect. It takes us to a place that's just being, just doing. *Jam Today Too* takes us to that place, between our so basic need for and love of food; and our need for and love of nourishing each other. Davies' daily inspirations about *what* to eat show us how home cooking becomes its own reward."
  —**Charlene Rollins**, Chef/Owner of New Sammy's Cowboy Bistro and three-time James Beard Foundation Awards semifinalist for Best Northwest Regional Chef

"Tod Davies, in *Jam Today Too*, teaches us how to have fun with food without throwing it. But, if you must, please throw this good stuff at me."
  —**Vernon Rollins**, Sommelier/Owner at New Sammy's Cowboy Bistro, one of *Food & Wine* magazine's "50 Most Amazing Wine Experiences"

"I'd just like a refill, please. A second cool, tall glass of *Jam*."
  —**Maggie Ruggiero**, Food Editor/Stylist for *Gather Journal*

Jam Today Too

THE REVOLUTION WILL NOT BE CATERED

TOD DAVIES

EXTERMINATING ANGEL
PRESS

Exterminating Angel Press
"Creative Solutions for Practical Idealists"
Visit **www.exterminatingangel.com** to join the conversation
info@exterminatingangel.com

Exterminating Angel book design by Mike Madrid
Typesetting by John Sutherland

ISBN: 978-1-935259-25-1
eBook ISBN: 978-1-935259-26-8
Library of Congress Control Number: 2014930139

Distributed by
CONSORTIUM BOOK SALES & DISTRIBUTION
(800) 283-3572
www.cbsd.com

Printed in The United States of America

Contents

Once again, for Alex,
the Beloved Vegetarian Husband

And in memory of Laurel Hansen,
great cook and great friend

"I hope very much that people will again make things, cook and bake for themselves, and for one another. Life is, after all, more real that way, more nourishing to body and spirit as well."

—*Joseph Wechsberg*

List of Recipes

Chapter Three: Food for Home

Foreword: Still Cooking

*Warning: Like the last **"Jam Today: A Diary of Cooking With What You've Got,"** this book still does not contain any jam.*

At least not the kind you put on your toast.

I'm still cooking.

I'm still cooking, and still thinking about what I and my loved ones like to eat, still keeping a diary of what I've got and what I do with it. I still meditate daily on my place in the world, and it's still a joy to talk to friends about their views on their own places. Especially when those talks revolve around food. Because it's still true—even more true than when I wrote *Jam Today: A Diary of Cooking With What You've Got*—that what we do in our everyday lives affects the structure around us, and that what we choose to eat, how we choose to source it, cook it, serve it, enjoy it, is more than a statement about our individual lives. It's even more than a political statement about our place in the polity. It's a potential for creativity, for creating the possibility of more joy in the world, and using that as a jumping-off point for making the world back into the garden we dream it once was and still could be.

Seriously.

There are a lot of people I love and admire for participating in that kind of creative process, undoubtedly more than I can name here. But I did want to mention some...local stuff, you might call it. People and places and foods that I found from looking around myself, and which made my life better. I still owe a lot of my vegetables and fruits in season to The Indigo Ray, of course, and her art project of a garden. I owe some of the best restaurant meals I've ever eaten to Charlene and Vernon Rollins, who together serve forth what must be the best food and wine in the known world at New Sammy's Cowboy Bistro. And if that's a prejudiced exaggeration, it's no hyperbole to say that their sourdough bread, New Sammy's Sourdough, delivered warm to our local markets by Charlene's brother Ken, is the best sourdough bread in the world. Truth.

I still use Pisces Tuna, fished by the husband and wife team of Daryl and Sally Bogardus (PO Box 812, Coos Bay, OR, 97420, USA. Cell phone 001 541 821 7117). After I wrote about them and their tuna in the first *Jam Today*, Sally tracked me down via the telephone directory and told me they'd gotten a lot of orders that quoted the book. The system works!

About halfway through the writing of this book, Dawn the Egg Lady, alas, was forced, in a household move, to give up her chickens. But my egg source has been replaced by my dear friend, electrician, rancher, and rural Renaissance woman Cindy Warzyn, whose freezer is, as you will see if you read on, a never-ending source of challenge for me. Then there have been so many meals I've gratefully shared with Teri Lewyn Thomas; her constant support of my food experiments, allied with her ability to share real conversation about real things, has provided me with a friendship, and dinner companion, I could not do without. Special thanks to Lanny DeVuono, who saved me from homesickness when I moved my kitchen, for a time, far away from Teri's encouragement. And to my wonderful sister-in-law, Cindy Daniels, who not only takes the place of the sister I once longed for in a childhood full of (admittedly great) brothers, but who also read through this manuscript in record time and gave me some excellent notes when I needed them.

Then there is the list of friends, which surely would be too long to list complete, but you all know who you are, yes? A lot of you are in here, in *Jam Today Too*, and without you the fabric of my daily life would be less iridescent, less cleanly woven than it is with you. And given that during the time I worked on *Jam Today Too*, I was involved in not one, but TWO floods, I don't know how I would have kept intact my sense of humor, let alone of enjoyment, without friends. Thank you, all, for insisting as usual that we enjoy every moment we possibly can.

If there's one thing my friends and I do agree on (and thank goodness we disagree so fascinatingly on so many other things), then it would be to enjoy every day right here right now. We agree with Lewis Carroll's Alice, when, no matter how many times the Queen insists that it's only jam yesterday or jam tomorrow, we keep laughing and say, "Listen up. We're not worrying about yesterday or tomorrow just at the moment, thank you. Right now it's still Jam Today."

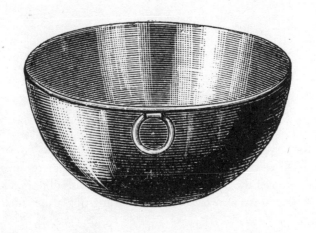

Food for Disasters

DISASTER AND BASICS

I never thought I would see the day that I would hate to cook. Maybe not feel in the mood to cook. Maybe be tired of my own cuisine. But actually hate to cook, loathe it, dread it, the way I've been absolutely sure any healthy human being would not actually feel—no, I never believed I would feel THAT.

Then I lived in an RV for a month. And I learned why so many people hate to cook.

Let me back up a little here. So our kitchen flooded when we were away (don't ask), and we had been living out of suitcases in various vacation rentals and motels, the dogs and me and the Beloved Vegetarian Husband, while the contractors and the insurance company put us back together (thank you, State Farm). Then we got sick of that, of moving around, and we rented an RV and parked it in the meadow in front of our house. We lived there for about a month, and more about THAT in a moment.

Right now I want to talk about how I learned why people hate to cook.

When the bedroom in our flooded-out house was finally ready for occupancy (just barely), I found myself sitting and waiting for the nice RV people to come and take it (finally) away. Since we were about a month out from still having a kitchen, and I was going to have to make do shortly with a toaster oven plugged in on our deck (and more about THAT in a moment, too), I was cooking a big pot of pasta on the little RV stove for the very last time. I planned to cool and mix the pasta with a vinaigrette dressing, and then dole it out over the next few days, spruced up with differing ingredients so it would be as if we were eating different things. First up: tuna/scallions/celery/parsley pasta salad.

As I sat watching the water boil, I found I was so sick of cooking I could

1

hardly recognize myself. Could this be the same woman who so cheerfully has urged dozens of her careworn friends to get back into the kitchen?

Well, it could. And it's interesting to me (as well as salutary, sorry anyone I bugged about this on a particularly fraught day of yours) to contemplate what the differences are between cooking in this RV, and cooking in my home kitchen—or in any home kitchen. It's interesting because it tells me a lot about BASICS. About what is the absolute minimum you need in your kitchen in order to cook in pleasure and in peace.

(At this moment in my thinking process I rose to toss the drained pasta with the vinaigrette: smashed garlic clove, vinegar and olive oil in a 1-to-3 ratio, salt and pepper.)

Which brings me to the first basic:

A good kitchen set-up is one where everything is close to hand. You should be able to move from refrigerator to sink to prep space (from which, without moving, you can toss things into the garbage can or compost bowl) to stove in just a few balletic movements, unimpeded by kitchen islands, dogs, husbands seeking beer, children drawing on paper on the floor, and guests. The ideal is a triangular arrangement, where it's only a few steps from one of these places to another. If you have to move between a stove in an RV and a refrigerator temporarily sheltered in the living room of the house halfway up a meadow from that RV, you are not going to have the fun you deserve. I know it won't happen often that someone will have a stove in an RV and a refrigerator in a house up a very long rural driveway from said RV, but you know, some of these new designer kitchens I've been in make it seem almost as far. You do not want a designer kitchen if it means you don't have a nice snug well-ordered corner of space in which to prepare the food. It doesn't matter how much internet access the room has if you're lacking that.

You do not need a lot of space for this—two of my favorite kitchens of the past were almost dollhouse in size—but it needs, as in so much else in life, to be well ordered.

(And pleasant. It needs to be pleasant. One of my main requirements for *a kitchen is a window that looks out onto something green—even if it's only a window box full of geraniums. Or rosemary. Definitely rosemary. It's essential to have a bit of the natural world around, again as in so much else in life.)*

Which leads me to the bare minimum of equipment and foodstuffs that you need in this well-ordered kitchen of yours.

For equipment:

◊ First, and most important, at least one good, sharp knife. Preferably three knives: one a small paring knife, one a medium-sized sharp bladed knife you'll use for most things, and one a serrated bread knife for cutting loaves of bread and hard cheeses.

◊ One big solid pot with a lid, in which to cook soups, stews, pasta, rice…anything that needs a lot of space. It should be ovenproof so it can do double duty, on top of the stove and inside too.

◊ One medium saucepan, also with lid, in which to cook smaller amounts. Helpful to have a steamer insert for this as well.

◊ One big skillet.

◊ One small skillet.

◊ One small saucepan in which to melt butter and warm single cups of hot milk, as well as make single helpings of breakfast oatmeal.

◊ A colander, or a big mesh strainer that can stand on its own, for pasta and such. A small mesh strainer you can hold by its handle to drain small bits of things, like capers, or to strain the seeds out of squeezed lemon juice.

◊ A selection of wooden spoons and spatulas. They don't scratch, and they can be used for anything.

◊ Two cutting boards, one for garlic and onions and foods that don't mind contact with garlic and onions. The latter for fruit and bread, and anything else you don't want tasting of garlic and onions.

◊ A wire whisk.

3

◊ A potato masher.
◊ A box grater (essential, do not even THINK about doing without this one).
◊ A good can-opener.
◊ A good vegetable peeler (a cheap one will only make your life a misery).
◊ A large mixing bowl that can double as a salad bowl.
◊ A small mixing bowl that can double as a serving bowl.
◊ A Pyrex measuring cup for liquids.
◊ Metal measuring cups for non-liquids, and metal measuring spoons.
◊ Tongs.
◊ A good mortar and pestle for mashing garlic cloves, mixing salad dressings, etc.
◊ A peppermill.

Then, for food basics, THAT was easy to figure out. It was everything contained in the cardboard box I ended up carting around from temporary housing to temporary housing, just to make sure we were always going to have something good to eat. The list of things turns out to be, unsurprisingly, what I consider the bare minimum for a pantry set-up. Like so:

◊ A good oil. I like a good olive oil I can use both for cooking and salad dressings.
◊ A good vinegar. Any kind you like: red wine, sherry, balsamic.
◊ A head of garlic.
◊ A couple of onions.
◊ A can of tomatoes.
◊ Some bags of pasta.
◊ Some oatmeal.
◊ A jar of salsa.

◊ A can of tuna.
◊ A can of anchovies.
◊ A jar of honey.
◊ A bottle of soy sauce.
◊ A bottle of hot sauce (we have to have two or three kinds in our pantry set-up).
◊ Some flour (I use Wondra, that quick thickening flour that comes in a small carton, but then I don't bake—this is for thickening sauces or dredging things to be sautéed).
◊ Some sugar (I use a brown sugar because I like the deeper flavor).
◊ A good kind of salt.
◊ Peppercorns (for the peppermill).

There are many things you can add happily to this skeleton set-up—more pots and pans, a wok, a blender, even a Cuisinart, as well as the little stuff: nutmeg grater, cheese grater, food mill, lemon reamer, etc.—and for the foodstuffs, of course, there are all sorts of bits and bobs you can personalize your emergency food choices with, as well as the fresh goods (lemons, parsley, butter, milk, yoghurt, parmesan cheese, etc.) you'll have to buy when you can, but this is the gear and the cardboard box pantry I cooked with for that month in the RV, the set-up I found I couldn't do without. It was the RV that I could have done without.

A MEDIUM-SIZED DISASTER AND CALAMARI STEAKS

However. To look on the bright side: it took that medium-sized disaster to teach me how to really cook calamari.

The flooded-out kitchen was not a small disaster—like a fender-bender—or a large disaster—like illness or injury—or, fortunately, the kind of mega-large disaster which we can all imagine and shiver at, and which I will hurry past. No, this was a garden-variety medium-sized disaster, where you and your loved ones are inconvenienced but not harmed. This has its own repercussions at meal time, since meal times are a particularly good time to knit up the raveled sleeve of care, laugh away frustrations, reaffirm that you are all whole and well and safe and relatively sane, and remember how lucky you are to be all that when so many people aren't.

The lovely woman helping me with my insurance claim had been steadfastly amazed that we would rather live in cheaper digs and make our own meals, than in the (insurance-reimbursable) local hotels with all our restaurant meals paid-for. But, while we like to dine out very much, it is not the same as dining in. And it is definitely not the same as the healing power of dining in while you have the bruises and scrapes of a medium-sized disaster.

As always, I learned things from thinking about what we were going to eat, and then preparing it, and then sitting down with the Beloved Vegetarian Husband to dine.

Hence the calamari.

Now, why calamari, you are saying. Or perhaps you are even saying, what calamari? What IS calamari? So I'll start with that. Better to be blunt and have it out immediately rather than trying to put one over on you. Calamari is squid. Yep. Those little things with tentacles. Except in this case, calamari is calamari steaks, which are, presumably, cut from the bodies of REALLY BIG SQUID. These steaks are white, and oval shaped, and scored for tenderness, and they're usually fairly inexpensive as seafood goes. I know they're sustainable…at least they are for the moment, who knows for how much longer with those computer-driven industrial-sized nets dragging every inch of the deep sea floor these days?

But for now, we can enjoy calamari steaks unmolested by guilty thoughts of using up every fish in the sea. Which also adds to a pleasant dining experience.

We both love calamari. In the days before our kitchen was a construction site, I would dry and lightly flour the steaks, sauté them quickly in hot oil and butter, then take them out and keep them warm while I deglazed the pan with a little white wine and some vinegar from the chopped-up capers I added at the last minute with some paper-thin lemon slices. A swirl of butter melted in the sauce as I took the pan off the heat and turned the steaks over, a sprinkling of chopped parsley, and the Beloved Vegetarian Husband was very happy. I usually served this with a little steamed brown rice, and some sliced tomato, or corn on the cob, or, in the winter, a pile of buttered peas (cooking frozen ones here is perfectly acceptable, as a matter of fact).

Here's the thing about living out of suitcases in a variety of vacation homes: the pot/pan/condiment situation is sketchy at best. You're dealing with an eccentric array of cooking equipment, and an odd choice of leftover gourmet flavorings left behind by previous guests. This means that I keep that box I told you about with us through every move, one that includes some olive oil, some vinegar, some honey, a bottle of soy sauce, two bottles of hot sauce, a packet of dried red pepper pods, a jar of garlic salt, and, of course, a pepper mill. Also a few packages of pasta and some cans of tomatoes. A jar of hot salsa, naturally. Then every time we go near a market, I buy a lemon, an onion, miscellaneous veggies and fruit, and at least two heads of garlic.

This gives me enough choices for what to dine upon, as it interacts in my imagination with the pan too small to easily boil pasta, the cheap aluminum wok, and the ancient, scratched-up, Teflon-coated pans that you always find in these rentals.

Of course, there are always baking dishes. Lasagna pans. Every rental of any kind I've ever been in had a Pyrex lasagna pan.

So we had been living off the usual salads, and pasta dishes (arrabiata being a favorite fallback position—tomato sauce with garlic and red pepper), and baked potatoes because there's always a toaster oven and I could always go home and get butter out of my freezer, which was then plugged into a wall in my living room. Tortillas with melted cheddar and salsa. That kind of thing.

I was getting a little tired of the old standbys, but we were exhausted after a day of more than usually tedious errand-running, so I whipped through the market as our last errand. I was wistfully hoping for some seafood. Something for a change. But everything in the market—the EXPENSIVE market in town, too, so there was no excuse—had been packed, literally, days before, or, in the case of the halibut packed that day, cost an outrageous twenty-five bucks a pound.

Forget that.

So on my way to the wine section—I really needed a bottle at this point—I had a look in the freezer section. And there were these calamari steaks at a more reasonable $7 a pound, so I threw those in the basket, grabbed two bottles of rosé, and headed for the checkout. On the way there, I caught a whiff of freshly baked bread, and saw, to my delight, that Ken of New Sammy's must have just delivered their sourdough bread. It was still warm. I grabbed a loaf of that (who wouldn't have), and was out of there in record time.

Back at the rental, though, I realized I didn't have my usual calamari cuisine accouterments. No flour, first off (which is why I now advise a carton of Wondra for that skeleton pantry). I scoured the cupboards, but all I could find were packets of gelatin (what could they have been doing, making jam?), and some microwave popcorn. And I was uneasy at the sight of those Teflon pans. They were so old and scratched I had my doubts about being able to unstick the fish, let alone about what kind of chemicals might come with it when it did get unstuck.

Also, the fish was still frozen, and it's just about impossible to get a nice brown crust on a calamari steak that's still frozen. Too much liquid.

8

Then to top it all off I realized I didn't have any rice. I did have some leftover cucumber/tomato/onion/lime juice salad. And I had bought some corn on the cob. So that was okay. But it seemed like we needed something more...

I got another whiff of that lovely bread as I prowled the kitchen. It smelled wonderful. And I thought, what a shame to have such fresh bread and not use it for something. And then I mentally hit myself on the forehead with the heel of my hand, and said, silently, "Idiot!"

Calamari sandwiches. Of course. It wouldn't matter then how brown the steaks were, just how they tasted. But then it occurred to me: those old Teflon pans were NOT for high-heat sautéing. No, sirree. So I rooted around in the cupboards and found the aforementioned lasagna pan. As I stood there contemplating it, a vague memory floated through my head, a memory of Sunset magazine's fish book (a very sensible and useful thing to have in any kitchen), where, among the many ways to prepare fish of all kinds, they recommend something I believe they call 'ovenfrying.' I was not completely clear on their instructions, since that cookbook, like so much else at that time, resided in one of the many white boxes littering my living room back home, but what I seemed to recall was that it involved heating the oven to 500°, putting a pan with oil in it till the oil sizzled, then cooking the fish quickly.

Well, it was worth a try, I thought. Why not? So I tried it, with olive oil, and with a lot of chopped garlic thrown on the steaks when I turned them over, so the house smelled incredibly of Spain. And I served them as sandwiches, on slices of fresh sourdough bread, one side of which was buttered, and the other spread with spicy salsa from a jar.

Oh, and I almost forgot—I found the heart of some escarole lurking in the fridge, and I sautéed that, and spread the cooked greens on the buttered side of the bread, put the calamari on top, closed up the sandwich, and served it with the cucumber/tomato/onion salad and some hot corn on the cob.

It was unutterably delicious. And browned. And garlicky. And messy as hell. The next day, I rooted around till I found a steel-wool pad, and set to work returning the lasagna pan to its former clarity. An impossible job, it's still a little golden in spots from the high heat of the oil, but this is what happens to pots and pans in rental accommodations. Or should. I personally think it's nicer to see evidence that a kitchen was in happy use before I get to it.

And this is how to make **Calamari Sandwiches with Braised Escarole and Salsa in a Vacation Rental.**

Ingredients for two:
◊   Four slices sourdough bread
◊   Two calamari steaks
◊   A half head of escarole
◊   As much fresh garlic as you please
◊   A jar of hot salsa
◊   Butter
◊   Olive oil

Take Pyrex baking dish, or similar, that will hold the calamari steaks flat. Add enough olive oil to cover the bottom.

Put in oven.

Heat oven to 500°.

On top of oven, heat a wide frying pan to medium-high, and add a little olive oil.

When oil is heated, add a crushed garlic clove and the escarole, washed and chopped (don't dry it, it will cook in the liquid left on the leaves).

Stir escarole around to coat, turn down the heat, put a lid on if you have one (or a cookie sheet, or something to help the veggies steam), take off the heat when tender. Salt.

If calamari steaks are unfrozen, dry on some paper towels, then add to the oil in the oven. If frozen, don't bother drying, put them in—you'll just cook them twice as long; it won't hurt them at all.

If unfrozen, cook for three minutes, salt, then turn and scatter chopped garlic on top. Salt a little more. Cook for another two minutes—they should be done quickly, too long and they'll turn rubbery. If frozen, just increase the time to five minutes on each side.

Butter two slices of bread. Spread salsa on the other two. Spread escarole on the buttered halves.

When the calamari is done, scoop it out and put one piece each on the escarole-spread bread. Sprinkle whatever loose garlic cloves and olive oil is still left from the baking pan. (Careful! That oil is HOT.) Cover each sandwich with its other half, cut in two, and serve with lots of paper napkins—this is messy.

Messy food is so delicious. And it's worth trying to scrub that dish back to pristine shape. You won't be able to manage it, but you can think as you do about how good all that garlicky oil and salsa and squid and greens tasted all squished together the night before.

And it almost makes it up to you for being kicked out of your own kitchen by fate. At least, it did for us.

PIZZA WITH ONE BOWL AND A PAN (and a cutting board)

Or, "Cooking in an RV." Shudder.

When we had our disastrous flood, and the kindly insurance company insisted on paying for us to stay in other places, and the kindly contractor insisted on us going to other places so we wouldn't be under his feet and the kindly feet of his various helpers, all of us (dogs included) were more into making lemonade out of lemons, and treated it all as an adventure at first. Another La Quinta to explore! A week at the beach in our favorite room on the edge of a cliff! A vacation rental that had once been the home of a close friend, now rented out after his death by our neighbor, close to home and with a tremendous view of our valley (that was the best). But after a month of it, we were absolutely homesick. The Husband would go home every day to work in his little hut in our meadow, and I would come up in the morning to walk the dogs behind the house in our forest (actually, literally our forest... yours, too, since it's National Forest. Thank you, Teddy Roosevelt). Even though the Meadow House, where we had been staying, was kindly, and our late friend's spirit was welcoming, and there was a picture on our bedroom wall of three cats I had particularly liked (long gone now), we were homesick. We wanted to go home. But there was this big hole where our kitchen had once been, and no wall between the kitchen and the bedroom.

So that was why I rented an RV.

A monster RV, it looked at first sight. Huge. Immense. Quasi-luxurious. The nice man who delivered it (an ex–gold miner, he told us as he propped up its various sides with scraps of wood cadged from the nice Christian carpenters working on our house) had quite a time fitting it on our meadow, but he seemed to enjoy the challenge. And I kind of cautiously looked forward to cooking in it (hah!). A new adventure, after all. The kitchen itself was quite compact, but looked serviceable: three-burner gas stove, oven, a microwave I would never use, a two-sided sink. Small refrigerator. It would be okay, I figured.

What I didn't reckon with was the presumed market for these RV things. The people who use them for fun don't seem to be really interested in cooking. The microwave said it all with its spelled out settings: "Popcorn." "Hot dogs." "Chili." "Pizza."

I just laughed when I saw that. Surely no one actually COOKED like that? Aside from the lack of nutritional value, surely people don't like to be treated like they're robots eating robot food, do they? DO THEY?

Well, I don't know. Maybe they do. It's a depressing notion, and goes along with a lot of other depressing notions, but maybe they do. I contemplated this as I struggled with the sink that didn't drain (and when it did, drained into the bathtub in another room, until the Beloved Vegetarian Husband figured out how to release the water onto the meadow); with the oven that was impossible to light and, when you finally managed it, burned everything from the bottom through uneven heat distribution; with the cupboards that made no sense, the drawers that stuck, and the total lack of anywhere to put anything down except on the sole table.

But there was a sound system. A pretty good one too. Speakers all through the RV, and, to my husband's great amusement, speakers outside so you could listen to your CDs while you sat under your awning, presumably eating your microwaved hot dogs. I, feeling a bit more flustered as I tried to cater for two people and two dogs used to eating home-cooked meals, was slightly more irritable on the subject.

After a couple of acerbic comments from me about the value of a living space that privileged a sound system over a basic cooking space, I got to work trying to figure out how to make the most meal out of the least space.

"This place is like a reverse Tardis," the Husband remarked as we did a little dance when he tried to get a beer out of the refrigerator while I was reaching for a head of garlic I'd stashed in a bowl on the table. "It looks huge on the outside, but inside…"

"Hermph," I said, thinking dark thoughts again, as I often do, about things and systems that seem to be designed with more attention to how they look than how they function.

"Welcome to America!" my English husband said gaily, as he went out with his beer to enjoy the sound system under the stars.

Until it started to rain. Husband and dogs retreated into the Tardis, underfoot, while increasingly hungry Wife decided what to do for dinner.

But, as often happens when you find yourself dealing with limited resources, I discovered a nice little trick that ended in a delicious little dinner. How to make pizza topping in a single bowl, and then make the pizza on a single pan.

I had this ready-made pizza crust, distributed by the same people who make my favorite bread (New Sammy's, so there). The idea is you spread it with sauce, then with toppings, then with cheese, then pop it into a 500° oven until it all melts together. Good idea.

Only I didn't have any sauce. And I certainly wasn't going to make some in a trailer with a husband, a beer, Mozart, and two wet dogs, with rain pelting down outside.

What I DID have was a bag of oven-dried tomatoes from my initial experiments with the oven. I had bought a bunch of organic Romas, but space being at a premium in that RV, I quickly discovered I had nowhere to store them. So I sliced them in half, put them on some aluminum foil on a cookie sheet, dribbled them with olive oil and coarse salt (once I could remember the space/time continuum closet space I'd hidden these in originally), and set them in the oven at the lowest heat I could manage (once the Husband and I could figure out how to light the pilot—a two-person job, the RV guy on the phone assured me, and he was right). I had found out then about the burning-stuff-on-the-bottom aspect of the stove, but got the tomatoes out in time, a few hours later, so they were dry and concentrated and easily storable in the refrigerator. I had mushrooms. I had garlic (I always have garlic). I had green onions. I had Jack cheese. I had more olive oil. I had hoped I had anchovies, but somehow the tin I was sure was there had been swallowed up by a black hole or something. But I did have a little bit of salami (which the

Beloved Vegetarian Husband refers to as 'Carnivore's Anchovies' since it has the same salty/umami kind of flavor), and I had emergency permission from the Vegetarian to add a little bit to the pizza for pizzazz.

So here's what I did:

First, I got the Husband to help me light the pilot. (He lights match, crouches down, reaches to back of oven, trying to reach tiny space where gas presumably enters, then tells me to push in the knob above. I do, we both wait: nothing. We wait longer. Aha! Success! I hold in the knob for a while to get it to catch, and then can turn the oven on. Were they insane, the people who developed this oven? A two-person job to light an oven in an RV? And it has to be lit every time you want to use it? That settles it: they must have been sure that the only people who would ever eat in one of these things would only use the microwave.)

Set the temperature to 500°.

Unwrapped the pizza crust, put it on a cookie sheet, dribbled olive oil on it, spreading the oil out with a paper napkin.

Took out a bowl. A cutting board. A knife. And got to work.

Slivered the dried tomatoes, about six of them. Tossed them into the bowl.

Thinly sliced the mushrooms, about a half-pound. Tossed them into the bowl.

Chopped four green onions. Tossed them etc.

Four garlic cloves. Minced one, thickly sliced the others. Tossed etc.
Six or seven thin pieces of salami. Diced. Tossed.

A few branches of fresh thyme from the garden, stripped into the bowl.

Salt. Olive oil. Stirred it all up with my hands.

Spread the whole thing on the pizza crust, mounding all the mushrooms up. I didn't worry at the huge mound of mushrooms; I knew they'd cook down.

Sliced some Jack cheese and arranged it on top of the mushrooms.

Shoved the pan into the oven with a heartfelt sigh, and gratefully watched as a sympathetic Husband poured me a honking big glass of red wine.

"Cheers," he said. And we both laughed. It was cozy, after all, in the Tardis with Mozart playing and the rain pelting down, and soon it smelled deliciously of mushrooms and garlic. I managed to get the pizza out just as it was beginning to burn on the bottom, and just as the cheese was melting all golden on the top, and we had slices with cucumber spears on the side, on paper plates so all there was to clean up was the pizza pan, the bowl, the cutting board and the knife. And you know what? It was the best pizza I'd ever made. I can't figure out why I'd made such a hoo-ha about it before. And it was about a thousand times better than any microwaveable pizza I've ever tasted, and that's not being snobby, that's just a fact. There was enough for both of us, and for lunch the next day too.

There, that wasn't so bad. Not bad at all.

(And just in case you want to know how to dry those tomatoes—a very neat trick, and a lot less expensive than buying those cellophane-wrapped ones in the stores—I believe I've described it before, but it's worth repeating, so here's how:

Take as many firm organic Roma tomatoes as will fit, split, on cookie sheets in your oven.

Split the Romas almost in half, leaving the halves connected. Spread them open and deposit on foil-covered cookie sheets.

Scatter coarse salt atop.

Dribble some olive oil on top (this is optional, but so good you'll probably never do it the low-fat way once you've tried it).

Put in a low-temperature oven, say 200° or 250°. You don't need to fuss about this; if you have something else cooking at 350°, don't worry, just watch the tomatoes a little more carefully.

Now leave them alone. For hours. Well, two hours, say. What you want is a dried tomato that is flexible but not leathery. I've left them in overnight at the lower temperature without visible harm.

When you've reached this perfect stage, just pile the tomatoes in a bowl (I usually use the foil they were cooked on to cover them) and stick in the fridge. They'll keep, if not forever, at least a long long time.

And they are good for so many uses: pasta sauce, bruschetta spread, the aforementioned pizza, salads. So go wild.)

TUNA IN A TOASTER OVEN

Tuna in a Toaster Oven. It sounds kind of awful, put like that, although I love the euphony of the name—the sheer alliterative bliss of it. Well, as it happened, the dish itself was pretty blissful, too. Tasty and easy and good for you. And it helped me through another evening of being kitchenless and stoveless, for which it was hugely appreciated.

We were by this time RV-less. The bedroom was habitable, and, as it was summer, the front deck became the kitchen and dining room. There on the deck was our toaster oven, plugged into the wall, and this obviously limited my cooking options and our food choices. I'd thought we were going to be doomed to another night of supermarket sushi. Supermarket sushi! That's how low I had fallen. It was hot, I was sick and tired of trying to come up with things to make for dinner that didn't involve kitchens or much washing up (since any washing up needed to take place in the bathtub), and we had, with relative success, more or less enjoyed eating a selection of rice/vegetable/seaweed rolls from the local market, along with a cucumber salad I had quickly mixed up (peeled, thinly sliced, tossed with soy sauce and a little mirin). It hadn't been great, but it hadn't been awful either, which is why I say it shows how low I had been laid by being without my kitchen. I was willing to settle for 'not awful.' This is a terrible thing, this settling for 'not awful,' and we do it all the time. This was the time that brought that home to me. Horrors. Well, I'd worry about such matters later. First need was to get me and the Beloved Vegetarian Husband fed.

But then I got to the market, and I just couldn't bring myself to head straight to the deli counter. Not that this would be an admission of failure (although during my more smug, kitchen-rich days, it would have been), but because I just yearned to wander through the supermarket in my 'old' way, as if I could peek at a bit of this, and contemplate a bit of that, and compose a meal in my head that would be served up later. I missed those days. To tell the truth, the reconstruction of the house was dragging on so long I was beginning to doubt those days would ever come again. So this was almost more nostalgia than actual shopping.

When I got to the fish counter, I noted, to my cynical amusement, that this, the 'expensive' market in town, had taken to marking its fish with an expiration date rather than a 'packed on' date. It's much more difficult to assess the freshness of the fish when the only info you have to go by is when the supermarket feels it should jettison the product as unsalable. I mean, you have to count on their awareness. And since in the marked-down bin this particular day there were packs and packs of salmon that had just hit their sell by date, and since I can't think of anything you can do with marked-down stale salmon except possibly serve it to the cat, I was wary of this store's judgment.

But then, what did catch my eye, but a series of wrapped packages of albacore with a reasonable enough price and an expiry date far enough away to make me skid to a halt and moon over them nostalgically. Albacore, a type of tuna, is one of the fishes that flourishes on the Oregon coast, as Oregon fisherfolk and fishlovers can attest, and by golly, this had all the look of local albacore wrapped within a day or two. Probably the day before I gazed on it, but this is the secret—if it's local and came straight out of the water, even sitting a day in the market's fish section isn't going to harm it appreciably. And it will certainly be fresher than that tilapia from Indonesia nestling seductively beside it.

That was when I thought of my lone cooking source these days: my toaster oven, sitting faithfully on my deck. And why not broil the tuna in the toaster oven? I had certainly done that before when said oven was in its proud position on my old kitchen counter. So I grabbed a package of it. Brought it home, and put it in a dish with some soy sauce, some of that wonderful Japanese sweet cooking wine mirin (about a 3-to-1 mix), and a good squirt of wasabi all mixed together. Left it till dinner time.

And turned the toaster oven to 'broil,' covered a toaster oven pan with foil, laid the tuna on that, basted it with a little more of its marinade, and stuck it in. Since the fish was about an inch thick, and the general rule of thumb for flaky fish is ten minutes to an inch, and since albacore (especially local albacore) is at its best rare, I set the timer to seven minutes. I had no plans to turn the fish, since I wanted it nice and browned on top, and who was going to look at the bottom? So even easier. Another advantage. Then I laid out two plates on our rickety but pleasant plastic table on the deck, spread what was left of the green clover sprouts I had in the fridge, dividing them between the two plates, and put out soy sauce and a tube of wasabi. Right before the timer went off, I got a little package of supermarket cucumber/avocado/rice rolls out of the fridge and onto the table. I called the Beloved Vegetarian Husband up for supper. Then I put each portion of fish on its own bed of sprouts and squeezed a little lime over that. And served it forth.

Timing is everything in these cases.

True, we hadn't been that hungry—a particularly sustaining lunch at the Best Restaurant in the World had taken care of that—but the Husband's face lit up nonetheless at the sight of that albacore. "You cooked!" he exclaimed. "You must really love me!"

"I do really love you," I said as we sat down and tucked in. "And here, let me give you some of my specially prepared vegetable sushi, bought just for you with my fair hands."

"I accept," he said happily, for his mouth was filled with tuna, and it was the small coup of having surprised him with something home cooked that almost made the happiness just that much more complete. Though he would have been happy with store bought sushi. He's not fussy. But, on the other hand, he's not stupid either.

ZUCCHINI WITH SOY SAUCE AND WASABI

Here's what you do when a medium-sized disaster has rendered your kitchen useless: salads. At least, that was what I did. And the easier to throw together, and the tastier once thrown, the better. Oh, and the fewer dishes/utensils used even better still. So that flooded-out summer, I ended up making a lot of salads. Good thing it was summer when you want a salad anyway—and, making lemonade out of etc., I discovered a couple of salads that are indeed a breeze to make with minimal equipment. My favorite being: thin-sliced zucchini with wasabi and soy.

This can only be made with the freshest possible zucchini, preferably small ones, picked in the last three days from your own garden or a neighbor's, or bought at a farmer's market stand.

Take as many zucchini as you like.

Slice thinly.

Stir together a mix of soy sauce with a dash of mirin (or sugar or honey— some sweetener), and as much wasabi as you like. We like a lot, since we like very strong flavors, but you might like a subtler mix. The amount of soy sauce has to be judged by the eye. You want just enough to coat the zucchini, but not so much that the vegetables drown. Mix the three ingredients. Taste. Adjust.

Then start adding it to the zucchini, tossing as you go, until the veggies are just perfectly coated.

Chill.

Sit down with a bowlful and some chopsticks on your deck, or in the back yard in the summer, and enjoy.

KALE SALAD

And while we're on the subject of foods you can make without having a kitchen in which to make them...

So I had coaxed a couple of out-of-town guests to stop by The Indigo Ray's garden, promising that it would be worth their while to drive the mile or so down her rutted driveway. And it was worth their while. And fun for me, too, the way it always is to watch loved friends enjoy loved places. We wandered dreamily through the Zen garden, and past the hundreds of lilies, and past the immense bank of raspberry bushes (but not without catching raspberries from said bushes in our hands and popping them into our mouths).

My own secret mission was not just to show all this lushness to my friends, but also to bag a few beets. Since the kitchen disaster had left me with that lone toaster oven sitting on my deck, I had found baking beets to be an excellent use of that space.

(And the single best way to cook beets: Wash and wrap in aluminum foil, bake hell out of them at 400° to 450° for about an hour, or even an hour and a half, until you can smell them in the next room—this is a reliable method to tell when something is done, when it smells like the cooked food you're trying to achieve—turn off and let cool. When you're ready to use them, just slip off the skins and proceed. If the skins don't slip off easily, you haven't cooked hell out of them, put back in the oven until skins do. Then proceed. Rumors I have read in other cookbooks that you should use the cooked beets immediately turn out to be exaggerated. I have shoved these things, still in their foil, into the refrigerator and turned them into glorious beet salads up to three days after the initial roasting. So there.)

I informed Indigo of my quest, and she said, "Oh, the kale looks great today. Take a lot of it." Alas, I said sadly, no stove. Must cook kale, mustn't we?

At this, my friends' dreamy looks as they inhaled the smell from a bush covered with tiny pink roses turned startled.

They turned and looked at me, and chimed a simultaneous protest:

"Kale salad!" they said. And then they both—mother and daughter—gave a reminiscent smile.

Indigo and I looked at them curiously. "Don't you have to cook it?" I said cautiously. "Isn't it too tough?" Indigo asked.

They tumbled all over each other, laughing, telling me the recipe.

"No, no, you just let it marinate enough, olive oil and lemon and ANCHOVIES are great, capers maybe, shred it, toss it with those, chop the anchovies, oh, and garlic of course, that almost goes without saying, a little feta cheese maybe? Some grated Parmesan? Then let the whole thing sit for a day or two in the refrigerator; that's when it gets really good!"

I grasped the concept immediately with the kind of gladness one only feels on discovering a new and simple way of cooking a loved ingredient—and believe me, this feeling doesn't come to me much anymore, a loss I feel as strongly as some middle-aged male writers feel over their loss of the delights of first love. (And my sense of loss is a lot more rational, I feel.)

"Kale ceviche!" I said triumphantly. Meaning, of course, those wonderful raw fish dishes where the fish is cooked by its marinade.

They beamed at me, mother and daughter. "Exactly," one of them said.

So we went down to the end of the garden where the kale grew in huge bunches, and I picked an armful, and the daughter said, "What I love about this salad is that you can keep it in the refrigerator and it just gets better."

The mother said, "What I love about this salad is how great it tastes."

And what I love about this salad is that from now on when I make it, I'll think about that morning when the three of us went on a sunny summer's day to Indigo's garden, and how I came out of it with a new way of cooking that was shared with me by a friend. By two friends, now that my friend had introduced me to her daughter.

A story that never ceases to amaze me, and to make me contemplate its applications to the way we live now, is that of the Irish Potato Famine. As you doubtless know, this was when a rot hit the potato crop, which was the main foodstuff of the peasantry of the Ireland of that day. People starved by the thousands. And all of this while seafood of all kinds teemed in the sea around that island. But seafood was a low-class thing to eat. And people weren't used to cooking it.

Not just seafood abounded. There were sea vegetables of all kinds. Seaweed. And while this famine was going on, men were vying for the low-paying, hardscrabble job of harvesting seaweed and turning it, laboriously, into iodine.

It never occurred to them to just eat the stuff. Or to just feed it to their starving children. Which seems astonishing, almost unbelievable. Until you look into the history of food everywhere, and find these instances abounding. When settlers of the American West starved because a plague of locusts ate their harvest, to the point where they cooked and ate the leather of their own shoes, and wrote pathetically about shooting coyotes who came in hope of finding them in a weakened state, it never occurred to them to eat a) the locusts themselves, a good source of protein, or b) the coyotes they shot. Instead they ate their shoes. And starved.

Now how could this be? Surely the urge to survive would trump any old stories people told about themselves and their surroundings. But that doesn't seem to be the case. In fact, the case seems to be the opposite—in stressful situations, we cling to the stories we tell about ourselves and about how we can manipulate our world ever more tightly.

I thought about that when I ran out of ideas for what to cook without a kitchen, with just a few utensils sitting on my house's deck, when all I could think was to go out to dinner and have someone else do the thinking for me. I'd looked at that lush row of kale at Indigo Ray's, and only sighed. It never occurred to me to do anything with it but what I had always done—which was braise it in olive oil with sliced garlic and crumbled red pepper, and then squeeze lemon over it.

But, fortunately for me, my friends chorused, "Kale salad!" And I saw a little light bulb go off, and amended my story. But would I have ever thought to have done that without their nudge? I don't know. Which made me thoughtful. How many other assumptions, ruts, and blind spots are all around, trapping me in a life that is less rich than the one I could have if I opened up a bit more? And how much is that true of our culture, too?

Isn't it true that we have our collective hand caught in a collective cookie jar, grasping a fast-decreasing amount of cookies, but with such a terrified grasp that we can't leave the thing where it lies and go looking for more nourishing ways of being that lurk just outside our present vision? I suspect it's very true. But until we let go together, I can't know for sure.

24

THE MANY LESSONS OF KALE SALAD

That kale salad idea is wonderful. And just what I like: healthy, inexpensive, easy to cook, and, above all, flexible—you can play with it a lot, and it's very forgiving. No matter what you throw at it, it wants to help you enjoy yourself, which is a trait I like in a person, let alone a foodstuff.

So I played with that kale salad idea the first time it invited me out. Well, I had to. I had grabbed what I thought was a ginormous amount of the green stuff—Tuscan, lacinato, dinosaur, whatever they're calling it now—out of The Indigo Ray's garden, but found, after I'd made the dressing, that it wasn't as ginormous as it had looked when gathered as a bouquet in my arms. That's the way of greens: when you've gotten them ready, they're a lot less present than they were in the garden or the store.

I'd made a dressing of a pounded garlic clove, a whole can of anchovies and their oil, a few capers, and some black pepper, and a squeeze of half a lemon, all pounded together in the mortar that was sitting in the makeshift kitchen on my deck. And I wasn't paying as much attention as I should have been, which was and is a common enough failing when I'm doing two or three things at once (and who isn't these days? though I think we should really try to stop, and tell you what, I'll start with myself).

I stripped the long dark green leaves off their stems, and then rolled them up approximately cigar style, then shredded them, slicing thinly all the way down. I added them to the bowl where the dressing lurked.

My first mistake.

There just wasn't enough kale to handle all that anchovy and garlic. I pushed the envelope a little too far that time. The problem was I just got cavalier, my default setting was "You can't have too much anchovy and garlic," which proves once again, as if we needed proving, that default settings need to be checked and reset from time to time.

This was such a time. There was DEFINITELY too much anchovy and too much garlic.

Hhhhhmmmmm. Well, I thought. You have to leave this salad to sit and soak up the dressing anyway, so see how it tastes tomorrow (and mentally I decided not to serve it till the day after that—give it and me some time to mellow and get used to each other).

Next day, still way too salty, too garlicky.

Thinking it over, and mulling over the eccentric contents of my refrigerator, I lighted upon a half of a baked potato shoved in there a few nights before. It had been a ginormous potato, and I hadn't been able to eat the whole of it. But it might just be the thing to soak up some of that salt. So I scraped out the pulp, fed the overly hard skin to the dogs as a treat, chopped the pulp and added it to the salad.

Next day, it was definitely better. But still not optimum. That was when I had my brain wave. A can of tuna. Why not? When I thought about it, the dressing I had made was what's called an anchoïade, a garlic and anchovy dip as they serve it in Provence, and of course they're always mixing the stuff with tuna over there. So I added a can of drained tuna, and then added a couple of dashes of sherry vinegar (since I didn't have any more lemon), and a dash more olive oil. Stirred. Put back in the fridge to ripen before dinner.

Served with a beet salad, and a tabouli salad, and a couple of glasses of rosé, it was perfection on a too hot day. We both had seconds, then the Beloved Vegetarian Husband had thirds, which I always like to see.

Once again, another one of those lessons I can't seem to get often enough: when something goes wrong, don't panic. It can always be fixed. And sometimes the fix is much much better (and in this case tastier) than the perfection I set out to achieve.

Luckily.

(Oh, and another lesson, which I have to keep reminding myself, since I am the salt queen and should start trying to abdicate that particular position: when you've added too much salt, judicious addition of something that can soak it up, like cooked potato, pasta, rice, or similar, will often help, as will the even more judicious addition of more acidic tastes, like vinegar or citrus juice. Just to put a mental Post-it on my mental kitchen bulletin board.)

And then there was the disaster that just missed us, though not our neighbors...another flood, the greatest flood in a hundred years, only this time not in our kitchen... The Beloved Vegetarian Husband, aka Alex, now works part of the year in Colorado, and where he goes, the dogs and I go, too. Home is where we all are together, so that's home too. That summer, I stayed longer in Oregon to finish fixing the house, which had been damaged in our own personal flood. Then, as I was driving back with one of our dogs to reunite with him and our other dog in Colorado, the rain came. And flooded all of the town where he worked, turning it into an island, and a muddy one at that... So when I got to that place, all I could do was make:

FLOOD SOUP

It was a king-sized disaster for way too many, but for us, a small one. The worst part was the anxiety we felt when Alex got caught at our home in the biggest flood in Boulder's history, and I was caught on the way there, unable to make the last 100 miles because of road closures and detours. We had a flooded crawl space, but that put us in among the lucky ones. We didn't lose our home, or even any rugs, and we were both safe.

I managed to get home in the break between storms—amazing how the roads clear suddenly, and then, when the rain comes again, clog and close just as fast. But I did get home. Tired and spacey after driving 1,300 miles with my little dog, but happy to be there, happy to see my loved ones, happy to be home...since home is defined as where your loved ones reside. The Beloved Vegetarian Husband had thoughtfully gone out and bought some grocery-store sushi rolls for lunch, so I wouldn't have to think about feeding us. And he suggested we go out to dinner down the street at the local pub, which invitation I accepted gratefully. During dinner we lent a sympathetic ear to stories from our wait-staff about how they had to watch, helpless, as the water roared down the street in front of the restaurant—"right down to where most of us live." Then back home we went, and exhaustedly tumbled into bed.

Next morning, I looked blankly into the refrigerator. Well, there was almost nothing there. "What have you been living on for the last six weeks?" I asked, though, amused, I was pretty sure I knew the answer.

"Oh, you know. The usual. Cheese and salsa sandwiches and granola and bananas for breakfast."

Ah. Thought so. I laughed and started to make a grocery list.

Then it started to rain. Again. Hard. Continuously. You could almost feel the collective anxiety of the county begin to rise. For the moment, it was foolish to think of going outside on the unstable roads, with the sheets of water pouring down. But life goes on, people need to be fed. We were hungry. I'd bought a jar of pickled okra on my way across the country, and we had some of that, with Alex's cheese and the Triscuits he'd been living on. That was lunch. But what were we going to do for dinner? I considered my possible courses of action.

And then, of course, I did what I always do in these circumstances. I rooted around to see what we had. And I made something out of that.

Here was what we had:
◊ 1 old, wrinkled turnip (but turnips can keep a long time, as long as you shave the wrinkles off, they're always good in soup...)

28

◊ 1 almost equally wrinkled potato, with sprouts (see above comment about turnips)

◊ Half a bag of baby carrots (obviously bought as a salad course for the Beloved Vegetarian Husband's cheese sandwich meals)

◊ One wilted celery heart (obviously left from a bunch bought as a … see above)

◊ Half a bottle of spicy tomato juice

◊ A can of beets

I don't know what that says to you, but what it says to me is soup. Especially on a cold, rainy, potentially dangerous day. Soup. Definitely soup.

So this is what I did:

I peeled the old turnip deeply, until the bit left was white. Then I sliced it thinly, and cross cut the slices until they were minced.

Did the same with the potato. This is an excellent thing to know: sprouting potatoes are fine as long as you cut away all the sprouts and green areas. What's left is a great addition to soup.

Cut the brown bits off the celery heart and sliced what was left.

Chopped the baby carrots.

Sautéed all of these in olive oil. Added a little dried thyme and some salt. Wilted them.

Added the juice drained from the beet can. Added some spicy tomato juice.

Added a little juice from the pickled okra jar.

Cooked on low heat until…

All the veggies were tender.

Then I sliced the sliced beets again, and then cut up the slices.

Added them, and rinsed out the beet can with water, added that.

Tasted.

Added a little more spicy tomato juice.

Turned the soup off and waited till dinner…

Then the rain died down, and the water that was knocking at our back door gave up and sank back into the river that was running through our back yard.

To celebrate, we sat in front of the fire, he with a beer, me with a glass of wine.

We toasted the end in sight of the flood. We toasted luck to all those who had lost so much that day. We toasted each other being safe.

Then we sat down and ate our soup.

And Alex looked down at his empty bowl contemplatively, and said, "I'm glad you're home. I was starting to get tired of cheese sandwiches and carrots after all."

This just seems the right way to end a chapter on Food for Disasters…

CHICKEN LIVER MOUSSE AND HIGH ANXIETY

One year, we experienced the worst Christmas Day of either of our lives, and the best Day After, when one of our little dogs got into a neighbor's toxic butter and marijuana pail (?! yes, that's right, and I don't know what it's for either, anyone who does please email me) and disappeared Christmas Eve. He must have thought he was dying, at least judging from the reaction of the other two dogs who had gotten into the same pail, though not quite as greedily. His instinct must have been to go to ground somewhere.

I'd made all sorts of nice things for us to eat Christmas Day. Needless to say, when it started to rain, then threatened to snow, and still no sign of the poor dog (even though we made about a million trips up and down the icy road yelling ourselves hoarse), neither of us could enjoy any of the feast. Well, except for the Christmas whiskey. But that was what you might call comfort food in this sort of situation.

One thing I'd made the day before was Chicken Liver Mousse. The plan was to have it as an appetizer, along with a lot of other little bits and bobs, before dinner, which was roast duck and potato pancakes with sour cream and salmon caviar. But lunchtime came around, and we both—even the vegetarian, mind you—wanted more protein than the planned tomato soup had to offer.

So I toasted a couple of pieces of New Sammy's Cowboy Sourdough, and put them out with a hunk of blue cheese, the pot of chicken liver mousse, and a big pile of cornichons. Tomato soup in mugs at the side.

I couldn't even finish the soup. And the tastes of everything else dulled down almost to sawdust. But there was something comforting about a piece of toast slathered with the mousse, and dotted with pickles. If it wasn't the taste delight it would have been on a happier day, it was soothing to eat. Even the Beloved Vegetarian Husband thought so. At least, so I assumed, as we sat there munching in silence and anxiously looking out the window to see if a little black and gray dog had returned.

We ate the planned dinner, but without much zest, and it was probably the first time in history that Alex didn't compliment me on my potato pancakes. Also the first time in history that I only picked at a small piece of roast duck.

More whiskey after dinner, and then to bed for a night that was punctuated—at one a.m., four a.m., and seven—by drives up and down the road, looking for paw prints in the snow that had begun to fall.

By morning, the snow was a blizzard, and we had just about given up hope, when a neighbor called to say they'd spotted the dog coming out of their woodshed. Ten minutes later he was home, still shaky and groggy and red-eyed, but alive, and, shortly, well.

We cried and laughed with relief, and fed him brown rice cooked in broth, and decided to have Christmas all over again.

And you know what? That tomato soup with toast and chicken liver mousse on the side tasted fantastic. And cold roast duck was a treat that couldn't be beat.

So I give the dual-purpose chicken liver mousse recipe here, as a medicinal lagniappe, and a festive snack, along with wishes that everyone have a safe, happy year, and that no one dear to you or dear to someone you know is harmed.

Chicken Liver Mousse *(you can call it pâté, or spread, or chopped, or whatever your inclination, as long as you enjoy it):*

For one honking big pot of mousse, enough to feed six as appetizers (with toast, crackers, celery sticks, whatever):

◊ 1 lb. chicken livers
◊ 2 cloves of garlic
◊ A sprig of thyme
◊ A bunch of butter
◊ A little cream
◊ A swish of Irish whiskey, or brandy, or port, or sherry, or wine open on your kitchen counter
◊ Salt and pepper

This is easy:

Melt about a half stick of butter in a sauté pan. Trim the fatty bits off the livers. Toss the livers in the pan, and cook at medium heat, turning the livers. Cook about 3 minutes on each side—you want them still pink inside, and smooth (not crusty with heat) on the outside. Add two chopped cloves of garlic and a stripped sprig of fresh thyme (or a little bit of dried). Toss to mix. Add a little cream and let it cook down (this happens fast). Scrape into a food processor, or a blender, and whoosh until smooth. While this is cooling, heat the pan, add a swish of the liquor of your choice, and deglaze what's on the bottom left from the livers. Add that to the smooth chicken livers. Mix. Salt and pepper. Add softened butter to taste, till you get the texture you like. I added about another tablespoon.

Decant the whole thing into a little pot. Melt some butter and pour over the top to make a seal. This will keep it from discoloring, and it just adds unction when you finally dig in.

It keeps about five or six days in the fridge. Take my advice and be sure to have some pickles handy (cornichons are the best, I think), when you finally get around to spreading it on a piece of toast or a cracker. Pickles on top.

(And my own special hint: try spicy Dijon mustard spread on the toast before you add the mousse. Yes.)

You can always tell your vegetarian loved ones that it's made from tofu. Not to fool them, just to give them an excuse. It always works around here, anyway.

By the way, it's great with a little tot of whiskey on the side. But then, practically everything is.

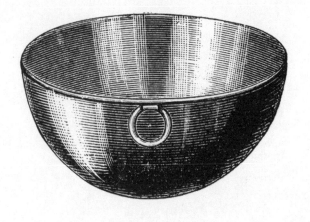

Food for Grief

And then, one of my oldest friends—truly, my best friend, if you rate best friendship by how often and how unjudgmentally the person is there for you, for how many, many years—he and I talked about the death of loved ones, of friends and family, and how it makes us need to nurture ourselves and our loved ones, whether or not this makes rational sense. He laughed and told me that a beloved cousin of his was dying, and that was not why he laughed, but at what he had done when he got home that day from work, after a few days spent going back and forth to the hospital. "I made a pot roast," he said. "Red wine, and carrots, and onions and garlic—you know. And it tasted so good, that before it was done, I'd eaten all the beef, and just left the sauce." He laughed again. "Pretty good gravy I made, though."

We talked about all the friends we had in common who had died, and we remembered the first in our group, an artist, who died from a rare cancer, which it turned out his surgeon father was one of the few specialists in. And even more sadly, oddly, tragically, the same cancer had killed his wife's mother, when his wife—also our much-loved friend—had been just ten years old.

"Do you remember when Bruce died?" my friend asked, as we talked on the phone, me on my deck in the country evening, he in his kitchen in the midst of the city. "I think you were in Oregon then, and you didn't come down here."

I was in Oregon then. I vividly remember hearing that Bruce had died, the first death of someone I knew and loved, and I remember taking to my bed, the conflict being so great inside me I had no other recourse. Whatever had killed Bruce, my body, alarmed, realized for the first time, would kill me too—and I wanted to get out of my body at once. That I couldn't caused pain, and fatigue, and brought me one of my first pieces of valuable wisdom: that it was terror of death that caused so much of what I found inexplicable

35

in the world around me. Because I had that terror then, through and through, and I could see what it would mean.

Ever after, I couldn't look at a skyscraper or a monument without thinking, "Terror of death. They wanted to get out of their bodies, those people who made that thing there." And of course, I wasn't wrong.

"Do you remember I called you from his house?" my friend said. This would have been the house of my dead friend and his wife Tish. Tish, who I had once been in love with the way you are with someone of your own sex who is so much what you are not—a house I had lived in, too, once a very long time ago. My friend went on: "And I said, 'Alison is cooking dinner for us all.'"

No, I said. I don't remember that. I did smile to think of Alison, who also loved Bruce's wife, and who I had known since I was ten years old, and still remember as the sunniest child to ever pass through our school. She was, and is, a sunny adult now, with warmth to spare—just sitting with her makes you smile. I smiled then to think of her, but I didn't remember that Alison had cooked for everyone the night that Bruce died, in the house where we had all lived with Bruce, and with Tish, who is now long dead herself. No, I didn't remember that small part of the scene.

"Then you don't remember what you said back?"

No, I said, and had another meditative sip of wine, wondering would come next.

"You said: 'I wish I was Alison right now.'"

Oh, I said, laughing. Did I say that? That would have been exactly what I thought, what I felt.

And we were both quiet then, thinking about many things that had come and gone, and many things, I think, that would come again…

36

THE NEIGHBOR MEAL

Even in the most devoted cook's life, there comes that inevitable time when, for reasons of anything ranging from the worst tragedies to the simplest ennui, you just can't focus on fixing a meal. Even for those of us who love to cook, and think of it as a high point of the day—sometimes you just wake up and can't do it. Or sometimes someone who lives around you wakes up and just can't do it. Maybe someone broke a limb, or a car broke down, or you've just spent a week cooking for a house full of guests. At any of these times, what comes into its own is the Neighbor Meal.

The Neighbor Meal is one of the warmest, best, and simplest ways of connecting yourself in...well, the neighborhood, however you define that. And you can define it a lot of ways. The immediate vicinity. A group of friends. A group joined together by a common interest. Any group, really, that is connected by a thread of community. And the best way of strengthening that thread is to give or exchange food.

We have a lot of Neighbor Meal traditions in the little alpine valley where I live for most of the year. When a woman has a baby, we do a roster so that she gets enough food to feed the rest of her family for a short period while she settles in with the newborn. (My split pea soup—see below—goes over big here, especially with families with kids. And you can freeze it ultra successfully.) When someone is ill, we all go on the alert and bring food. If someone goes to the hospital, we leave food at their home for the remaining family. All of these things.

I have noticed, in the preparation and presentation of the Neighbor Meal, that the person getting the most out of the gift of food is not always the recipient Neighbor. Quite often, it's me. I'll never forget the courtesy with which The Indigo Ray, in the hospital for a cancer operation many years ago, received a demented, distracted box of lemon squares. I'd completely forgotten that she didn't eat white sugar or white flour, in my total freakout that she was in the hospital at all. But she accepted the gift for what it was:

a way of soothing myself, while I fooled myself into thinking I was soothing her. And I suppose just the fact that I had brought something and was trying to hide my own upset strengthened the bond, too.

And then there was the year when I went to a friend's house, where she was slowly dying of a terrible disease. She couldn't eat solids any longer, she who had loved food as much as I do. I spent two days making three different kinds of soups, liquidizing them carefully, with a necessary obsessiveness: any little bits left unstrained would be a positive danger. The next time I saw her, she could no longer speak, but she wrote out appreciative thanks about the soups, which she claimed to have eaten for a week after I went back to the States. I didn't believe her. I knew those soups had been pecked at by her distracted husband, and then thrown away. But I loved her even more for the grace that knew I needed to be needed right then, and that the only way I could express my own love was in the kitchen. I loved her all the more for knowing and acknowledging that, and the last time I saw her, the day before she died, she wrote vigorously on her white board again about the soup and how good it was. That was all for me. I had meant to comfort her, but she was comforting me. Although maybe, now I think of it, her comforting of me was a comfort for her, too.

So the tapestry, complex and beautiful, is woven from these loving threads.

I thought of this one night when, tired of myself, tired of my own productions, even (gasp!) my food, I gratefully turned to a hamper that my neighbor across the street brought over on Christmas Day. Homemade tamales. Spinach enchiladas. Spicy Spanish rice. Salsa verde. I heated them all up, tossed what lettuce I had with a diced avocado, minced green onions, walnut oil and a squeeze of lime, and crowded everything on a plate. And it was not just entirely delicious (I'm lucky to live in a neighborhood of Extremely Talented Cooks), it was comforting, too…to think that she had packed that basket and brought it over just when I needed it. I had needed it, and the fact of being a part of that neighborhood web fed me as much as the delicious food on my plate. And I think she liked bringing it, too.

In case you want a simple Neighbor Meal to take to someone, here is my recipe, cadged off a bag of split peas, for:

The Perfect Neighbor Meal Split Pea Soup

◊ A pound of split peas
◊ 1 cup chopped celery
◊ 1 cup chopped onion
◊ 1½ cups chopped carrot
◊ A bit of dried thyme
◊ A bit of red pepper or cayenne powder
◊ A bay leaf
◊ Salt
◊ Pepper

Wash and sort the split peas. Put in a large soup pot with 8 cups of water, celery, onion, carrot, thyme (rubbed between your fingers), red pepper, and bay leaf. Bring to a boil, and then simmer for about 45 minutes to an hour, until the peas are tender. Salt. You can mash the peas with a spoon, or blend the soup in a blender or processor, or (what I usually do) just leave them the way they are, since when you reheat the soup, the peas will cook some more and start to dissolve on their own. (It tastes best at this stage, and best of all after you've frozen the soup, thawed it, and reheated.) At the last minute, add fresh ground pepper, and serve with grated cheddar or a dollop of sour cream on top.

If you want, you can add a ham hock to the start of the process. But it's absolutely swell without, and that way you don't have to inquire if the neighbors at the receiving end eat ham.

There is no child in the world who doesn't love this soup. Trust me on this one. And it will comfort you to make it almost as much as it will comfort them to eat it. Trust me on that one, too.

ON GRIEF AND TWICE-BAKED POTATOES

There's this thing about grief: you need to eat what you need to eat when it hits you. But you also need to feed others, if that's the role you have, and this is a juggling act. In my case, I have a Beloved Vegetarian to feed, and I'm happy to do so—but when grief, or indeed, any other trauma, hits me, I have to go with what nourishes me. Which is, in this order: Blue cheese. Unsalted butter, Sourdough bread. Red meat. And that last is the one that is usually most readily to hand.

So, when someone dies—and in the most recent case (though goodness knows, we've seen a lot of death around here the last few years), the someone was my father, after a traumatic week of his being constantly, conscientiously, and painfully attended by the medical profession—I really really really needed some red meat. And some wine. Together. Yes. In a vegetarian household.

You may know the way I serve myself here. A big salad (on this particular night, a garlic/sherry vinegar/walnut oil dressing mixed with diced avocado, diced tomato, one scallion, torn basil and marjoram, roasted pine nuts, and grated Parmesan, tossed with greens), accompanied by a seared piece of rib steak topped with a garlic clove mashed into a tablespoon of butter. Well, that was for me. The Bereaved. Also accompanied by a honking big portion—indeed, a half-bottle portion—of beefy red wine.

But for the loved one. No matter how carried away I get by my own grief, or even my own worries, I still constantly consider the meals of my Beloved.

And this was no exception. *So this is what I did:*

TWICE BAKED POTATOES TO BE SERVED TO ONE'S VEGETARIAN LOVED ONE ON THE EVE OF ONE'S FATHER'S DEATH:

Shove three potatoes into a toaster oven at 450°, after they have been scrubbed and pricked with forks to keep them from exploding.

Make the salad dressing, add the greens on top of crossed salad implements to be tossed at the last minute.

Sit down for an hour or so while the taters cook and have a few glasses of red wine. Speak freely about the Loved Dead.

When the potatoes are done (and they are done and stay done for a long time in the oven, so don't fuss too much about timing here), take them out of the oven, split them, and scrape out the potato insides. Mash these with a mashed garlic clove, some sliced mild onions of any kind (scallions, onion tops, chives…shallots…whatever you have), some chopped herbs (parsley? cilantro? whatever's in the fridge), some butter, some milk or cream or both, whatever you have, salt and pepper…and then pile these mashed insides back into the potato shells. Sprinkle with paprika, or, better yet, smoked Spanish paprika. Ten minutes before dinner, put back in a 350° oven to reheat. Stick under a broiler if you want browning on the top.

In the meantime, if you are a worried carnivore, broil your steak.

Then serve your Vegetarian Beloved with salad and potato, and yourself with steak and salad.

Glasses of wine for both of you, at will.

Most important of all: turn off the phones and computers.

Eat in silence, appreciating the flavors, and each other, and the fact that you're both alive.

And then sleep well before heading out for the funeral, and all that entails.

Bon appétit.

SKIRT STEAK

When I was a little girl, there were certain foods that meant festivity to me, and that I still crave when feeling a bit battered by life. Inari sushi, rice balls wrapped in fried tofu skins, is one—ever since the day Teruyo, the kind woman who cleaned our house, brought the five-year-old me a box as a surprise. Soy-sauce-baked chicken, as made with the frequency you would expect from a harassed mother of a large and greedy family, which I always thought was a heritage dish from her Asian past, until I discovered it in James Beard's *American Cookery* as one of the quick 'n' easy dishes that newlywed wives of the Fifties turned to in a similar pinch.

But most of the dishes, I find when I think about them, were my father's. In true Fifties husband fashion, he only cooked on Sundays and holidays, so his cuisine had an unfair advantage over my harassed mother's. (Now that she's not forced to cook, her cooking has changed completely, being innovative and delicious, another clear and compelling reason why no one should ever be forced to do things for duty that they could do, if everyone would just relax, for pleasure.) I still remember his raisin sauce for ham, his wilted lettuce salad (heavy on the bacon and green onions), his sage-seasoned turkey stuffing, and, of course, his navy bean soup—made the day after the feast with the remnants of the ham. Then there was his Yorkshire pudding, which rose higher than any Yorkshire pudding I have seen since (except that of my brother Peter, who seems to have inherited the knack—see his recipe p. 224).

What I remember most, though, and have always craved, is his way of cooking skirt steak. This is a cut from the meaty part of the cow's diaphragm, kind of looking like a pleated accordion—the pieces are long and thin and marbled with membrane holding it together. For the longest time between my childhood, when this was the dish most requested for birthdays in our house, and my adulthood, you couldn't find a piece of skirt steak at a meat counter anywhere. Out of fashion, I guess. I don't know why it went out of favor and disappeared, but somewhere in there, about twenty years ago, it started showing up again, this time wrapped in pinwheels and skewered into shapes, to be cooked…well, I was never sure how. I didn't care. I just bought the pinwheels, unraveled them, and happily went back to recreating my father's dish.

What he had done was cut the long strip into smaller, manageable pieces, just big enough so three was a wonderful helping for a hungry child, four even better, and five leading to the kind of repletion we all associate with festivals. And then he would sauté them in a mix of butter and oil (or, more probably, margarine and oil, since that was what we ate in those long lost days of the early Sixties), using the lovingly-cared-for, square cast-iron pan in which he cooked many of his magic dishes. When they were browned and savory, he salted them, and turned them out onto the plate, glistening and beefy.

They were deliciously livery, unlike any other cut of beef I had then or since. But when I did finally find them, all pinwheel-constricted in my supermarket's display case, and released them into my own sauté pan, conscientiously frying them quickly over high heat, so that they were wonderfully browned on the outside and rare on the inside, the way I liked all my beef, they just didn't taste…quite right. I couldn't figure it out. I tried again and again. They were good. But they weren't the skirt steaks of my childhood.

I tried cutting them in bigger pieces. Then in smaller pieces. I tried different kinds of oil. But there was something missing.

I called my father.

"Oh," he said. "The thing about skirt steak? You have to cook it till well done. Not dried out—but not rare either."

"You're kidding," I said. "But…"

"AND," he said, not letting me finish. "The secret is: you have to use GARLIC SALT."

Gasp.

I was going through a phase at that point where I could out-food-Nazi any passing food Nazi. I knew exactly what kinds of dishes you were supposed to eat if you were in the slightest bit in the know, and I knew how to cook them—so I thought, with that wonderfully obtuse tunnel vision of the Young Cook. Garlic salt was a complete no-no. All those preservatives. Tsk. And well-done beef? What, was he crazy? Was it possible? How could my father tell me this, who had hovered over every roast beef of my childhood with loving care to make sure that it never got past a certain rare phase of rosy goodness?

Still, when I tried to cook those deconstructed pinwheels my way, I had to admit, it just wasn't working out.

Then one day in the local Co-op I found a jar of ORGANIC garlic salt. Hallelujah. I was freed from worrying I would be letting down the side by just going to Safeway and getting one of those red-capped jars filled with chemicals (by the way, I never bothered to read the ingredients lists on those jars; for all I know they are pure garlic and salt—ah, youth!). At this point, I was willing to go all the way. So I bought another one of those pinwheels, unraveled it, cut it up into pieces, and, sprinkling it with the PURE garlic salt, proceeded to cook it in a cast-iron pan, in a mix of butter and oil, to a beefy glistening striped brown on both sides. Then I held my breath, turned down the heat under the pan, and cooked till well-done.

Put it on a plate. Dug in—cutting lengthwise, the way I'd always liked it as a child, rather than across the grain of the meat, the way every book told me I was supposed to.

And there it was: the skirt steak of my childhood. In all its glory. I can still see the testimonial in a handwritten book of what I cooked each day that I used to keep back then: "Against all odds," it admitted, "the garlic salt was the secret."

There's a postscript to this, though. Years later, I was discussing skirt steak with my father. And he shook his head wisely, and said: "Of course, the only way to cook skirt steak is very quickly, so it's still rare. That way it's tender."

I looked at him, astonished. "But...but...you told me the only way to cook it was well-done."

"Did I?" he said. "Then I must have changed my mind."

So now I cook it both ways. And it's true: well-done makes it taste particularly livery, which I love. And rare...makes it tender and wonderful. Both ways are great. But now that my father is gone, when I want to remember him and the way he would cook my favorite dishes for my childhood birthdays, I cook it well-done. With garlic salt.

Like this:

Take a nice piece of skirt steak, about half a pound per person if you're planning on wishing you'd made more. Two-thirds of a pound per person if you're serving real skirt steak lovers. (Fortunately, this cut has come back into fashion, and you can find it at any decent butcher's. What a relief.)

Cut the long strip into manageable pieces, say three to four inches across.

Heat a good heavy skillet on the stove. Cast iron is the best. No need to use nonstick for this.

When it's hot, add some oil and a dollop of butter. Sunflower oil is good. Peanut oil would be fine. Olive oil, while untraditional, tastes great in my opinion.

When the oil/butter sizzles, add the steaks. Salt generously with garlic salt, or sprinkle with garlic powder and salt. Brown to beautiful bronze stripes.

Turn over. Keep over the high heat for a minute, then turn down and cook till well done, still a little rosy in the middle, but not dry.

That's the classic. If you like it rare, just sear the other side and cook for three minutes at a higher heat.

Turn out and enjoy.

It's lovely poured with the juices over shredded lettuce and sliced avocado. Totally against tradition. But then, as my father pointed out, who needs to be shackled by that?

(And by the way, ignore those cookbooks that say this is a cut better braised. I mean, it might be fine braised, but why do you want to bother with all that, when this is the dish that five out of five Catholic children agreed was their idea of a true feast? I mean, why?)

CANDIED WALNUTS

And while I'm on the subject of foods that are more than just something to eat, something that conveys more than nutrition, conveys love, the best example of that in my own life are my Aunt Celia's candied walnuts. Delicious. Sugary. Buttery. Addictive. Somewhere back in the dim fogs of my childhood, she made these for all of us, and the response was so wholeheartedly in favor, she was doomed to make them for the rest of her life—with love. As she was my godmother, I felt a particular right to demand them, and so just before every Christmas, no matter where I was, a small parcel would arrive in the mail containing a tin of her candied walnuts.

Somewhere in my early forties, my tastes changed somehow, and the walnuts tasted too sugary to me. I never had any trouble getting other people to eat them, though—they were still as delicious as ever; I don't know what had happened to my taste buds. And I wondered—it was so much trouble for her, this shelling of the walnuts every year and the sugaring of them, and the packing of them in a tin, and the mailing them off to me—maybe I should find a way to let her off the hook she had been on for, oh, probably more than twenty years at that point.

The Beloved Husband and I discussed this seriously. And we concluded (and how glad I am that we came to that conclusion) that the point of the candied walnuts was not calories, but Love. With a capital 'L'. Neither of us was willing to give up that manifestation of it from my godmother. It had come to mean Christmas to us both.

Then, as mysteriously as my tastes had changed, they changed back again, somewhere around when I turned fifty. And I loved those walnuts every bit as much as I had loved them as a child. The Beloved Husband found the same mysterious change happening in him. Like magic. How glad we were that we had never said anything in those strange, puritanical years where we had a lurking feeling that sugar was an enemy! (And so it is, like so many other things, when there is too much of a good thing.)

Before she died, when she knew she was dying, my godmother typed up the recipe for candied walnuts, as well as for her Green Mold—another well-loved feasting dish in our family (see recipe below, p. 166). And she made copies for all of us, and signed them, and gave us each our own—a farewell present from the most loving woman I have ever had the luck to have known, and been cared for by.

The first Christmas after she was gone, every time we drove past our mailbox three miles up the road, we would both say, "How can it be Christmas? There isn't going to be a tin of candied walnuts in the mailbox from Aunt Celia." Still, it was Christmas. But it would never be the same. Fine, yes. Lovely, too. But not the same. Which is the way it is with the years, isn't it?

But I still have her recipe. And here it is, as she typed it herself:

Candied Walnuts

Have 6½ to 7 cups of shelled walnuts ready.

Butter a large platter or a large piece of foil.

In a big pan combine: 2 cups dark brown sugar
1 cup granulated sugar
½ cube butter
5½ oz. evaporated milk

Cook over medium heat, stirring occasionally, until mixture forms a sticky ball when dropped in cold water. Say a Hail Mary. Remove pan from heat, add walnuts and stir so that walnuts are coated with the sugar mixture. Turn onto buttered platter (or foil) and separate nuts.

Cecilia F. Torres

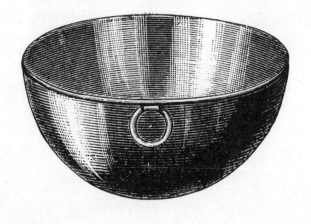

Food for Home

SEX AND FOOD

Really, there's nothing nicer than having sex with a loved one, followed by a lovely meal à deux.

All the better if the lovely meal is in your own home, and you can both sit down to it wearing your bathrobes.

And even better if the lovely meal scents the house increasingly with enticing food smells during the actual act.

I mean, think about it. What's wrong with making love before dinner, rather than after, when you're both probably too full and too tired anyway, or one of you wants to get on the computer, or one of you wants to finish reading the paper, or you both just would rather call it a night? It's nice, every so often, to make some time special for…er…interaction. And, as always, to follow it with a very nice meal.

This of course means you've got to clear the decks. Kids have to be sent off to slumber parties, grandma's house, etc. Phones turned off. Cares dispelled (as much as possible, even if only temporarily). Then you've got this space to concentrate on each other and provide a playground for the two of you.

Naturally, this is another one of those happy moments where you realize that we really are better off than the richer Victorians. Imagine having all those servants and trying an evening like this? You'd have to give them all the day off. And the cook would want to know, suspiciously, what you'd been up to in her kitchen while she was gone.

But you don't have to worry about any of that. This is the good thing about not having master/servant relations in a culture. So don't let me catch you fantasizing about having enough money to hire unlimited help. Who's going to manage that help, I ask you? Better to just concentrate on managing ourselves, I reckon.

And on having a very good time on our time off.

To which we now turn.

I don't have the slightest intention of giving any kind of insight into what should happen in the more private part of this particular kind of festivity. You'll have your way, and I have mine. But what I can do is give you a couple of suggestions about what to cook for the dinner afterwards. That I know something about, that's applicable across all ages, classes, sexual orientations. I do know a practical thing or two about how to orchestrate that.

First off, you want something simple that can cook unattended for at least an hour. If not more. Without much fuss at the end (you're not going to feel like fussing in the kitchen, after, at least we hope not—we hope you'll be in a happy daze and more in the mood for drifting from one thing to the next). Also, you want something that will smell increasingly good as the time goes on. It adds to the total experience.

So you basically want a stew, or a casserole. Roasted meats are fine, but be careful about the ones that have to be basted. You don't want to all of a sudden think, as your loved one whispers sweet nothings in your ear, that you really need to turn the chicken on its side and slather it with some butter (well, maybe you do, but that kind of thing is beyond the scope of this inquiry). Chile relleno casserole, like the one in the first *Jam Today*, is a good choice here. It can go in the oven with the refried beans, after you've laid out a couple of plates with lime wedges and shredded lettuce waiting to receive it. The smells are great with that.

Roasted vegetables are another terrific option. Make a garlic mayonnaise before, to dip everything in. Shove a few scrubbed and pierced baking potatoes in the oven, with a pan filled with various other vegetable options tossed with olive oil, and let it all cook away. Serve with a simple salad and the garlic mayonnaise after. Go crazy with the garlic. After all, it's just the two of you.

A big vat of simmering soup's a good idea, too. Or a baked polenta dish.

Or…sliced peeled potatoes layered with garlic-infused cream and nutmeg. (Just chop the garlic up small or mortar it, and add cream, salt, and ground nutmeg.) Push the potatoes down in the cream. Turn the oven on to 400°. For a salad on the side, grate some carrots, mix them with some chopped parsley, squeeze some lemon over the whole. Sit down to a glass of wine with your loved one. When the oven is heated, pop the potatoes in, retire to the playground of your choice.

An hour later, the house smells of mildly roasting garlicky cream.

Emerge, rosy-faced and happy, in bathrobes (optional). Serve the potato gratin on a few shredded lettuce leaves. Carrot salad on the side. Another glass of wine.

Speak softly and pleasantly as you eat. Smile reminiscently from time to time. Don't be in a big hurry to turn the phone(s) back on.

There. Love and food go so well together. Why not? They're both as important to the human body as it is possibly important for a thing to be.

And, more importantly, they both mean home.

MIXED MARRIAGES AND THE SAUSAGE SANDWICH

By mixed marriages, of course, I refer to the one joining two wildly diverse sides: the vegetarian and the carnivore.

The other day, I had a chat with my butcher—my butcher!—about this. He was depressed, he said, because his girlfriend was a vegetarian, and she never let him hear the end of it.

That is sad, I consoled him. But not inevitable. Really, if there's going to be a fight about what you eat as a couple, there's probably something else going on, other than self-righteous belief in the rights of the cow, or aggressive condemnation of airy fairy highfalutin' food fads. These things tend to mask something much more creepy: a desire to dominate. I mean, if you can't let your loved ones go their own way, when it's not hurting you or them, you've got to ask yourself why. Why exactly is it so important to you that your loved one eats the same way you do?

Well, of course there's one practical reason. It's a bore to constantly cook two different sets of meals. And not only is it a bore, but it's actively disunifying. Having a meal together is not really about the food, if you know what I mean. It's about Having a Meal Together. This is why we teach children (or we should, anyway) that when they're invited to other people's tables, it is rude to make a point of their own likes and dislikes: just get on with liking what's on offer, and avoid anything that brings on allergic reactions. But you don't dictate to others what they're going to feed you.

Conversely, it is an act of kindness not to dictate to those you feed. A certain flexibility and partnership is what's called for here. In this, of course, as in all else in life, come to think of it. If you really love those you're feeding, you'll tend to be quite anxious that they get fed what they like, as well as what's good for them.

What's good for one person is not necessarily good for another, of course. So every once in a while, I just have to make, not two separate meals, but two separate courses, followed by one unified set of foodstuffs. It's the only way to deal with diversity.

Take myself and the Beloved Vegetarian Husband. He thrives, and I mean absolutely supernaturally thrives, on a diet of not too much fat, many potatoes, and lots and lots of vegetables. Accompanied by pints of artisanal beer and lashings of ice cream to follow.

Beer makes me feel like I'm drinking liquid bread. I can take ice cream in moderation, but not in the boatloads he happily downs (and never shows, by the way, something that would be very annoying if I wasn't so fond of him). I like potatoes, but they're not the Ur-Food of my people. I love fat, particularly full-fat cheeses. I adore vegetables. But if I had to live on them, I would turn, in a short period of time, into an anemic wreck.

This is just the truth. When I'm stressed, I need to eat some meat. I find I don't like to eat meat every night, but when I want it, I really have to have it.

Hence the conversation with the butcher. I had spotted a nice piece of hanger steak, which looked like, as I said to him, "A piece of meat just calling out to be eaten by the sole carnivore in the family while the vegetarian has a nice mashed potato/garlic/cream/cheddar cheese baked casserole." (And on the side, a big romaine/walnut/blue cheese salad, and a bit of beet and dill salad, too.)

That was when my butcher got all sad on me and said the bit about his girlfriend. As I say, I consoled him as best I could, but as I walked away from that market, I couldn't help think that relationship wasn't going to go the distance. I could see some nice tolerant girl who appreciated that he has an actually useful job snapping him up, and that other girl going on to run off with her yoga instructor.

Something like that.

And maybe the nice tolerant girl is a vegetarian, too. And maybe they have a really good time together (I started fantasizing about this, about how they'd hang out together on his days off from butchering, maybe having a drink of something in the back yard while the barbeque heats up). And maybe for supper one night, when neither of them felt much like cooking, they would make something that we have here once in a while: a barbequed sausage sandwich and a barbequed portobello mushroom sandwich. Both wrapped in pita bread that's been slathered with Dijon mustard and covered with fried onions. And on the side, some potato salad with dill, and a big green salad that includes chopped bits of whatever vegetables have been left in the refrigerator.

Like this:

◊ Sausages
◊ Portobello mushrooms
◊ Pita bread
◊ Onions
◊ Cheese (optional)
◊ Dijon mustard
◊ Olive oil
◊ A little soy sauce, salt and pepper

Heat the barbeque.

Slice thinly as many onions as you like. At least three for the two of you. Put them in olive oil on low heat in a heavy pan and let them cook for as long as it takes to get them smelling great and turning a nice mahogany color. You can always turn off the heat when they get there, and then turn it back on and give them a quick stir to reheat before the actual sausage/ mushroom event. (By the way, I like to add a little soy sauce before the final heat-up.)

Now, to proceed to said event:

Take the sausage of your choice. Better take two just in case.

Put them on one side of the barbeque.

Take the portobello mushrooms of your choice (definitely take two, at least, but more will never be harmful; they're great cold later) and roll them in some olive oil.

Put them on the other side of the barbeque.

While they're cooking, heat up as many pita breads as you think you're going to need. I generally just do two. I wrap them in foil and stick in the toaster oven at 325° for about fifteen minutes. Twenty-five minutes if they were frozen to start with.

When the sausages and the mushrooms are just about done, add some sliced cheese to the tops of the mushrooms you're going to eat that dinner. I like to crumble some blue cheese on top, since that's what the Beloved Husband likes best. Well, that and/or pepper Jack. Your choice.

Shut the barbeque lid to let the cheese melt. Spoon out the potato salad onto the plates. Toss the salad with chopped vegetables that have been marinating in the dressing (in this case, leftover asparagus, sliced). Put that on the plates. Put the pita breads out, slather with Dijon mustard, heap with onions.

Then on the carnivore's plate, plunk down the two sausages. Right on the onions on the pita bread. On the vegetarian's, do the same with the mushrooms.

Meanwhile, have your other half pour out the drinks preferred. (Beer for the vegetarian, in our house, and a glass of red wine for the carnivore.)

Sit down and have at it.

Congratulate yourself silently on your tolerance, and try not to be too envious of the other person's sandwich. Remember, you don't need to be doctrinaire about this. If one of you wants a bite of the sandwich across the way, we trust that Love and Generosity will prevail. On both sides.

As, we hope, it will in other areas of life as well.

Of course, since I live with a Beloved Vegetarian Husband, vegetables in many different guises appear in our household. And this is an excellent circumstance, since vegetables are a marvel of deliciousness, in my opinion. For example: cabbage.

IN PRAISE OF CABBAGE

A cabbage is a marvelous thing.

Not only is it beautiful—I mean, look at it, all pale jade and creamy white—and versatile—think, just think of the things that can be done to it (more on that in a minute)—and delicious (also more in a minute)—and readily available almost all year. Not only is it all of these things, but, as if these things were not enough, cabbage is not particularly hard on the budget. In fact, it modestly offers itself as a help to anyone eking out the last bits of their allotted cash for the week's food. Even organic cabbage. Really.

Cabbage is one of my favorite foods. It is, as M.F.K. Fisher would say, a friend. Now why is this? Well, all of the above. But mainly because it's delicious. It's even delicious after you've bought it on Monday, and forget you have it till the following Friday. It sits there, patiently, waiting for you to remember it—unlike more fragile lettuces. It's so forgiving. And so multicultural. There's not a cuisine in the world you can't use cabbage to enhance.

It's good sliced thinly and added to soups. Still sliced thinly, it's great wilting underneath hot cooked meats. Grated, it's fabulous as a crunchy element in a burrito or a rice wrap or even sushi. It's a welcome element in any stir-fry. Coleslaw, of course, in all of its myriad, delicious permutations. If you're willing to go the exotic distance with it, it makes terrific kimchi. And sauerkraut. Who could forget sauerkraut?

All of these things. My, how I admire the cabbage.

I thought of all this, and of how happy it makes me to have a cabbage handy in the refrigerator, one week when I didn't have time to spare from a full workload to go to town and stock up again on fresh vegetables. I had a few left, but it was going to be at least three days before I could head down the mountain again and buy some lettuce and zucchini and corn.

But there was the cabbage. And I used that cabbage for three completely different things. Each one of them superb in its own way. Easy. Delicious. Handy.

How I love the cabbage.

First was **Cabbage Cilantro Slaw**. Alas, I cannot remember where I first got the idea for this. I know it was a newspaper recipe, but what newspaper, when, and where the original has got to over the years I can't any longer tell. I do remember being struck immediately with what a good idea it was to mix cilantro with scallions and cabbage. And the dressing was so similar to one I used already for lettuce that I could taste it immediately on my mind's palate. That it was even better on my mouth's palate was just all to the good.

Like this:

Thinly slice a half a cabbage and two or three scallions. Chop as much cilantro as you think you're going to like (add more than you think you're going to like; it's even better that way). Mince a green chile if you have one, jalapeno or serrano. Put in a bowl.

Make the dressing: Mash a clove of garlic with some pepper and salt. Add a tablespoon of lime or lemon juice (I like lime the best here). A tablespoon of soy sauce. Two tablespoons of a bland oil (I use either sunflower or walnut oil, depending on supplies and how I'm feeling).

Toss.

This is terrific with any number of things. As one of an offering of different salads. Alongside a dish of noodles with peanut sauce. Next to a piece of soy-sauce-cooked chicken, or even just a simple grilled steak. And of course, it's excellent rolled in a heated whole-wheat tortilla for a quick lunch. That may be the way I like it the best.

Come to think of it, I like the second cabbage dish I'm going to tell you about rolled in a heated whole-wheat tortilla for lunch. Only this time, the tortilla is spread thinly with a little hoisin sauce and layered with a slivered scallion.

That would be **Sautéed Cabbage**.

Like this:

Slice as much cabbage as you'd like, but not thinly—about an inch wide is right, I think. Heat a wok or a skillet over high heat. Add the oil of your choice—anything is good here, olive or peanut or sunflower or even duck fat (it's been known to happen around here). Add some salt. Throw in a slice of ginger. When the ginger lets out a good smell, throw in the cabbage. Sauté over the high heat till it's covered in the fat, then lower the heat to medium, continuing to toss, until it's good and wilted. At this point, if you want, you can add as much Szechuan hot bean sauce as you like—if you like, of course (that should go without saying, but, on the other hand, it can't be said enough). Right before you're about to take it off the heat, season to taste with soy sauce. Let that cook just enough so it softens on the cabbage, but not so much that it burns.

Serve as is as a side dish. Or wrap in a tortilla with hoisin sauce and scallions as I suggested above.

Yummy.

The third way I used the cabbage was the simplest, but I am not sure it wasn't the best. I just shredded what was left and put it on a warm plate. Then I put a serving of roast duck on top of it. A quarter of lime on the plate. And when I'd finished the duck, I spritzed the lime on top of the cabbage, and ate it as a salad, with the warm duck drippings mixing with the lime in a particularly enticing way.

How I love the cabbage. Yes, indeed. How anyone could overlook it, or think it a boring vegetable, or even regard it with only tepid affection is something I can never understand.

Then there's kale. Which is another form of cabbage—or at least a first cousin. When combined with potatoes, what could be a better food for everyday? What, in fact, could be better than—

Potato and Kale Soup…or Caldo Verde…or Tuscan Potato Soup

Anyone who knows me knows this bedrock fact of my personality: I love anything that makes something big out of something apparently small. I loathe those dishes that include every conceivable expensive ingredient; I would have been hell at a Victorian dinner party, turning my nose up at everything but a dish of sautéed spinach, probably.

And one of the classic dishes that makes something out of practically nothing, the whole being way way way greater than the sum of its parts, is the Portuguese national soup Caldo Verde. Which boils, literally, down to this: Potatoes. Water. Cabbage.

Yep, that's it.

I love it. I loved it when we were in Portugal, where they serve it with every possible meal. They use a special kind of cabbage over there, and the basic concept is you boil hell out of the potatoes in water and olive oil until they puree themselves, then you shred the cabbage as thinly as you can (they sell specially shredded cabbage just for this in Portuguese markets), then right before you serve, dump the shreds into the boiling potato soup, cook quickly till done, not more than a few minutes, salt, generously pepper, and serve.

That's the basic dish.

I do fiddle with it, enriching it a bit at home, but it's still the same comforting, healthy, sustaining, economical dish it is in its homeland.

My version amps up the taste a bit. And I use my favorite kind of kale in place of the unobtainable Portuguese cabbage (though you can use regular drumhead cabbage, or other greens, as long as you sliver them as thinly as you can). My favorite kind of kale, of course, is called by various names: dinosaur kale, lacinato kale, black kale, Tuscan kale. That last is the result of the first few names not really making it from a marketing perspective.

My dear friend Teri and I have a joke about this. When you can't sell something, call it Tuscan. She once sent me a picture of a billboard advertising a Tuscan mobile home park. In Oregon.

So if I can't get you to make this soup when it's called Potato and Kale soup, how about when it's called Caldo Verde? You don't really need me to call it Tuscan potato soup, do you? I will, though, if you want me to.

It doesn't matter what you call it, as long as you enjoy it after all.

Here's how.

◊ Potatoes
◊ Olive oil
◊ A minced onion
◊ A minced garlic clove or two
◊ A bunch of Tuscan kale
◊ Salt
◊ Pepper

Take about 4 to 6 russet potatoes. Peel and cut up whatever way you like, add to water*, with two or more tablespoons of good olive oil, a minced onion, and a minced garlic clove or two. Boil hard to start with to combine the oil with the water, then turn down heat to medium. Cook to a fine mush, salting to taste. Feel free to mush the ingredients down to taste with a fork or big spoon or potato masher. Before serving, shred a bunch of Tuscan kale, de-stemmed, as thinly as you can manage. Add and boil for about three minutes till the kale is cooked. Add pepper to taste.

Delicious. Perhaps even more delicious is you add to it, as my friend Cindy does, sliced sautéed chorizo sausage. This is a matter of debate between me and the Beloved Vegetarian Husband. We agree, though, that whichever way you slice it, it's going to be good. Trust me on this one.

Happy eating.

*About that water. It's particularly good if it's water that you've saved from cooking vegetables. (All those vitamins! Saved! Add flavor!) What I like to do is cook a vegetable hash for one dinner, parboiling the potatoes and greens for the sautéed hash in the same water, which, after they're removed, I then leave on the stove overnight in its pot—don't worry, it's just veggie water; it won't go bad—throwing the potatoes, onion and garlic for this soup in the next day for lunch. Only one pot! Two meals! You don't even have to move it to the refrigerator! Save time, eat well! Another one of my many mottoes...

Then there are carrots. How I love carrots. Especially:

PICKLED CARROTS—Easy, Fun, Tasty, Do It Today!

We are one of those households that always has a five-pound bag of organic carrots sitting on the bottom shelf of the refrigerator. Why, you ask? Well, aside from the fact that we really, really, really like carrots, when in situ in our Oregon home base, we're also half an hour from the nearest store—and carrots keep really, really, really well. Also, in the winter, they brighten all that desperately depressing limp-looking produce that makes its way so flavorlessly from the central California industrial organic fields. (Does that industrial organic stuff ever have any taste? Well, it's good for fresh and organic when I can't get anything else, but if I can get something else, something local, even something more expensive and local, that's what I do. And I never regret it, either.)

Anyway, the best five-pound bags of carrots up here in the snowy winter wastes of southern Oregon come from a reasonably local, reasonably family-ish farm in northern California. They're more expensive than the industrial organic bags, but, as I say, they are so, so worth it. How worth it, you ask? Well, when I put out carrot sticks at lunch that come from the local bag, Alex, also known as the Beloved Vegetarian Husband, actually looks up from whatever he's reading and says, "Why do these carrots taste so good?"

From a man who has been known to eat disgusting plastic packaged sandwiches for days on end while traveling, not discriminating between cheese and pickle, and olive and cream cheese (and they are, indeed, hard for even a discerning palate to discriminate between, at least if said palate is blindfolded), this is praise of an extraordinary order.

So, needless to say, when these carrots are available (and they start to come in around mid-February), I buy them by the sack-load. First I fish out all the tiny, slender, pretty little carrots from the bag (they're all different sizes, usually), and serve them unpeeled but scrubbed alongside soups or sandwiches for lunch. I peel and shred the larger carrots, and put them on top of whole-wheat tortillas, under refried beans and chopped cilantro/green onions/avocado, with a little shredded cheese, also for lunch. Or I shred them and make them into a salad: lemon/thyme/olive oil dressing; or lime juice/soy sauce/chili oil; or lemon juice and walnut oil; or just a good plain red wine vinegar vinaigrette. Or I slice them and cook them in a little water and butter, add powdered ginger and brown sugar, turn up the heat and sauté till the water disappears and the carrots are nice and browned, then I toss with lots of chopped parsley...for a dinner veggie side dish. Or, of course, my favorite shredded carrots cooked in cream (see the original *Jam Today*; that recipe alone is worth paging through it, if I do say so myself). There are about a hundred and fifty other things I do with those carrots. But for now, I'm only going to tell you about one...one of the more useful ones, in fact.

This is for those carrots at the end of the bag. The ones that are starting to look a little tired, but not so tired that I move them over into the dog stodge bag with the ends and peelings of their fellows that will go into the dogs' food when I make it up. The carrots that are still good, but not perky enough to make me want to make them into raw salads.

Pickled Carrots.

This is a great recipe. I found it originally in a Mexican cookbook for pickled zucchini, which, given the zucchini situation around here at the height of the growing season, has always come in very handy. These aren't the kind of pickles you store in jars; these are the kind you make up quickly, stick in a glass bowl in the refrigerator, stir a little every day for one or two or three days, and then eat. Simple. Tasty. Cheap. My favorite kind of recipe.

First take however many carrots you feel like pickling. For two of us, and the way we use them, I'll usually use about five or six medium ones. But the quantity doesn't matter; it's the technique here, which is as follows:

◊ Carrots
◊ An onion
◊ A clove of garlic (or two or three)
◊ A few tablespoons of bland oil
◊ Vinegar
◊ Dried oregano
◊ Salt

Slice your carrots however thick you like them. (I like them thin because I like the vinegary flavor to penetrate all the way through.)

Slice an onion, or a part of an onion, if you have one handy.

Crush a clove or two or three of garlic.

Heat up a few tablespoons of oil in a skillet you can cover later. Throw in the carrots and the onion. Cook, stirring from time to time, over medium heat for about three minutes. Now throw in the garlic cloves.

Salt.

Turn the heat down to low, cover the pan, let the carrots cook till tender—this will depend on how young and what size your carrots are. Check them from time to time and give them a stir to keep them from sticking.

When they're tender, turn the whole mess out into a glass storage container to keep in the fridge. I like a shallow rectangular one for this particular use.

Now pour in vinegar—red wine vinegar is great—about halfway up the carrots.

Sprinkle with dried oregano. Make sure the oregano has got a good, strong, resinous oregano-ey smell. Mexican oregano is the best here, or good-quality organic oregano (though I have to admit, I like the stuff in the bags you buy at Mexican markets the best).

Give the whole thing a stir. Put in the refrigerator. For the next 48 hours, when you think of it, give the carrots another stir. After about two days, they're ready to eat…they're not pickled enough before that for my taste, but you'll have your own ideas.

And how do you eat them? Our favorite way is on top of refried beans on tortillas, with a little sour cream garnish, for lunch. But they're good as a side salad, too. Or mixed into a green salad. Or…or…or…

They're just plain good. And try it with zucchini, too…zucchini season will be here upon us before we know it. That being the way it is with seasons, after all.

Then there's…

ACORN SQUASH

I love acorn squash. It's my favorite kind of winter squash. (Although I can hear someone out there saying, "What kind of person HAS a favorite winter squash?") That means, you know, the hard shell kind that can keep for a bit longer on your kitchen counter before you cook them—though it's better to eat them as fresh as possible, as I have found this year. For some reason, there was a lot of acorn squash this autumn in the market in Colorado, where we live part of the year, and it proved in the cooking to be amazingly sweet. Even raw, when I tasted the little bits still clinging to the knife when I cut one open. (And be careful cutting them open: damn, they're not called hard shell for nothing.)

If I have the time, and I think of it, a baked acorn squash is a great cold-day lunch for the Beloved Vegetarian Husband and me. One of those little dark green and gold suckers cut in half (renewed warning: careful with that cutting), and smeared with a little butter or olive oil, and drizzled with a little honey or maple syrup or sprinkled with a little brown sugar, and then baked like hell for about an hour at 400°, and you have a lovely autumn bronze and orange dish in its own personal shell. You can cook it longer than an hour, and all it does is collapse in a comfortable sort of way. I like to baste it a little with the melted butter when it's near done…and I like to spear the sides with a fork so the buttery/brown sugary glaze sinks into the flesh.

Very nice.

I serve this with whatever kind of salad I have handy, usually a green one just easily tossed with some walnut oil and a dab of sherry vinegar (3-to-1, or even 4-to-1, that sherry vinegar stuff is STRONG). Or—I love this—a sliced celery salad mixed with a mustard vinaigrette (smashed garlic, salt, pepper, and mustard/red wine vinegar/olive oil in a 1-to-1-to-3 proportion).

Then there are the seeds.

In my never-ending game with myself of trying to find ways to cook most anything that comes my way, I learned years ago that the seeds from squash—acorn, butternut, pumpkin, you name it—are wonderful roasted on their own. Usually, when I'm making squash for dinner, these seeds end up being an appetizer. But for lunch, I cook the seeds from each half in their own little cazuelas, those tiny brown glazed ceramic dishes that Spanish tapas bars use to serve you tiny boiling-hot shrimp in garlic olive oil. I have a bunch of them, brought carefully home in hand luggage after a trip to Spain, and for the acorn squash seeds I do this: I scoop the seeds out, wash them to get rid of the gluey strings, separate them with my fingers, divide them between two little ovenproof dishes, douse them with a hit of olive oil, a shake of salt, and a shake of smoky paprika, stir them around, and then, when the squash is done but still too hot to eat, I stick the little dishes in the toaster oven where the squash lately resided, and cook till they're brown and sizzly. Then I put the little dishes on a big dish with the squash and salad and serve up.

A very nice lunch. And it makes you know that autumn is here. In a good autumn vegetable kind of way. Which is a very nice way indeed.

I know I'm going backwards here, bringing you out of autumn and back to spring, but I left this to almost the last, because I'm afraid of its reception, and I want to coax every reader to like, if not absolutely love…

OKRA

I love okra. I really do. And not just because it's a strange outsider, looked at askance by the modern world. I mean, I hate kidneys (one of the few foods I do dislike, after an unfortunate bout making a steak and kidney pie which left my kitchen smelling like a New York sidewalk on a summer day). Just because it is what it is. Pretty. Modest. Unpretentious. A riot of different textures.

I ate it a lot when we lived in England, since every Asian market carried it—bhindi is its name on the Indian menus that were always my fallback position in provincial towns where you took your life in your hands every time you went into a restaurant that didn't serve poppadum. I always ordered it. And at home, I cooked it in curried vegetable sautés on top of rice with lots of chutney (or 'pickle' in the UK).

But my favorite way to cook okra was and is Madhur Jaffrey's way, which she claims is Japanese. Very likely. Whatever its nationality it's terrific…and comforting, too. Also the perfect hot-weather side dish. So I was very pleased when a heap of the pale green stuff appeared at a local farmers' market. Someone's growing it around here. Thanks for that. Of course I scooped it up and brought it home to have for dinner.

This is how:

◊ Okra
◊ Soy sauce
◊ Mirin
◊ Wasabi paste

As many okra as you feel like having. It's easier if they're all around the same size. Madhur Jaffrey picks through the heap to find the smallest ones, and I do that too, when there ARE smallest ones. But it's still a pleasure if they're all medium to large.

She recommends about 24 okra for four servings, but that, I think, is REALLY a side dish, implying a lot of other side dishes to come…for us, 24 is the least we'll eat. On the other hand, we do, as I say, love okra. You'll have your own ideas.

Bring a pan of water to the boil. Doesn't have to be a big one, just big enough to hold all the okra under water. Add the okra to the boiling water, and bring back to the boil, boil for about 2 minutes—or until when you bite into one, it's just tender and nowhere near overcooked mush.

Drain. Rinse with cold water to stop the cooking. Drain again.

Cut into half-inch lengths, discarding the tops. Now you can either mix it with the sauce, or set it aside and mix at the last minute. Jaffrey says to mix at the last minute. But I kind of like it marinated a little.
Try it both ways and see what you think.

For the sauce for about 24 okra: 2 tablespoons soy sauce to 1 teaspoon mirin (that lovely sweet Japanese cooking wine), with a little smudge of wasabi paste mixed in. If I cook more, I adjust upward, of course.

It's good room temperature, but I like it best chilled.

And I like it really best chilled and nestled up against a tangle of hot linguine mixed with butter, soy sauce, chili oil, minced scallions, and diced, salted cucumber (just dice, toss with some coarse salt in a colander, let sit for about a half hour, then squeeze out extra liquid…add to the noodles at the last minute before you serve). That's what we had the other night. If I'd had some cilantro, I would have chopped that and added it to the noodles with the cucumber.

Extra soy sauce and butter on the table to add at will.

We'd both had a very hard day—hell, a very hard WEEK—and there is nothing like butter and soy sauce on noodles to comfort you at the end of a tough run of anything. Unless it's soy sauce and butter on noodles next to chilled okra, soy sauce, and wasabi. That's the most comforting of all.

THE WORLD'S SIMPLEST HOLLANDAISE SAUCE (*with continuing thanks to M.F.K. Fisher*)

Early asparagus is a thing of beauty, don't you agree? The first ones that show up in the market in what still seems like the dead of winter pull you up and whisper in your ear that the dead of winter thing is an illusion, and that spring is near. At least, that's what they whisper in my ear. And even though the bundles of them from Mexico are not nearly as tasty as the homegrown multi-sized ones later on in the growing season, they're still spring-like and delicious enough for me to bring home bunches and bunches of them through April.

So many bunches of them, in fact, that we start eating them, not just for dinner, but for lunch, too. Pretty sumptuous lunch. Easy, too.

One half-spring/half-winter day (snow flurries in the morning, breaking into brilliant, crystal-drop sunlight on trees afternoon), I decided to celebrate with such a lunch. Baked potato and asparagus. And since I was celebrating… and since The Indigo Ray had begun raising chickens and selling her eggs in competition with Dawn the Egg Lady, and had delivered a just-laid dozen and a half that very morning, without being asked or anything…I decided it was going to be baked potatoes and asparagus and HOLLANDAISE SAUCE.

Hollandaise sauce, you may or may not know, is sunlight on a plate. Sunlight and clogged arteries, sure, if you eat too much of it. But just enough of it, no more, no less, and a big pile of hot asparagus to dip in it at will, is just what you need to celebrate the end of the winter and the coming of the spring.

There's just one problem with it, normally. It's kind of a bitch to make. Especially for lunch. Especially if your morning goes as mine does: work, notice the dogs have grabbed their squeaky toys and are squeaking them for all they're worth to let you know it's way past time for a walk, walk, lunch, back to work. There's no time for planning, or for concentrating on your sauce, with all that squeaking going on, in the brief recreation times between work.

But I really wanted hollandaise sauce that day. And when you really want something, and you can really get it without too much fuss for yourself or your loved ones, I really think it's a good idea to have it.

So I tried an experiment. I decided to see if it was possible to make hollandaise sauce on the top of the stove while I went out for a walk.

And you know what? It turns out you can. If you know about a recipe M.F.K. Fisher passes on in her book *With Bold Knife and Fork*, anyway. This is a recipe she says was given to her by a dignified and pleasant older woman who liked to make hollandaise for one as a treat, now and then. It involves melting some butter in a custard cup set in a pan of simmering water, adding one egg yolk, some cayenne, and a little lemon, and stirring it now and then while the rest of dinner is cooking, making sure the water never gets hot enough to scramble the eggs, until it's nice and thick and hollandaise-y.

That gave me an idea. And I figured I had so many eggs, and that a lunch of just baked potatoes and asparagus and lemon would be luxury enough if my idea flopped, that I was justified in taking the plunge.

So this is what I did (for two people):

◊ Eggs
◊ Butter
◊ Lemon
◊ Hot Sauce
◊ And potatoes and asparagus to serve it atop

I scrubbed three smallish potatoes (that was all I had, but a small one is enough for me for lunch, and two are good for the Beloved Husband), pierced them so they wouldn't explode in the toaster oven, put them in at 475°.

Then I went back to work for fifteen minutes, until the dogs got bored and started squeaking their toys again.

Back to the kitchen:

I put two Pyrex custard cups in a heavy skillet on the stove, and added water up to half their size. A heavy skillet because I wanted the pan to hold the heat while I went for a walk—a thin, aluminum one wouldn't work here. Then I brought the water to a simmer, and cut about three tablespoons of butter into each cup. (M.F.K. Fisher recommends a scant quarter cup...four tablespoons...and normally I would have followed her advice, but I was avoiding that Clogged Artery feel, which I enjoy at dinner, but not at lunch…and besides, Indigo's eggs are smaller than the normal market ones…)

While the butter melted in the cups, I quickly set the table, snapped the ends off of about fourteen asparagus, and put them in a water-filled sink to soak. I filled my oval asparagus pan up with water, salted it, and put it on the stove to await action. Pulled out two plates, cut up two lemon quarters, one for each plate.

When the butter was melted, and bubbling a bit, I dropped an egg yolk each into each cup and whisked it with a small wire whisk. Added some hot sauce. Squeezed a bit from each lemon quarter into each cup, and put a quarter on each plate.

Now I hit the intercom to let the Beloved Vegetarian Husband know it was time for the dogs' walk. No need to speak; he could hear the frantic squeaking toy noise and knows very well what THAT means.

I gave the egg yolk/melted butter another whisk, then, seeing the BVH come out of his hut down the meadow, turned off the heat underneath.

Let the dogs outside ("drop those toys—no, NOW, inside, not outside!"), went out with them, put on my walking boots, and enjoyed the spring day for about a half an hour or so.

On the way back, I wondered: was this really going to work? And when I walked into the kitchen, shedding my coat and fumbling around in the cupboard for post-walk dog treats, I looked over at the stove. Oh no. Curdled. Scrambled eggs. Must have left the water on too high.

But how could that be? I'd left it at a simmer, and turned it off. The pan couldn't have held THAT much heat, could it?

Thinking things over, I turned on the water to boil in the asparagus pan, and when it did, added the asparagus. Then I turned my attention back to the custard cups. Taking the little whisk, I tried whisking one. I turned the heat on low just to warm the water up and encourage everything. And then, like magic, the more I whisked, the more that curdled looking egg thing turned into hollandaise sauce. Until it WAS hollandaise sauce. By the time the asparagus were done, and the potatoes, too, I had two small custard cups of, yes, that's right, hollandaise sauce. Just lifted them out of the water, wiped their sides and bottoms, deposited them on the plates with the lemon and the drained asparagus and the potatoes, and put them on the table.

And the BVH was suitably impressed. "You don't have to work this hard!" he protested faintly as he poured sauce on his potatoes and dipped an asparagus spear into what was left in his custard cup. "Want me to take you out to dinner tonight?"

Silly me, I told him how easy it had been. Melt butter in cup set in simmering water. Add egg yolk, hot sauce, lemon juice. Whisk. Turn off heat. Leave for about a half hour. Come back, turn heat onto low, whisk hell out of it, and voila!

"I'll still take you out if you want," he said earnestly. "But whatever we have, it won't be as good as this."

Which was really a very nice end of a winter/spring morning, and start of a winter/spring afternoon day.

A POUND OF GREEN BEANS, A HANDFUL OF SHALLOTS, AND MARITAL HARMONY

As far as I'm concerned, moving to a new place is a chance to invade a series of new markets. So when the Beloved Vegetarian Husband and I moved part-time to Boulder, Colorado, I immediately began my exploratory forays. I checked out a large regular-type supermarket (better than expected), two Co-op style hybrid-type markets (pretty good), one actual Co-op in a small Rocky Mountain hippie town (lovely but predictably expensive), one branch of Whole Foods (very disappointing, with miserable-looking veggies, at the height of summer!), and a terrific Asian market hidden in a strip mall, where the internet reviews said the owner was 'rude' and the products 'scary' (my kind of authentic Chinese market).

Of course the high point of these market trips is always the local farmers' market. Even the Beloved Vegetarian Husband, who loathes shopping on even a good day, loves checking these out with me. So there we were in a new town, and a whole new set of farmers' markets to check out.

We started our exploration of said markets in a nearby small town, which was VERY Norman Rockwell, at least if Norman Rockwell enjoyed iced green-tea lattes. Lovely place, lovely market. I especially liked the heap of what I thought was a bunch of tossed-out beet greens, but which proved to be the beets themselves.

"How much for the beets?"

"Oh, I don't know. Grab a bunch and we'll call it two dollars."

After I'd grabbed a bunch: "You call that a bunch? Go back and get some more, for God's sake!"

Excellent salesmanship in my opinion.

Then there was the stand that had heaps and heaps of green beans, including those purple ones that turn green when you cook them, alas, but which are such a pleasure to look at when you're preparing dinner (and that's important too, don't let us forget). I got a pound of half and half, and then I saw they had a small pile of shallots besides, and I can't really enjoy my green beans in the summer to the max without shallots, so they went in the bag too, along with mutual expressions of esteem for how well shallots go with green beans.

So there I was with the green beans and the shallots and a bunch of other stuff I'd foraged from all the other markets, and I was overwhelmed by choice.

What to do? There were so many things I could do, even in the 90-degree, "we don't want to eat anything but vegetables and maybe some anchovies" weather. The Beloved Vegetarian Husband and I had a serious discussion about this in the car on the way home. I love it when we do that. There was a time in our marriage when he felt that food was nothing more than fuel for work. Now he takes the kind of pleasure in our meals that does a wife's heart good, I'm pleased to say. He had his own opinions about how those green beans should be cooked on a hot summer's day.

All of those opinions, his and mine, started with the same step:

Top the green beans. Boil a BIG pot of water (green beans need a lot of water to bounce around in, no lid, that keeps them green for some reason, as long as you don't overcook...), salt it, add the beans, cook till they still have a little crunch, then drain and rinse in cold water. Drain well.

Now they're ready for all sorts of possible treatments.

In slightly cooler weather, I might combine them with minced shallots and toss them with butter over medium heat, and sprinkle them with chopped chervil or parsley or dill.

I might mix them with a little béchamel sauce, sprinkle with grated Swiss cheese and sliced almonds, and heat under the broiler till they have a nice little crust on top.

Or I might quickly stir-fry them with some chopped fermented black beans and ginger and garlic and serve them wrapped in whole-wheat tortillas spread with hoisin sauce.

But that day, it was too hot for any of those ideas. So it was green bean salad we finally settled upon. Which offered an even wider range of options, even when I started with those shallots, and even though, since this was a new kitchen for me, I only had one kind of vinegar—red—in residence:

Just to narrow it down a little, for all of these salads, I'd mortar and pestle a clove of garlic with some salt and pepper, add a spoon of vinegar, and a sliced shallot or two, letting the shallot sit and sweeten for about fifteen minutes or so before adding three spoons of olive oil.

After that, the only question is: what do we feel like eating?

Toss the dressing, and the beans, with:

For veggies—
Diced tomatoes?
Diced cucumber?
Diced avocado?

For protein—
Anchovies?
Tuna fish?
Hardboiled eggs?

For extra oomph—
Capers?
Chopped parsley?
Chopped green or red onion?

For a little carbo punch—
Diced toasted croutons?
Diced baked/steamed/boiled potatoes?
Cooked pasta?

What?
Then came dinner time. At that point, the algorithm by which I decide

what goes into the meal had kind of stabilized. It's always an equation of what I really feel like eating plus what the Beloved Vegetarian Husband feels like eating, divided by what we have on hand plus what time I have, plus how much time I feel like putting into the thing.

So this is what we ended up agreeing upon for dinner: Green Bean and Potato Salad with Anchoïäde, Basil, and Cherry Tomatoes.

Like so:

Put a big pot of water on to boil.

Dice as many potatoes as you are going to want to eat. (I diced four large ones, since I wanted enough left for lunch the next day.) Steam or boil them till just fork-tender.

Meanwhile, make the anchoïäde, which is really just a strong garlic vinaigrette with a can of anchovies, and maybe some capers, mashed into it. As usual, you don't have to be too fussy about this. In fact, I forgot all about the anchovies till after I'd made the vinaigrette (mashed garlic clove, pepper, salt, red wine vinegar and olive oil in a 1-to-3 ratio), so I just mashed them up with some more olive oil and a thread of vinegar, along with a bunch of capers and a little of their vinegar. I added that to the original dressing.

Mince a shallot or two and leave in the dressing in a big bowl while the potatoes cook.

Top a pound of green beans.

When the potatoes are done, dump them on top of the dressing, SAVING THE WATER IN THE POT. Sprinkle them with some white wine, or some lemon juice, or (since I had some open, hah!) some rosé wine.

Put the beans into the water you cooked the potatoes in. Boil briskly for as long as it takes for them to be still crisp, but cooked to your liking.

Drain them, sloosh them with cold water to set them and stop the cooking, drain well again.

At this point, I also added a handful of cherry tomatoes to the draining beans, rinsed them, and let them drain with the beans.

(You don't want much added water in this salad, or any salad, come to think of it. It kills the dressing.)

When the beans and tomatoes are dried off, add them to the potatoes, and toss the whole thing. Have a taste, have a look. Is there enough dressing? If not, you can just add a little more oil. Maybe squeeze on some lemon if you have it.

If you have some parsley, chop it up. I did. And I had a big basil plant, so I grabbed some leaves and tore them and threw them in, too.
I served it with some boiled corn. And a couple of glasses of rosé.

And the Beloved Vegetarian Husband gave that sigh of sheer happiness that you like to hear if you've talked over the menu with him in a companionable way, then cooked the dinner on a Sunday night, and you're hoping you've done enough to be a Good Wife and make sure he's well fed and happy at home, before he heads off next day to the second week of a completely new job.

SALT-GRILLED TROUT

Another excellent choice for a mixed marriage between a vegetarian and a carnivore—really, an excellent choice for dinner in any marriage—is fish, if fish is something you both eat. And one of the best and easiest ways to cook fish is the Japanese method called salt grilling. This is very simple and tasty (surprise!). You just salt the fillets or whole fish with coarse salt, and let them stand, an hour for fillets, up to overnight for whole fish. Wash off the salt, pat dry, and grill. Usually served with a soy and lemon juice sauce, it's one of those elegant dishes that make you feel like a tremendous cook with very little effort. The salt firms up the fish and gives it an extra savor that is quite exciting. At least it definitely is exciting to me.

While we're on the subject of salt-grilled fish, let me say it's a particularly good way to treat whole trout. Farmed trout, which used to underimpress me with its boring tastelessness, has gone through some kind of taste revolution: it's absolutely terrific, now, whenever I buy it. Tasty and tender. Now this may be because the two places I buy it in, i.e., Southern Oregon and Boulder, Colorado, have trout farms nearby to buy from, and those trout farms have been paying attention to a sustainable, good-tasting fish. Probably because said trout farms provide trout to trout fishermen in the area.

So the other day, I was doing errands in a far rural corner of the valley I live atop. When I'm in that particular corner, I like to stop at the local butcher shop, which is, truly, one of the last remaining of the great butcher shops (may their number shortly increase). These guys do game. They do local rabbit. They make their own sausage. They do stuff to order in the most charming way imaginable. And they're staffed by a bunch of cheerful young men, who give you hope that butchering is not going the way of the Lost Arts. For there is no charm in buying one's meat and fish wrapped in cellophane, its actual wrap date a mystery. No charm at all. So I like going to this shop and being able to ask about what I'm buying, and get recommendations, and hear the wonderful words: "Which one of those in the case did you want?"

There was this wonderful sign: "Trout. $1.99 a piece." A bargain. And since the local trout hatchery is about fifteen minutes away from the butcher shop, I had a pretty good idea why such fresh-looking fish, looking like it was going to leap out of the display case, arched and rainbow-colored, was lying there waiting for me to take it home. "I'll have those," I said. Then I paused, suddenly remembering I had hours to go with errands in a valley that was going to reach triple digits in heat very shortly. And the trout wasn't going to do too well through that.

Explaining this to the nice young man behind the counter, I was soothed to hear him say, "No worries. I'll wrap it in a bag of ice for you." And he wasn't fooling: he packed in so much ice that I had to act quickly to stop him from putting it in my shopping bag atop the dead-ripe tomatoes bought at the local produce stand in the parking lot.

We had that trout for supper that night, along with boiled corn bought from a farm stand along the way, and some crisp green beans stir-fried with crushed red pepper and lots of garlic. I salt-grilled the trout, and served it with a little soy/wasabi/lemon sauce, and it was terrific. Salt grilling does something to the skin of a trout that renders it ambrosial.

Like this:

◊ Trout, one per person
◊ Coarse salt
◊ Olive oil

For the sauce:

◊ Soy sauce
◊ Wasabi paste
◊ Lemon wedge

Take a trout (or two or three or four) an hour or so before grill time.

Slash each side diagonally three times down to the bone.

Sprinkle coarse salt on both sides, rubbing it into the slashes.

Let sit in the refrigerator for an hour. More won't hurt it; in fact, if you want to keep the fish fresh overnight, this will do it—just rinse more thoroughly to get rid of the extra saltiness.

When you're ready to cook, heat your grill, or your cast-iron grill pan (which is what I use).

Rinse the trout. Dry with paper towels.

Paint it with olive oil.

When the grill pan spits when you flick a drop of water in, add the fish diagonally—this makes no difference to the taste, but diagonal grill marks are very handsome.

While it cooks on one side (about three to five minutes, depending on how well-done you like your fish), mix a little soy sauce and wasabi in a bowl. Squeeze in a bit of lemon to taste.

Turn the fish.

Turn the heat down to medium and cook until it is no longer pink inside, but still moist.

Take the fish off the grill, put them on big enough plates so they're nice and comfortable. You can now let them sit while you make the rest of the meal; it's very good warm or at room temperature. When you're ready to serve, either pour the soy/wasabi over it, or bring the bowl with the sauce to table to be spooned over at will.

And don't forget a spare plate to put the bones on. What we usually do is eat the top half, blissfully enjoying the crispy skin. Then we just pull the whole spine, taking the bones with it, and put that aside on the spare plate. What's left behind is a lovely boneless fillet to finish up with.

Don't forget to suck the little bit of skin and meat at the tail end. That's always very tasty.

And you'll see what I mean about farmed trout—they're getting better and better these days. And it's wonderful to find something that is.

HARISSA, SPRING GREENS, AND ME

As you can easily tell, I like it when you spot a recipe you want to try and you just happen to have the ingredients on hand. But what I really love is when you have ingredients you want to use in a new way, and you spot a recipe that can be cut to fit what's on hand. Especially one that I recognize will cheer the Beloved Vegetarian Husband at mealtime. That cheers me too.

So it was with me last spring.

I'd been nosing around a local spice shop, and found a packet of their ready-made harissa spice mix. There are plenty of recipes around for this rather exotic (Ethiopian?) combination, but since I always like to get a baseline for what someone else thinks something new should taste like when I can, this seemed like an irresistible purchase. So I didn't resist.

This was their mix: roasted red japones pepper, cumin, coriander, two kinds of paprika, garlic salt and caraway, all ground together to a brick-red dust that smelled heavenly and tasted even better.

Then there were these shrimp at the market that looked so good…and these organic Roma tomatoes at a reasonable price for spring…and then, to top it off, the local farmers' market started up, and everyone was selling the first crop of the year, which is always spring greens. So I got a huge bag of the spicy mix (arugula, mizuma, red kale, more arugula, can't have too much arugula…).

And there I was. Shrimp. Spicy greens. Tomatoes. Harissa. All the signifiers for those ingredients dancing round in my head. How to use? Marinate the shrimp in oil and harissa, then barbeque, serve on a bed of spicy greens, save the tomatoes for another dish? Slice the tomatoes, layer on a pan, spread out the shrimp atop, scatter harissa and oil over the whole, bake and serve with a spicy green salad tossed with blue cheese vinaigrette?

Naw. Not. Quite. Right.

There were all these other things I could have done with the shrimp and tomatoes and the greens, things I was used to doing. But I was dedicated to learning something about that harissa.

So I wasted a little time I should have spent working, looking up recipes on the *New York Times* site before my free ten articles a month ran out.

And there it was.

The perfect recipe.

Sure, it required me to marinate the shrimp in a combination of spices I did not now and never planned to have. Sure, it called for big handfuls of spinach, which I only had in frozen form for those emergencies that can only be solved by having frozen spinach on hand.

But there you go, it was so easy. So adaptable. So exactly what I felt like eating. I wanted to jump up and high five someone. But there was no one there. No matter. There would be by the time I finished cooking.

Harissa-marinated shrimp, sautéed with tomatoes and spicy spring greens, on brown rice.

Here's how:

◊ Shrimp
◊ Harissa powder
◊ Olive oil
◊ Garlic
◊ Tomatoes (Romas work well here)
◊ Spring greens

Take your shrimp (about a pound for two people if this is a main dish, for four if an appetizer—and very good it would be as the latter, too). Mix two teaspoons or more of harissa powder with a pounded clove or two of garlic and enough olive oil to make a nice bright-red slooshy wondrously smelling slurp. Toss it with the shrimp. Leave to sit for at least a half an hour. An hour even better.

(And here's where I want to make a plea for sanity. Why peel and devein them when the shells add so much flavor? Sure it's messier to eat when you have to peel them at the table, but it's so much more tasty. And more fun, too. And you can save the shells in the freezer to make a great stock for risotto or arroce later.)

Cook your rice. (You can skip this step if you decide, instead, to wrap the shrimp in heated whole-wheat tortillas, another excellent decision to be made along the way.)

Dice your tomatoes, about four decent Romas, I think. Have on hand at least two big handfuls of the spring greens of your choice—more will never hurt.

When it's just about dinner time, look around to make sure all your forces and all your ingredients are properly marshaled, since things will go fairly swiftly from here on in.

(If you're using those tortillas, wrap them in foil now, stick them in a 350° oven for about ten minutes to heat…and as you get closer, continue with the shrimp…)

Just about ready for dinner? Heat a large skillet almost to smoking. Add some olive oil, just enough to slide around the bottom of the pan. Toss in the shrimp, and continue to toss like mad so that the spices don't burn, though they do sort of caramelize on the shrimp as they turn pink. (If you took my advice about leaving the shells on, this also helps to keep the succulence inside, another culinary advantage.) When they're halfway there (pale rose, say), throw in the diced tomatoes, continuing to toss like mad. Cook for a few minutes till the shrimp are a nice bright sunset pink, and the tomatoes have given up some of their juice and are kind of lying around and melding together with their pan-mates.

Then add your handfuls of spring greens.

Stir once or twice, just enough to wilt them into the sauce. And…serve!

On rice, wrapped in tortillas, on pasta…whatever you feel like.

By this time, I guarantee, even if there was no one around to high-five you at the start of the process, anyone within scenting distance will have wandered into the kitchen, saying something along the lines of, "What's that wonderful smell? Are we having that for dinner?"

Sit down and enjoy. And I do hope you took my advice about the shells.

(And by the way, I made this dish in the autumn too, but this time with smoky Spanish paprika replacing the harissa, a regular overripe tomato replacing the Romas, and a big bunch of autumn arugula, chopped and destemmed, to replace the spring greens. I served this version over shredded lettuce, with lemon wedges on the side. It was utterly delicious, though in a different way. We like that—doing something differently, but still enjoying it all the same.)

And speaking of brown rice…

IN PRAISE OF BROWN RICE

I know there are a lot of you out there who think of brown rice along the same lines as you think of Birkenstocks. Hemp clothing. Rasta locks on young white guys. And I know every time anyone mentions it to you, an inadvertent pained look crosses your face, and you respond automatically with defensive thoughts of double vodka martinis, rare steaks, potatoes, and chocolate cake.

But brown rice isn't like that. Not really. Not in its heart of hearts. If you knew brown rice like I know brown rice, you wouldn't just give it a chance, you'd welcome it into your home. Invite it to meet guests. Maybe even vote for it for high office.

Brown rice is absolutely terrific. And I say this as a person who really doesn't think all that much about health in my food choices. Wait, scratch that. I do think about health, but only in the sense of whether or not what I eat makes me feel good. I rarely take vitamins. They just scratch my throat and don't do much for me one way or the other. I do eat a lot of salads. I love the way they taste, plus they make me feel light and energized. And that, after all, is part of the pleasure of eating. Sometimes you like to feel full and like you can't move an inch before you've digested. Sometimes you don't. It'd be weird, I think, if you felt one way or the other all the time.

Brown rice, properly approached, will not just be your friend, it will be your friend for life. It has a nutty, deep, satisfying taste to it, when you make it right (which, by the way, all that moaning on the part of white-rice enthusiasts notwithstanding, is just not that hard), and you feel great after you've eaten it. It goes with a lot of stuff. And, as a lagniappe, it's allegedly terrific for you. So, I mean, what's not to like?

I like it a lot. I think I've made that clear. And after a lifetime spent loving white rice, I find, to my surprise, that when there's a choice, I spurn my former love. This is a taste thing, not a health thing. Trust me on this.

It's easy to cook brown rice. Just measure a cup of the stuff into a pot, salt it, and add two scant cups of water. Bring to a boil. Cover it. Turn the heat down as low as you can (I use a flame tamer), and set the timer for 55 minutes. After which, turn it off and let it sit for 10 minutes or so—you needn't fuss about this; just as much or as little time as you need to get the rest of the meal together. Fluff with a fork. Eat in any one of a number of ways.

Or: bring a huge pot of water to a boil. Salt. Add as much rice as you want (1 cup will feed two generously as a main course, or four as a side dish... or...). Boil till a grain is tender—about 45 minutes. Drain without being too fussed about getting all the water out. Put in a buttered casserole dish and stick in the oven, set on low, say 250°, till you're ready to eat it. Fifteen minutes, thirty minutes...it can wait this way an hour.

Now...about what you DO with it...have it plain with butter and soy sauce (I love this; they call it 'children's rice' in Japan)...use it as the landing for a stir-fry...put something on top of it, to soak up the juices, a piece of marinated broiled fish, a skewer of lamb kebabs, chicken adobo...

It was chicken adobo that made me want to tell you about brown rice. Our household is a tolerant one, and when I get a carnivorous urge, the Beloved Vegetarian Husband graciously (even voraciously) eats the many dishes I cook on the side.

In this case, I had to have chicken adobo. So I cooked a cup of rice to go with the original chicken dish, and then had all these leftovers. So to save it for a lunch when Alex would be away, I put the chicken I hadn't eaten on top of the leftover rice, deglazed the chicken pot with a half cup of water, poured THAT on top of the chicken, and, slapping a lid on it, stuck it in the fridge.

When I was ready for that lunch, hungry and distracted by work, I just stuck the pot in a 350° oven. After about a half hour, the house started to smell wonderful. After forty-five minutes spent virtuously at my desk, I pulled it out, spooned it onto a plate with some grated carrot salad, and had at it. Halfway through, I noticed I was making little noises of pleasure. That rice had soaked up the extra juices and steamed in them, and crisped a little bit at the bottom, and tasted not just heavenly, but the way dinner would taste in heaven after you'd had a long day cloud-jumping. I looked down at my plate and said a 'thank you' out loud.

(By the way, chicken adobo is a Filipino dish of chicken legs and thighs cooked in vinegar and soy sauce with lots of garlic and bay leaves and peppercorns until the chicken soaks up the liquid and browns in its own fat. The carrot salad I had with it, both meals, was just grated carrot mixed with minced green onion, tossed with a little sugar mixed in a little lime juice, plus a little fish sauce and chili oil. Terrific. Less expensive and infinitely better-tasting than any handful of vitamins, and probably a lot healthier for you, too.)

And then there's...

Garlic Fried Brown Rice

Not to go on about brown rice, but...

No, wait a minute. I AM going on about brown rice. Why should I apologize? It's better for you than ninety per cent of the rest of the food world, and it tastes great, too. This is something I have never understood: why is it that something that is good for you, or good for the planet, or good for anything at all, trails behind it this reputation for being wussy, or foolish, or not quite pukka? Why is that? It's enough to make you believe in the devil.

But that's way off the subject...maybe. Anyway, back to brown rice, and the brand that I particularly love, Lundberg's organic brown rice, grown by a family operation in California, so you can see the miles and miles of rice fields if you drive (as I unfortunately do now and then) up and down the otherwise monotonous and slightly alienating Highway 5. It's a relief to see those rice fields. Cheers me right up. Even better for that long drive from Oregon to Los Angeles than cruise control.

So our local Co-op takes a quite enlightened attitude toward food costs, and even though it's dead expensive for a number of items (don't get me started on how much they charge for whole-wheat pasta), it has this program called "Basic Pricing." Which means that certain key items throughout the store, which are themselves enough to sustain a decent level of delicious nutrition, are priced as low as the Co-op can manage to price them. Things like New Sammy's Whole Wheat Bread (delicious), certain kale and chard greens (also delicious), line-caught tuna (terrifically delicious), and so on.

Of course Lundberg brown rice, both long and short grain, benefits from this. Which makes it, per pound, half the price of the same rice in other stores in the vicinity. So all of us around here in my little Oregon alpine valley go to the Co-op and stock up.

Naturally, as is always the case no matter where you are, the local conversation frequently turns to food. It turned, the other night when I sat with two of my neighbors, to brown rice. The first neighbor remarked that she never cooks more than she needs for the evening, "Because there's really nothing you can do with leftover brown rice."

Well, it was as if an electric shock had gone through me and the second neighbor (this happens a lot, this kind of sudden animation and vehemence, in any food conversation, about any kind of food, anywhere in the world—it's always a great topic if you can't think of anything else to say to a stranger). We both sat up straight and said, almost at the same time, "Nothing you can do!"

"Oh my God," the second neighbor said. "I make a huge pot of it on Sunday, and reheat it all week when I get home. You just put a little water in a pan, dish as much rice out as you need, mix it all up, and stick it in a 350° oven till dinner's ready."

"Fried rice!" I said vigorously. "With mushrooms and fish sauce and scallions and cilantro and shredded lettuce and egg and frozen peas!"

"Rice salad! I toss it with salad dressing and leftover veggies and take it to work for lunch…"

"Rice pancakes," I said, more dreamily this time. "Mixed with a little egg and garlic and milk, fried in butter…"

"…sometimes I wrap it in a tortilla or stick it in a pita bread with some lettuce and yoghurt…"

"Reheated refried beans and leftover brown rice wrapped in whole-wheat tortillas, topped with avocado, shredded carrot, a little sour cream…."

"Rice pudding! Oh my God, I love brown rice pudding with heavy cream!"

"Savory rice pudding! Add onion and cheese instead of brown sugar and cinnamon! And if you add frozen spinach sautéed in olive oil…"

"Pilaf! Mix it with butter-sautéed almonds and raisins, some minced parsley, more melted butter, heat it up…"

"Layer it with sour cream and green chilies and Jack cheese, bake it till it's bubbly, serve it with corn tortillas and salsa and guacamole…"

The second neighbor and I looked at each other, and burst out laughing at our own enthusiasm. And the first neighbor admitted defeat, and accepted that there were a lot more options than she had at first perceived. We finished up an amiable glass of wine, hugged each other good night, and they went home, leaving me to fix my solitary dinner.

Then I went to the refrigerator and looked at the comforting pot of cold brown rice on the top shelf. The Beloved Vegetarian Husband was away that night, and so I made for myself:

Garlic Fried Rice with Bacon and Eggs

For one:

◊ 1 thick slice of bacon
◊ Peanut oil
◊ Leftover cooked rice, about a cup and a half
◊ 2 eggs
◊ 3 cloves of garlic, sliced thinly
◊ A little coarse salt

I had a very thick slice of bacon—the one lonely slice left from a thrifty package of bacon ends—in the freezer, so I took that out and cut it into thick batons. Fried that in a little peanut oil while I sliced three cloves of garlic (you can use just one clove, but in my opinion if you're going to have garlic fried rice, then you should have GARLIC FRIED RICE), which I then gently fried along with the bacon until the bacon was crisp on the edges, and the garlic near golden.

Then I scooped the bacon and garlic into the bowl I planned to eat out of when it was all done, and left the fat in the frying pan. Added as much brown rice as I thought I could eat that night (about a cup and a half, cooked), salted it, and turned it around in the fat until the chill was off it and the clumps unclumped. Then I added back the bacon and garlic, and turned the heat down to low.

Two eggs. I cracked each one carefully into a cup, to make sure it didn't break (half of the charm of this dish for me is the unbroken yolk spurting out over the garlic rice when I stick a chopstick into it at the table), and then even more carefully slid each egg into slight depressions on the top of the rice. Sprinkled a little coarse salt over the eggs, clapped a lid on the pan, and set the timer for 7 minutes. Poured myself a glass of water (which is the best drink for this recipe, except for, maybe, beer—wine is just too genteel here) and got out a pair of chopsticks. Rooted around in the fridge and found a jar of pickled peppers, which I like to spoon on top of the rice with their vinegar, the way they do in the Philippines, and put that on the table with the water and chopsticks.

At seven minutes, I checked the eggs. The whites were done and the yolks barely set, and I silently thanked the food gods that my timing was right. (Otherwise I would have left the dish on for a minute or two more, all the while anxiously hovering to make sure it didn't get to that horrible point where the yolks, instead of being unctuously liquid, turn hard like little yellow tiles.) Well, it was right. In fact, it was perfect. And I sat down with my chopsticks and my vinegared peppers, and my glass of water, and a good book (Elizabeth David's *French Provincial Cookery*), and was as happy as it's possible for a solitary diner to be.

And all this thanks to brown rice. So I really can't be blamed for going on about it, after all.

(By the way, the vegetarian version, where you just leave out the bacon, is particularly appreciated, too. At least, it's appreciated by the vegetarian around here.)

And what about the good old recipes? Who speaks for them? I do, and with all my heart...

Retro Quiche

There are some foods that at this point feel about as quaint and retro as a beanbag chair. Fondue, for example. Uno bars. Ridged potato chips with sour cream and dried onion soup dip.

Not that they're not delicious. (Actually, I love all of the above, along with canned dried onion rings, La Vache Qui Rit, and grapes mixed with sour cream and brown sugar. Not that I would admit it to anyone.) They're just mated permanently in our minds with some specific time and place. The more au courant they seemed at the time, the hipper, the more up-to-the-minute...well, the more they go together in your memories with black octagonal plates. And of black octagonal plates, the less said, the better.

But let's not be put off by guilt by association. Some of these retro foods need to come out of the closet and take their place in the sunshine where they belong. They need to cast off the old reputation for quaint provincialism. They need, in short, to reinvent themselves.

Such a food is quiche.

Even the word quiche can make you wince, and make you think of the various stodgy and overpriced messes perpetrated in its name. Instead of thinking—as you would, if you were thinking of the quiche you make to suit your own tastes in your very own home—of a comforting, warm, creamy custard enrobing a savory marriage of flavors, all enclosed in a buttery, tender crust.

There. That sounds so much better than something you would take out of an avocado-green kitchen, being careful not to spill anything on your leisure suit. Doesn't it? Much better than that tired excuse for a vegetarian entree, served in buffet-lunch restaurants around the world, mainly to get rid of all the odd vegetables in the kitchen left over from unsuccessful salads.

Quiches fit all my requirements for a meal. They're inexpensive. They take well to improvisation. They're delicious. And they're easy to cook.

If the crust thing bothers you, there are two ways to deal with it: 1) buy a readymade crust at the grocery store. They're pretty good. Or 2) make a hardy tart shell that is practically foolproof, especially if you have a food processor and are even half paying attention to what you're doing.

Here's how for the shell (thank you, Marion Cunningham):

◊ 1 cup flour
◊ 6 tablespoons chilled butter
◊ An egg yolk
◊ A few tablespoons ice water
◊ Mustard or honey to brush on the crust (depending on if the filling is sweet or savory)

Mix 1 cup of flour (or 2/3 cup white flour and 1/3 cup whole wheat flour) with some salt. Put in the bowl of your food processor, and cut into it 6 tablespoons of chilled butter. Pulse this up and down until the butter looks like a variety of differently sized crumbs. Then mix an egg yolk with a couple of tablespoons of cold water. With the processor going, pour this in from the top. The dough should mix and form a ball around the blades; if it doesn't—if it still looks crumbly—add a little more cold water to the cup you mixed the yolk in, and add it, little bit by little bit, until the dough DOES mix and form a ball etc.

Take the dough out, wrap in plastic wrap, and shove in the fridge for at least twenty minutes.

When you need it, take it out and put it in the middle of your quiche pan. Mind you, this does not have to be a quiche pan, purpose-built and bought from a department store with the words "quiche pan" on the side. It can be a pie plate. A Spanish cazuela. A tart pan. Anything ovenworthy that will be big enough to hold the finished product.

Now push down with the heel of your hand, and, using the heel and your fingers, push and pull the dough until it covers the bottom and sides of the pan. Don't worry if the crust tears. Just pull a bit off where you don't need it and use that as a patch. Make sure you don't leave any too thick spots, especially around the edges—that'll make the whole thing a little stodgy when you're done.

You see why this is a good recipe. None of that floured surfaces and rolling pin stuff, and then the crust sticking to the rolling pin, and then the worry that if you work the dough too much, it'll come out tough. Nope. This crust is friendlier than that.

If you have time now, cover the crust, and put it back in the fridge to rest. When you're ready to proceed, preheat the oven to 425°, take the pan out, and, with a fork, pierce the raw crust all over its bottom. This is so it doesn't swell up in the oven. Then, with a pastry brush if you have one, or just a wadded up piece of paper towel if you don't, paint the bottom of the crust with mustard (if you're making a savory tart), or honey (if you're making a sweet one). I find this keeps the crust from getting soggy later, when it's filled.

At this point, you can fill it with anything you like (and I do emphasize that verb 'like'...this is not the place, if there ever is one, to get rid of all the odds and ends you can't figure out any other way to use). What do you fill it with? Whatever tastes good to you. Sautéed mushroom. Sautéed onions. Sautéed mushrooms and onions. Chopped buttered cooked spinach. You get the idea.

Whatever you fill it with, that gets enrobed with a basic custard:

◊   3 eggs
◊   1 cup of milk
◊   ¼ cup of cream
◊   Salt

You can start with this recipe for a good custard: 3 eggs mixed with a cup of milk and a quarter cup of cream, salt added. But you can fiddle with that, too. 4 eggs and ¾ cup of milk. 3 eggs and ½ cup milk, ½ cup yoghurt. Substitute sour cream for some of the liquid. Etc. Pour this atop the filling.

Paprika the top, if it's a savory custard. That looks nice. If you think of it, put little dabs of butter there, too, or dribble on a little oil. Bake at 425° for fifteen minutes, then turn the oven down to 350°, and bake another thirty minutes. It should be brown and puffy when it's done, and smelling of its ingredients. If you have any doubts at all, stick a toothpick in the custard and see if it comes out clean. Let the tart sit for a few minutes on your counter to settle—a good time to have a little appetizer at the table. Serve slices with a green salad on the side.

Delicious. Comforting, too. And your family thinks you're great for making that piecrust. If you bought it, just don't bother telling them. You deserve some credit, after all, for restoring quiche to its rightful position.

(This is what I did the other night: Anchovy/Mushroom/Cheddar Cheese Quiche. I sautéed a handful of mushrooms in the olive oil from a can of anchovies. Salt. When they were done, I turned off the heat and tossed them with minced parsley and garlic clove. I cut a few slices of cheddar cheese into small dice. Scattered half on the bottom of the pastry shell. Spread the mushrooms on top. Laid the anchovies from the can on top of the mushrooms. Scattered the rest of the cheese over all. Poured on a custard made of 3 eggs, 1 cup milk, ¼ cup cream, salt, and liberal dashes of hot pepper sauce. Dribbled what was left of the anchovy oil on top. Sprinkled paprika. Cooked as per instructions above. While it sat, we had a salad of grated carrot, minced parsley, and marinated herring. Then served the quiche with a little green salad. Absolutely divine.)

Retro Green Beans

Speaking of retro foods that need to be reestablished, there was that night I had a surplus of green beans, having bought a huge bag at a bargain price in a year where obviously green beans were popping out all over. I'd used half of them for a stir-fry with whole garlic cloves (did that on the barbeque grill and served them with a whole barbequed fish stuffed with cilantro and garlic chips). But it was almost a week later, and some of them were looking rather sad. Well, the sad ones just would end their lives in the compost bin, but the others were still begging to be eaten. Just not eaten flash-fried—you really want extra fresh for that. And anyway, who says I always have to cook veggies till they crunch? Okay, so maybe somebody did, but does that mean I have to listen to them? Of course not. All I need to do, as in so many other situations, is nod courteously and then consult my own common sense and desires.

My desires last night said: long-cooked green beans with bacon.

I don't know where this desire popped up from. Some atavistic childhood memory of those luscious vegetable dishes that graced the Thanksgiving tables of the Fifties and early Sixties? Was it the chill in the air promising an October snow that reminded me of the harvest food of my grandparents?

Whatever it was, it prompted me to something truly delicious. As delicious as that stir-fry of fresh green beans with garlic cloves. Just different. And since what we want (don't we?) is a world of poly rather than mono experiences, that was a very good thing.

Even the Beloved Vegetarian Husband, who normally likes his veggies as close to raw as possible, and without the slyly added bacon, said, "Man. That was good." Of course, I made sure to tell him the bacon flavor was there after picking out the bits of it to eat myself. He still said it was good.

And it was.

Here's how:
◊ Green beans
◊ Thinly sliced onion
◊ A thinly sliced garlic clove
◊ Bacon slices
◊ A little olive oil
◊ A dried red pepper pod (optional)
◊ A very little salt (the bacon takes care of most of it)

Take as many green beans as you fancy, say a pound. They don't have to be the freshest or the sweetest, but get rid of any mushy or bruised ones.

Top and tail them, and cut them into manageable pieces. Again, don't fuss about that too much—it doesn't matter if they're all the same length or not.

Thinly slice an onion and a garlic clove.

Put a little olive oil and a couple of whole slices of uncooked bacon into either a skillet or a casserole dish (depending on whether you want to cook on top of the stove with the former, or in the oven with the latter). Add the green beans, the onion, and the garlic. (I popped in a whole dried red pepper for zest, but you don't need to if you don't like it.) A little salt. (You don't need too much because of the bacon, which, though added raw, releases its flavor as everything cooks together. Also, while I think of it: you don't need to add liquid—the onion and the water clinging to the green beans take care of that.)

Now for the magical bit:

Cook for at least 45 minutes, maybe an hour, maybe an hour and a quarter, until the beans are meltingly tender and thoroughly imbued with the onion/garlic/bacon taste. Don't take them out too early. And don't let them turn to total mush. In between those extremes, be my guest to make the beans adapt to your schedule rather than vice versa.

You see what this means? You can cook in a skillet on a low flame for a long time. Or you can stick the casserole in the oven with the baking potatoes or whatever, and, minimal fuss later, have a dish that will have your family raising their eyes joyously to the heavens. I cooked mine in a 375° oven, next to a pan full of halved yellow potatoes rolled in garlic/parsley/olive oil, and a casserole of sliced carrots mixed with a little butter, water, and a tiny bit of sugar. That was a complete and wonderful dinner in an hour, and in that hour I got to sit in front of the fire reading Trollope and having a glass of wine.

The smells were terrific, too. It felt like autumn, with winter coming on.

And if you're warm and well fed, that is a very nice feeling to have. One I'd wish for everyone at that season.

And what did I leave to last? What did I think I was going to have to sneak by all my gourmet friends? What did I think would stand tall and proud as a great everyday kitchen staple? And what did I think would immediately sink my cred to be even a moderately successful gourmand? Yes! It's…

FROZEN VEGETABLES ARE YOUR FRIEND (Some of Them)

It's true. There are a few frozen vegetables that the well-equipped freezer should seldom be without. They are a) versatile, b) handy, c) as good as or even better-tasting than the unfrozen versions.

In my experience, there are three more than worthy of your close attention: Spinach (either chopped or leaf form). Green peas (especially the baby 'petit pois'). And edamame (yes! that's right! the sushi-bar favorite available now in your grocer's frozen food section!).

(Some people would add corn kernels to that list. And yes, I agree, they're quite nice and good layered in, say, a Mexican-style rice/sour cream/rajas extravaganza. But I don't add them to my list since that's about all I can think of to do with them. And because they don't even begin to touch the taste of fresh corn on the cob.)

Spinach is the first. You just really owe it to yourself to have a bag of frozen spinach available for emergencies. Or even for nonemergencies. It tastes great. It's easy to fix. It's easy to add to about a kazillion dishes to add both color and flavor. Not to mention (did I mention?) it's damn good for you. And as you probably know by now, easy, tasty, good for you are my trinity of Food Traits of Excellence.

How many things can you use frozen spinach for? Ah, let me count the ways:

You can defrost it at room temperature, and squeeze the water out of it (don't be foolish, save that water for soup or to add to vegetable juice or even to cook your dog's food in—all those vitamins. Yum.) But you don't necessarily have to defrost. You can just cook it up, still frozen, like regular spinach. Just add a little butter to a skillet, melt over medium heat, add the spinach and stir till it's defrosted and heated through. Salt. Squeeze lemon on top. Serve as is, or use as a filling in the dish of your choice. Crepes are nice. Casseroles, definitely. Tossed with pasta, garlic and grated Parmesan. Mixed with the scooped-out insides of baked potatoes, spooned back in the skins, gilded with cheese and baked till warm through.

And then there's creamed spinach. How I love creamed spinach. And with frozen spinach, you can have creamed spinach whenever you want (and "whenever I want creamed spinach" turns out to be "quite often"). Melt some butter in the skillet as above, add a little finely minced onion. Sauté. Add a tablespoon or so of flour (Wondra flour is good here). Sauté to get the floury taste out, but keep it pale gold. Add the spinach (defrosted and squeezed is best here, since you don't want any added liquid) and stir to blend it all together. Then add a couple of splashes of heavy cream. Not the right consistency? Add a little more till it is. Cook to heat through and thicken the cream. Now (and please, I pray you, do not skip this step no matter how tempting to skimp) grate a little fresh nutmeg into the cream. This is easy. Whole nutmegs are cheap in the spice section of your supermarket. And they're easy to grate on a fine grater. Really. Trust me. You need this fresh nutmeg. PLEASE. Salt. Pepper if you like. Decant.

Serve it forth.

That is probably my favorite thing to do with frozen spinach.

Now. We move on to frozen peas. This is the one vegetable I have discovered is better frozen, ninety-nine times out of a hundred, than fresh. Unless you grow your own, you just can't get peas in the market that are still as sweet as they were when picked. They just turn to starch too darned fast. BUT here is one place where modern technologies work wholeheartedly in your favor. The peas get picked by someone else and frozen immediately, and they stay as youthful as the day they were picked. Petit pois, even sweeter, even better (if a little more expensive…your call). To serve them simply, just boil a little salted water, and dump in as many frozen peas as you want (water should just cover). Bring to the boil. Drain. Add a pat of butter and serve.

Fantastic on the side of a piece of grilled fish, might I add.

Or, you can add them to, say, a sauté of mushrooms you want to put atop some pasta. Just add them frozen and continue to stir the sauté; they'll cook just fine.

In other words, don't worry about that defrosting thing, no matter how many recipes urge you to feel anxiety here. Trust me. And if they give you any back talk, those experts, just refer them to me. I'll handle them for you. You just go on with doing things as simply as you can to get the best outcome possible. That's the general rule.

Which leads us to frozen edamame. These are soybeans, whole, in their pods, as served in sushi restaurants worldwide. Ever wonder WHY they are served in sushi restaurants worldwide? I mean, including those ones popping up in strip malls everywhere? It's because they're so damn easy to prepare, is why.

You take your bag of edamame. You boil enough water to cover as many pods as you and your guests are likely to eat your way through. Add salt. You open the bag. When the water boils, you pour the chosen amount into the water. (Any left in the bag? Just use a rubber band to close it up and toss back in the freezer to await developments.) Bring the water back to a boil, and boil for three or four minutes, stirring, long enough to heat the pods through and cook them a little. Then drain thoroughly, decant into a bowl, anoint with enough coarse salt (kosher is best, I find, just the right amount of crunch) to indicate its presence without unnecessary aggression. Take that bowl of edamame out to your guests, as well as an empty one for the pods, put them in their midst, and sit back and receive contented compliments as said guests pop the pods and strip the hot beans into their mouths. They'll be happily astonished at your savoir-faire; at least until they figure out how easy it would be for them to do it too.

But that's okay. The point is not the showmanship after all. The point is to eat well and to have a good time doing it together.

And frozen vegetables can help! Who would have thought it?

Food for Friends Too

Yes, I know I had a chapter called "Food for Friends" in the first *Jam Today*, but what can I say? Food is a way of connecting, connecting is another way of nourishing, and I am nourished in all sorts of ways by my friends—ways that may not always be so evident as the kind of nourishment that comes at meal time, but which are deeply satisfying all the same.

THE WORLD'S BEST UPSIDE-DOWN ADULT HAMBURGER

There's been something of a shift in our rural populations the last twenty years or so, as cities have grown so gargantuan that some civilized souls have felt the need to flee and seek a different, maybe even better, way. If you look around, you'll notice people living in the country have a different kind of gloss to them: they're a long way away from the old country mouse cliché. You see more and more young people moving out to states, and towns, and counties we didn't use to hear about in the *New York Times*, trying mushroom farming, goat ranching, cheese- and wine-making—all manner of nonvirtual activities. All manner of real activity. And we should be very grateful for that. A large part of our humanity is being preserved in these experiments, in these lives.

My neighbors, Cindy and Drew, are like that. They live on a ranch they built just south of me, in the house they designed and put up, next to the barn and the workshop, fitted around the garden and the woodpile and the henhouse, beside the acreage where their cattle graze. Both of them can do things, much to the benefit of the neighborhood. Cindy is an ace electrician, much in demand, and Drew is, among other things, a farrier. If you need some help of a practical kind, they are so there. Cindy recently fixed the generator for our volunteer fire department's station when the electricity kacked out. For example.

She grew up in a Midwestern college town; he grew up in New York ("I believe I was the only boy who actually hunted in the parks of Manhattan"), but they individually felt a pull west, and moved till they got to Oregon, where they met and joined families and built the ranch I mentioned, with the house with the screened-in porch where we sit when I go down to visit at wine time, using my need for eggs as an excuse (now that Dawn the Egg Lady is moving house, and has given her hens away). Cindy and I share a lot of interests—thrift stores, and cookbooks, the local fire department, and solving the mystery of why people aren't happier given all the riches and pleasures of a simple life well lived. We discuss these interests over another shared love—affordable, preferably beefy, red wines. I've spent many a pleasant pre-dinner hour sipping one of Cindy's finds out of a glass tumbler. Cindy and Drew tell great stories, too, of the kind that show the storyteller is fully engaged with his or her life, and since those are the stories I like most to hear, I always enjoy myself over there. (Drew's story of herding, on horseback, a bunch of cows who'd gotten loose on the freeway, "while those damn trucks whizzed by at eighty miles an hour, swear to God, it was like I was invisible to them," seems to me like some kind of metaphor for our lives right now.) I enjoy it there even when the talk turns sad, as it did once when Cindy and I talked about death, which her family has had a full and deep experience of, in a way all families pray fervently never to experience. And she said, "You know, I think that one of the things that makes life joyful is death." I agreed with her, and we sat quietly thinking about that, and sipping our wine.

That was a good day.

Anyway, one summer week I went down there at wine time, needing a dozen eggs, and wanting a couple of packages of the hamburger that Cindy has in the huge freezer in the shop, ground from the meat of their own cows. We went out there after a good-sized glass of a Rutherford Zinfandel. This had been drunk in the screened-in porch during a sudden unexpected downpour that made the dust smell rise up and liquefy, and made all your senses suddenly relax. So we were both in an amiable mood. She gave me the hamburger, and said, "Oh my God, you're going to so love this hamburger, I ended up putting all sorts of cuts in it: chuck and steak and…"

"I loved that last batch, too."

"No, no, this is TONS better than that one. You'll see."

When we got to the freezer, she felt inspired, as sometimes happens, to toss a bunch of other packages into my cloth bags: a bit of lamb, some elk neck, and about eight pounds of oxtail. I laughed and said, "You'll come eat some of this with me, right?" And she promised she would. I started thinking hard about what I would do with that oxtail. I went home to eat her eggs fried with bacon strips so the bright yellow yolk was still runny, served on top of a bed of lettuce and sliced avocado.

The next night I remembered what she'd said about the hamburger. I also remembered that my friend Teri loves hamburger, and that I love to have my friend Teri over for a (frequently carnivorous) girl dinner, just the two of us. I called and asked if she could come over that night. I was lucky. She could. And she did.

Fortunately, I had been wise enough to store one of the packages in the refrigerator, while all the rest went to the freezer below, and that one pound of hamburger was just perfectly, gently defrosted. So I took it out, and found I had a nice ripe avocado in a bowl on the counter, and some lettuce greens, and a leftover portion or two of a tomato/cucumber/cilantro/scallion/lime juice salad (just chop as much as you want of the ingredients and squeeze lime juice over to taste. Salt. Fantastic). After a moment's thought, I went back to the fridge and got out a jar of Dijon mustard.

Now I don't eat hamburger very often, and the main reason for this is that I like my beef really, really, really rare, 'bleu,' as the French so rightly say, and you just can't get good flavor, let alone assured food safety, out of most store-bought beef cooked almost raw. And many restaurants are reluctant to do them as rare as I like for the same reasons.

But here I had enough for two patties, half a pound each, of the most perfect hamburger you could ask for—ground from cows I had actually known in the pasture. And the people who raised them, and slaughtered them, and turned them into something we could all eat—they are my friends. You can't get better meat than that.

One thing I didn't have was any bread. But I didn't feel like eating any starches, anyway—I just wanted to enjoy the meat, and it turned out that, luckily, Teri felt the same way. I found I wanted fried onions on top, lots of fried onions (I like fried onions, and when I inquired, found Teri does too). I thought avocado, and lettuce, and a little bit of Dijon mustard on the side to dip pieces of meat in cautiously at will, would be just the ticket, and once again, Teri agreed. When we discussed it all further, we found neither of us wanted all of these things precariously balanced on top of the patty so that they kept sliding off.

Then I had a brain wave—why not put them under the burger, instead of on top? Oh, not the fried onions. Fried onions piled extravagantly high atop a burger, and falling lavishly off it to the sides, is part of the joy of eating a hamburger, as far as I'm concerned. But the lettuce, and the sliced avocado. Why not put them underneath, where they can soak up all the excess juice?

Why not indeed?

At the last minute, I sliced up a Roma tomato I had hanging around, and arranged it, and the sliced avocado, on two plates on top of the lettuce leaves. Lime wedges to the side. Divided what was left of the tomato/ cucumber/ cilantro/green onion salad and nestled it up against the lime. A spoonful each of Dijon mustard.

Then I made my burgers.

This is how (for two):

◊ Sliced onions, as many as you like
◊ Olive oil, butter
◊ 1 lb. grass-fed hamburger
◊ Salt and pepper

First I fried my onions. One onion, sliced thin, scattered in a cast-iron skillet, jolt of olive oil, small bit of butter. Low heat. I went outside with Teri and we drank a glass of my wine together while I waited for the inevitable smell, at which point I came back in and stirred the slices around till they got nice and browned.

Now I was ready. Halving the package of hamburger, I pushed the two lumps lightly into two very thick patties—two, maybe two-and-a-half inches thick. Then I pushed the onions to one side of the pan, turned up the heat underneath, and turned on the vent overhead. When the pan was sizzling, I laid the patties in, right over where the flames were licking the pan hottest. I let them sit there for a good three minutes, and then I turned them over. They were all browned and crusty at that point, so I turned the heat down, added a little more butter and oil, and cooked it another three for me, and then taking one of the patties off, another three for Teri, who likes her hamburgers a bit better done. Turned off the heat. Scooped the burgers up and onto the lettuce/tomato/avocado beds I'd made for them.

The kitchen smelled heavenly from burger and fried onions. We inhaled appreciatively, because that's a part of dining, too, and because Teri is always wonderfully appreciative (which is one of the reasons among many that she's so in demand as a dinner guest). I poured us two more glasses of wine. And we carried our wine and the plates outside to where I'd set the little table on the deck.

It was indeed the world's best hamburger. The beefiest, tastiest, tenderest burger imaginable. We ate it with great appreciation for it, the cow it came from, and the friends who had made it. And Teri and I toasted the little alpine valley where we live and have such neighbors who would raise such a miracle of beef.

Afterwards, when Teri and I had hugged good night and I had watched her contentedly amble home, I settled down with a pile of cookbooks and investigated ways to cook that oxtail. I was feeling so cocky after those terrific burgers, and I thought, why not share all that meat with friends? Teri and Cindy, of course. And Deidre and Laurel, too, while I was at it. There were eight pounds of it, after all…

And after thinking about them, and plotting, what became a reality was…

THE MONUMENTAL OXTAIL STEW

I should've known.

When Cindy said, "You want an oxtail? It's filling up my freezer." And I said, "Sure, of course!" Little did I know.

But I should've.

When she piled the three enormous white-butcher-paper-wrapped freezer bags into my arms, I should've at least suspected.

But I was blithe. I was thoughtless. Perhaps I was even a touch arrogant ("I can cook anything, can't I?"). Also, I suppose I was deluded. I mean, the word 'oxtail' did not conjure up an actual, real oxtail from an actual, real ox. I just thought, and vaguely, too, since this oxtail exchange took place after those couple of glasses of nice Alexander Valley Zinfandel on Cindy's screened-in porch that I mentioned before—well, I had a picture in my head of those cellophane-wrapped portions of store-bought oxtail. Nice, neat, red and white little rounds. I'd never cooked them. But they certainly had looked intriguing.

I should've known.

So when I got home, and realized there was, as I've said, eight pounds' worth of that stuff, I still didn't tumble to the reality of the situation. Instead, being temporarily without the Beloved Vegetarian Husband, and having a brand new restored kitchen to show off, I called up those four women friends—Teri and Laurel and Deidre and Cindy—and asked, do you want to come over and inaugurate my kitchen with a girl dinner of Oxtail Stew?

"I've never had oxtail stew," Laurel said.

"Neither have I," I admitted. "But I figure when you have eight pounds of oxtail in your freezer, that's the time to try."

We agreed she'd bring me some polenta, since I didn't have anything in the house to put the oxtail stew, once cooked, upon. A cup or two of dried polenta cornmeal, and I thought I'd cook that in the oven (the only way to cook polenta unless you want to spend an hour tied to the oven stirring it—one cup, four cups of water, salt, a bit of oil or butter, poured into a gratin dish, cooked for about an hour, stirred from time to time: thanks, Paula Wolfert) while I reheated the oxtail stew, which I would have cooked the day before.

Now that was lucky. I mean that I thought I should cook it the day before.

The day before THAT day before, I started thinking about the whole thing. Well, I thought idly. Red wine. Cook 'em in red wine. But I remembered that eight pounds of butcher-paper-wrapped meat dubiously, and who knew how much red wine it would take to cover all that? So I thought: well, I'll add water. That would've been okay, I'm sure, but then I had an inspiration of sorts.

There was meat and saved-up bones in the freezer. The Beloved Vegetarian Husband had been forced to go back to Colorado, while I had to stay in Oregon to make sure the kitchen got finished. So I was taking the opportunity to be a bit more of a carnivore than usual. Not that he nags me or anything, but…well…you know.

Anyway, he'd been gone for a couple of weeks, and I'd saved some chicken bones from one dinner in a bag in the freezer, just to make stock with. And then there was that pack of beef short ribs I'd bought on sale when they'd hit their due date at the market. Beef short ribs! I'd never cooked those. So then I thought: Tod, you love boiled beef. Put those short ribs in a pot with some sliced onion and a stalk of celery, a clove or two of garlic, and a sprig of thyme. Add those chicken bones. And simmer gently till you have both boiled short ribs for a meal, and a lot of broth—for the oxtail stew, and, who knows, maybe even another soup dinner.

Good idea, Tod, I said, patting myself mentally on the back. So I did that to the short ribs. I normally would've added a carrot, but I only had two left in the fridge, and I planned on putting them in the oxtail stew. This is Oregon, after all. Here I'm half an hour away from the nearest market, and it is amazing how that changes your shopping and cooking habits. When I'm in Boulder, I think nothing of running down to the market BECAUSE I CAN. (I'll never forget my amazement the first time I left a duck roasting in my Boulder oven, with the giblets covered with water on the stove top, and I went down to the wine shop to buy a bottle of something to go with the meal, and came home BEFORE THE WATER HAD BOILED. That was a red-letter day, all right.) I normally would've added a bay leaf, but in the recent kitchen disaster (see above), my bay leaves had gotten thrown out, and never replaced.

But I did have a big, beautiful bush of thyme in the Beloved Vegetarian Husband's garden (thank you, Alex). So I just grabbed a handful of that.

I gently cooked those short ribs, then put them in the refrigerator overnight, and skimmed the hardened fat off the surface the next day. Then,

114

looking at them, I just couldn't resist. I turned the heat on gently underneath, and went out to walk the dog. Came home and had them for lunch. I was only going to have two of the four—I did, after all, have an ear of boiled corn to eat beside them—but you know how that goes. I ate two, with coarse salt sprinkled atop, and Dijon mustard for dipping, and cornichon pickles on the side, and well, I just had to eat the other two as well.

I can't say I regretted it, either. And then, there was all this nice beef broth left behind. I thought I'd have that for dinner, maybe with an egg cooked in it, and the seaweed/cucumber salad that was left over in the fridge on the side. That sounded nice.

But first, the challenge of the oxtails. They were calling me. I was looking forward to putting them together in a nice stew, putting it on to simmer, and feeling, truth to tell, smug.

I should've known.

I hauled them out of the fridge, having put them there from the freezer a couple of days before to defrost. The outsides of two of the packages were getting bloody, so I handled them a bit gingerly.

First, brown the things, I figured. So I poured some Wondra flour in a bowl, salted it, and unwrapped the smallest package. There they were, little red and white rounds, just the way I'd pictured them. Humming, I heated some olive oil and butter in the biggest Le Creuset Dutch oven. Floured and salted the little suckers and popped them in the hot fat.

While they were turning a nice golden brown, I opened the second package. And blinked.

There, sitting on the butcher paper, was an enormous—nay, a ginormous—hunk of...what? Something red and white, certainly. But this was...what, seven inches across? What was this, a piece of a dinosaur?

Suddenly suspicious, I opened the biggest package of all. And stood there for a moment, stunned. Until I started to laugh out loud, so hard tears came to my eyes. Dinosaur tail! Yes! Huge hunks of meat, hacked at by someone who obviously finally gave it up as an impossible job. Massive, large, monumental pieces of…well, it must be oxtail. Cindy said it was oxtail. Also, there were two or three skinny long little pieces that…er…must be…the…END of the tail.

I should've known, I thought to myself, wiping my eyes before I got to flouring the epic mountains of meat, and putting them in the pot to brown. I mean—OXTAIL. What did I think? It was going to look like tea party food? Like finger sandwiches?

Well, maybe if the sandwiches were made from real fingers.

But do you think I would admit defeat? Admit defeat and fall back on a frittata to feed my friends? Never! Forward march to oxtail stew!

Two principles guided me: Anything cooked forever in red wine is going to get tender and taste good…eventually. And, as my brother Peter always says, "Anything tastes better if you add more garlic." I am a true daughter of my natal family, and that is a mantra for me.

So, lucky I had lots and lots of garlic…and lucky I know I have understanding friends. No matter what happened, I reckoned, we'd all have a good laugh together. And I could always make a frittata at the last minute.

But I wasn't ready to admit defeat. Never say die. So the oxtail stew braised gently in the oven all that day.

This is what I did (for six):

◊ Oxtail, about eight pounds
◊ Wondra flour
◊ Garlic salt
◊ Olive oil/butter
◊ 2 minced carrots
◊ 1½ minced large onions
◊ A minced stalk of celery
◊ 2 minced garlic cloves

◊　A head of garlic, cloves separated and peeled, left whole
◊　A diced tomato
◊　A little tomato paste
◊　A third or more of a bottle of red wine
◊　A basin full of broth
◊　Sprigs of fresh thyme

I browned that meat. Rolled the pieces in Wondra flour mixed with garlic salt, and browned them in heated olive oil/butter in a Dutch oven, a few uncrowded pieces at a time. Removed the browned pieces to a plate.

When all the pieces were browned, I poured out all but about 3 tablespoons of fat, and sautéed the two minced carrots, one and a half minced onions, a minced stalk of celery and two minced garlic cloves until they were soft.

Then I added the diced tomato, since I had one in the refrigerator almost overripe, and no plans to do anything else with it—and tomatoes always are a nice addition to any stew. After thinking for a moment, I added a tablespoon of tomato paste. One tomato just didn't seem enough tomato power to me.

When I'd cooked this for another minute, I added what was left of a bottle of red wine I'd been drinking for the last few days—about a third of the bottle. Could've been more, probably wouldn't have been good to be less. I brought that to a boil for a moment.

I looked at the huge mound of oxtail on its plate, and decided the skinny ends of tail should go to my dog. I gave him one of the pieces, which put him into ecstatic communion with the universe immediately, at least judging from his expression. I packaged the other two to give him later.

Even with that subtracted from the lot, I realized that was a lot of oxtail to just dump on top of the vegetables. So I spooned out about a cup of the wine/veggie mix. My idea was I would add that atop the packed-in meat once I had it all arranged.

I considered my options. And vaguely remembered a recipe that had seemed so wonderfully romantic, probably from Richard Olney, who is always Food Romance Personified, where the meat was layered with whole garlic cloves and innumerable sprigs of fresh thyme.

So I peeled a head of garlic, mainly by squishing the cloves with a knife and popping them out of their papery skins. And I went back to the garden and cut down a veritable sheaf of thyme (thank you again, Alex).

I packed the dinosaur...er...oxtail...into the Dutch oven, biggest pieces first, fitting all the other littler bits around them. As I packed, I scattered whole garlic cloves and sprigs of thyme.

Then I poured the wine and veggies I'd saved on top. THEN I took a ladle and ladled the beef stock from the short ribs over everything, until all the oxtails were almost completely submerged.

Lid on top. Put in a 325° oven. An hour and a half later, a heavenly smell began to sneak through the house. I began, well, not to relax exactly, but to look forward to seeing...to tasting...the end of the story.

For who knew what dinner would be like?

THE MONUMENTAL OXTAIL STEW PART TWO

I should have known. But of course I just blithely went into cooking those oxtails, sure I could just navigate my way around their immensity. And I didn't do my due diligence. While I did go through a bunch of recipes, I was a little cavalier about it. I didn't read those recipes at all closely, which is what I usually do in going into strange ingredient territory: read every recipe I can find, and pull out the basic pattern that all of them seem to follow, and then dress that pattern up according to some algorithm made up of how I feel that day combined with what I have in the house.

But I didn't read those recipes except in their broadest outlines, really just to reassure my overconfident self that I knew what I was about. Only after the big pot in the oven was giving out heavenly smells, and I pulled it out and tested the meat, and yes, it was testing tender, so I let the pot cool and put it in the refrigerator…only after that did it occur to me it might be helpful to have a closer look at what other people had to say about those oxtails. Well, again I was feeling pretty smug. Most of the recipes I had found by flipping through the books on my cookbook wall pretty much said to do what I had done—albeit with less garlic, and not so many sprigs of fresh thyme.

Then I got to Richard Olney.

His recipe was for an oxtail and pigs' ear stew. I had one brief, wistful moment of regretting I had no pig's ear hanging about in the pantry. And I shut that book and went to bed.

I think it was about two in the morning, which is a time I frequently wake and, all too frequently while going over the events of the day, ruefully remember some misstep I hadn't noticed in daylight. And this line from Olney's recipe floated through my mind: "Remove all excess fat from oxtails before browning."

A picture flashed through my mind there in the dark. All those oxtails. And the really big pieces coated in nice white fat. An inch thick.

Oh well, I laughed to myself. There's no mistake you can't fix—and that's the truth. That's another nice thing about getting older. It doesn't panic you quite as much as it does when you're young to make a mistake. You just laugh at yourself, generally, and move on to thinking about what can be done, instead of brooding over what has been done.

(I still remember my upset at the ruin of a lovely boeuf à la mode I was trying to cook for guests when I was in my twenties. The recipe called for it to be wrapped neatly in twine, in order for it to keep its shape, which instruction I followed religiously. Of course, I should have noticed the twine I used was string coated in some kind of plastic, which burnt smell started coming from the pot fairly quickly into the process. Ruined! Ruined! I wailed, and cried, and threw the meat out, went out to the store and bought another roast we could ill afford and began the whole process again. What would I have done today? Laughed (I hope), thrown out the sauce, cut off the outside of the roast where the plastic had melted and stuck, sliced the roast, and made another kind of sauce to coat the slices, layered these, and covered the whole with bread crumbs and minced garlic and a little Parmesan, before nestling it back in the oven to make an appetizing gratin. That's what I think I would have done now. There are, as the novelist Barbara Pym once said, some compensations for being fifty that a twenty-year-old woman may not suspect. For one thing, many a fifty-year-old cook does not bother wrapping the damn pot roast in any kind of twine. Why not let it be comfortable? is the way the older woman's mind works…mine, anyway.)

I went back to sleep, serene in the knowledge that I could and would deal with that ridiculous amount of fat in the morning. "And besides," I murmured to myself, "cooking it with the fat will just add flavor, yes?"

In the morning I pulled the pot out of the refrigerator. And yes, indeed, there was the fat hardened on top of the sauce—about a good four inches thick of it. This is why you make these dishes in the day before the party. It's easy to pull chilled fat off the top of a stew, much easier than skimming it while the stew is still hot…and you are, too. Much better to be leisurely about these things, letting everything and everyone cool down. The end result tastes better, too.

So I scraped the fat off into a bowl, and saved it to add, bit by bit, to the dog's food, since I'm well aware this kind of thing makes him grunt with delight (but not too much, not as much as he'd like, very rich it is—very). And got down to the gelled sauce underneath, all rich and unctuous, and with the minced carrot suspended inside it like a scatter of jewels. All that beautiful sauce, and these weirdly and variously shaped pieces of oxtail. Well, an oxtail IS weirdly and variously shaped; what on earth had I expected?

So now the challenge was to tame the dish and make it respectable for company. This meant pulling the meat off the bones in nice, tender chunks of varying size. I proceeded to do that, greatly impressed both with how tender and tasty the meat was (you didn't think I was going to be able to do this without tasting, did you? that would be so, so unlike me), and at what an enormous amount I managed to get off those bony bits.

I have noticed (perhaps you have too?) that the tastiest meat comes from the boniest bits. The taste comes from the bones and the fat and the skin. You know those packages of pallid-looking skinless boneless chicken breast? No taste. No taste at all. You might as well be eating protein powder, in my opinion. And it would be kinder to the chicken if you did. Would YOU want to have spent a life of torture only to end up as something mindlessly prepared and eaten just because it was cheap and, supposedly, healthy? I wouldn't.

So now I was getting enthusiastic about this oxtail stew. I put all the pieces of meat I had scavenged off the bones back into the pot with the sauce. But then I looked sadly at the bones sitting there forlornly in a big bowl, nice jellied bits of the same sauce still clinging to them, and I thought, "How awful to waste all that flavor! How sad!"

That was when I had a lovely brain wave, which I have to admit I bragged about at dinner that evening. If I was going to reheat the stew in the oven while I cooked the polenta, I was going to have to add some kind of liquid to it that could cook down in the heat—the sauce was at that perfectly thick state already, and heat wasn't going to improve it. I had an open bottle of white wine in the fridge, and that was all, my having used the last bit of red in the original dish. So I was going to use some of that. But what I did first was pour some white wine on top of those sauce-covered bones in the big bowl, and then I swished the bones around and rinsed that sauce right off them into the white wine. And then I added THAT wine to the pot.

I was quite proud of myself for that one.

Nevertheless, I held my breath. The guests arrived—Laurel with the promised polenta, along with tomatoes from her garden, and a lovely ripe cheese with crackers. Teri with lemon squares and mineral water. Deidre with a deep-flavored red wine. And Cindy with some of her eggs, and an enormous bouquet of herbs from her garden—basil and dill and parsley—that looked so beautiful it went immediately into a flower vase. We had our wine on the deck in the late summer evening sun, and ate the cheese (Rogue Creamery Lavender Blue! Superb!). As the smells from the oxtail stew wafted out, you could feel a tiny tremor of curiosity about the dinner to come.

Me, too. I was curious too. Curious, and nervous, as a good hostess should be, I suppose. At least a good hostess who is about to serve her friends an oxtail stew.

And you know what? It was absolutely delicious. Everyone, dubious about the oxtail (except for Cindy, who serenely awaited the stew, but after all, it had been her ox), gasped with pleasure when they smelled the red wine/garlic/thyme sauce and saw how beautiful the stew looked on the gold polenta, scattered with chopped parsley. Everyone had seconds, and this time they skipped the polenta so they wouldn't waste the calories. My friend Teri said, "When you said it looked like dinosaur, I got worried. I kept thinking it was going to taste like a dragon or something. But then I remembered I've always been happy at dinner at your house, and I calmed down."

I shouldn't have mentioned that dinosaur thing, I realized then. No. I should have said something like, "Ah, a special stew from Cindy's own beef, fragrant with herbs, flavored deeply with wine." Something like that.

I should have known.

But in the end, it was all right. My four women friends and I had a jolly evening, and we all toasted Cindy, and celebrated the ox.

THE AFTER-PARTY

The day after my dinner party featuring that unctuous oxtail stew, I was in the mood for something a little simpler and more modest in scope. That's the time when I think about an omelet. And so it was that evening. I made myself a little two-egg omelet with a bit of cheese, and sliced a tomato, laying it out on a white plate and topping it with torn basil leaves, coarse salt and olive oil.

With the omelet and the tomato salad, I had a glass of sparkling water mixed with the small bit of white wine left in a bottle from the night before.

A beautiful, satisfying supper. And as I ate, I suddenly realized:

The eggs and the basil had come from Cindy.

The cheese in the omelet had come from Laurel.

The sparkling water had been part of Teri's contribution (we polished off her dessert, nothing left).

And Deidre's wine, well, we'd finished that the night before, but it left a satisfying memory, which was part of my nourishment the day after.

So my 'solitary' dinner was really by way of being an After-Party. I thought about how lucky I was to have four friends to share a meal with, and then to think about the pleasures of sharing a meal with them when I dined by myself, apparently alone. But not alone, not really. You're never really alone when you have a rich store of evenings like that.

With friends like that at home in Oregon, I was a little sad when we moved, part-time, to Boulder, Colorado. Would I find friends like that? How could I? How could there BE friends like that anywhere else? And yet, there are friends of all kinds to be found everywhere. But most of all, there are always friends who like to eat and drink and make a modest merry, if only one looks to find them...

DINING WITH A FRIEND

It was a snowy day, and the Beloved Vegetarian Husband was off somewhere or other in another clime, and I was homesick for my hearth in Oregon, and for the friend there who I liked to sit alone with on winter evenings, drinking wine and talking about things that really happened and thoughts we really have—a rare conversation, generally. How many times do you talk about what's really going on with someone who will tell you what's really going on with her?

I had almost given up hope of finding a friend of that kind in the new place we were living in, although why I should want to find the same friend I'm sure I don't know—friends being unique, irreplaceable. It was a lapse. But there I was feeling sad, although we had a new hearth in the new home in the new place (gas, of course, less fussy than wood, more…urban). I had invited a woman I had met only twice before to come share my dinner, but she lived an hour away, and it was, as I've said, snowing. I was sure she wouldn't want to come. And I wanted to let her off the hook. So I called her up.

"Don't feel you have to come if you don't want to. And you can wait till evening to decide."

"Is it snowing? Really? I have a cold, and I'm in bed. I'll worry about it later, if that's okay with you."

"Of course it is. And here are your choices, if you do decide to come. I've just been shopping, so I can give you 1) macaroni and cheese, with a celery salad dressed with mustard, 2) sautéed trout with brown rice and vegetables and wasabi butter, or 3) roasted vegetables with thyme, and a beet salad."

There was a considering silence for a moment. A perfect kind of silence, actually. She was weighing the options; she was taking them seriously in a way I thoroughly appreciated.

"Won't the trout not keep?"

"Naw, don't worry. I've put it in a teriyaki marinade; it'll only get better. Alex and I can have it tomorrow."

More thought.

"I think," she said—and you could tell she was really thinking about it, and the thought was really giving her pleasure, so it gave me pleasure, too—"since I'm sick, not the macaroni and cheese. Too rich for a cold. I vote for the vegetables."

"Veggies it is. If it's not snowing too hard. And you still want to come." I was sure she wouldn't want to. It was snowing harder and harder outside, and if it had been me...

An hour before dinner, the phone rang.

"I'm up. I've been in bed all day and I feel fantastic. Looking forward to those veggies."

I was pleased. "Don't bring anything, okay?" I said earnestly. "Anyone who has to drive an hour in the snow to dinner is exempt."

Chopping the vegetables and strewing them with thyme, I remembered I didn't have anything sweet in the house for dessert. I'd meant to buy a couple of chocolate bars, but forgot. I always think you should have a little bit of chocolate for dessert. Damn.

When she arrived, she was holding a bottle of wine, and a bar of chocolate. "You should have a little bit of chocolate for dessert," she said earnestly. I smiled.

I offered her a Kir Framboise. "Oh yes," she said. You know a Kir Framboise? It's a Kir, which is a French aperitif made by dolloping a heart of liqueur into a glass of wine—but with raspberry liqueur, framboise, instead of the cassis usually called for. You put a small capful of the deep-red/purple stuff at the bottom of the glass, and fill to the top with white wine. Delicious.

And beautiful, too.

I brought those out along with a few celery and carrot sticks, and a little bit of blue cheese smooshed into some Greek yoghurt for dip. And we curled up in the matching huge chairs Alex and I have by the fireplace with those rosy drinks, with the smell of the vegetables—fennel, carrot, celery, onion, garlic cloves, and sweet potato, all diced and mixed with olive oil and branches of thyme that I dug up out of the snow in the garden—filling the house.

And we talked about things that mattered: the things that mattered to her, and the things that mattered to me, and the things that mattered to us both. Love and art and solitude and companionship, and a few intellectual back roads I was delighted to find she enjoyed a meander on once in a while. We meandered on them together and sipped our pink glowing wine.

When the vegetables had cooked so long that they were nice and browned and caramelized, we sat down to them and a little more of that rosy aperitif, because it was so tasty that neither of us wanted to move on to red wine, and the snow came down outside, and everything was warm and kind and good.

Afterwards, we had a little piece of chocolate or two, because we both know you should have a little bit of chocolate after dinner, and then we said good night, and I sent her on her way ("That was a breeze getting here, even in the snow! We'll have to do it again soon!"). And as she turned to walk off the deck down to her car, she paused and said, "Those vegetables were delicious. They kept me from regretting I didn't ask for macaroni and cheese after all."

"Next time," I promised, with a laugh, and waved as she drove down the snowy street. And I went inside, quite pleased, because I knew there would be a next time, and I didn't feel sad anymore. And I slept wonderfully well, all night long.

HOW TO MAKE ROASTED VEGETABLES FOR A NEW FRIEND WITH A COLD:

Take whatever vegetables you have at hand, but always remembering to include onions and whole peeled garlic cloves. As many veggies as you think you'd like and can eat. That night I had a couple of sweet potatoes bursting out of their papery skins. I had an ivory and emerald bulb of fennel; I had celery stalks. I had carrots (of course, I always have carrots), and an onion, and garlic, and lots of parsley. And I had the beet greens that came with the beets I baked for our salad.

So this is what I did:

◊ Veggies
◊ An onion
◊ Whole peeled garlic cloves
◊ Olive oil
◊ Branches of fresh thyme, or a scattering of dried
◊ Coarse salt

I chopped the onion.

I diced the fennel, the celery, the carrots, the sweet potatoes, all about the same size.

I chopped the beet greens. Chopped a handful of parsley.

Peeled about a dozen garlic cloves.

Mixed all of the above in a big ceramic casserole, anointed them with enough olive oil just to coat, not to drown, salted with coarse salt, and then threw in about five or six branches of fresh thyme. Swooshed the whole thing together with my hands, and put it in a 400° oven for about an hour and a half, which is just the right amount of time to prepare a couple of Kirs Framboise for a new friend, and sit with her by the fire and talk about the things that matter to you both. Then wait till the veggies get nice and browned and caramelized. Serve with a salad—in this case, sliced beets baked in the same oven, dressed with a mustard vinaigrette. A little piece of chocolate for dessert is always nice.

Talk, sip, serve, and sleep well, knowing you've dined with a friend.

SALT COD AND CREAM

So that was such a success, we planned another girl dinner…and I sent her this email:

"Are we still on? What time?

And if so, here are some of your choices for dinner:

Shrimp/greens/tomatoes/smoked paprika. Probably with a salad of some kind.

Salt cod baked with potatoes in garlic cream.

Macaroni and cheese. Celery salad.

Smoked salmon frittata with undetermined veggies/salad.

I could go on, but maybe there's something in the above you like?

T."

As she voted for the salt cod, that's what we had. It was on the list because I've taken to making my own salt cod quite often in Boulder. For some reason, we get frozen cod from Alaska quite cheaply here, and salting it oneself is even more of a satisfying economy, anywhere from $2.99 (yes, really) to $5.99 a pound. I happened to have some salting in the fridge when we made this plan.

This is how to salt cod:

Buy some cod fillets. As many as you like. Between two-thirds of a pound and a pound will feed two, depending on what you do with them.

Lay them in a casserole dish that will hold them flat without too much space around them.

Salt heavily on both sides. Use any kind of salt you like for this: coarse, Kosher, or plain table.

Cover with plastic wrap (this is so the fish doesn't smell up the rest of your refrigerator).

Refrigerate.

Next day:

Pour off the water that's accumulated around the fish. Salt again on both sides.

Repeat the last step until the day when no more water appears, and the filets are nicely coated with salt.

You can use them any time, you don't have to wait for that step, but once they are dry and salted, they'll keep for a couple of weeks at least.

I do not have specific time frames about this one since I've never been able to keep them more than a few days.

The day before you're going to eat them:

Rinse off the salt.

Put them back in the casserole and fill with water.

Refrigerate.

Change the water once or twice in the next 12 to 24 hours.
When you taste the water, and it's not salty, the fillets are ready to cook.

Now, the big question. How to cook? There are so many ways salt cod is so astoundingly delicious. And comforting. And good for you, too (there's a reason those Basques kept it quiet that they had discovered America's cod fisheries about two hundred years before Columbus started enslaving its Indians). You can make brandade, the celestial mating of garlic, mashed potatoes, and cod. You can make Portuguese salt cod and potatoes, the equally celestial orgy of olives and (you guessed it) garlic, cubed potatoes, and salt cod with a little parsley thrown in. But of all the celestial cohabitings of salt cod, the most Olympian of all is:

Salt Cod Baked with Potatoes in Garlic Cream

Here's how:

First, jettison all personal worries about eating too much dairy and too many calories. Just this one dinner. Come on. Live a little. Add a glass of red wine on the side, and you'll be glad you did.

Next, invite someone to share this delightful orgy of garlic and cream. Someone you like to talk to. This dish will cook undisturbed, bubbling happily by itself, for an hour or more while you chat.

Now, construct the casserole. This can be done earlier in the day, and left to sit till ready to pop into the oven.

Like so:

◊ Salt cod fillets
◊ Peeled, sliced russet potatoes
◊ Garlic
◊ Butter
◊ Cream
◊ Nutmeg, grated
◊ A tiny bit of salt

Put the salt cod fillets flat in a skillet and cover with cold water. (If you've thought of it earlier in the day, you can make a little court bouillon by boiling some carrot, celery, garlic cloves, and parsley, then letting the whole thing cool before adding the cod). Turn the heat onto low. Watch carefully for the first sign of bubbling. At this sign, turn off the heat and let the cod sit from five to ten minutes, until it flakes easily. Careful: overcooking leads to woolly cod, for which there is no remedy. I've been there. I know.

Peel twice the weight of the salt cod in russet potatoes. Slice very thinly (I use the slicing side of the grater).

Mash up as much garlic as you like. I recommend about three cloves for a pound of cod and two pounds of potatoes.

Add garlic to cream along with a little salt. Not too much salt, the cod should take care of that.

SPECIAL WARNING: Now get out whole nutmeg and a nutmeg grater. You don't need to do this, but if you do, you'll never regret having learned this step and applying it to this particular casserole.

Butter a casserole dish that's just big enough to hold all the cod in one layer. By coincidence, you should have one handy, if you've washed and dried the dish the cod was salting in. Butter it well. As Nigel Slater once memorably said, "You're only hurting yourself if you don't."

Make a layer of half of the potato slices. Pour garlic cream on top. Now, very important, GRATE A LITTLE NUTMEG atop. I repeat, you will not regret this.

Now layer the salt cod. Add more garlic cream. If you've used up all the garlic cream, just add more cream. It will all meld together in the end anyway.

A little teeny bit more grated nutmeg.

A final layer of sliced potatoes.

More cream. Press down on the potatoes. Does the cream just cover the top, lapping gently at the sides? Good. Now if you want, put the dish on a cookie sheet so if in process the cream bubbles enthusiastically over, you have something to catch it in.

Now put it in the oven and turn the oven to 400°. You can preheat if you want, but I can't see the point here. It's just fine if you let the casserole heat up with the oven, in partnership as it were.

Cook for about an hour, until the cream is absorbed by the potatoes, and the top crust is nice and browned. A little longer won't hurt it. Don't take it out before cream absorption, though. It'll still taste good, but not celestially good.

Let sit for a moment to settle while you toss a nice green salad. Cut lemon wedges if you like them to put on the side. Pour out red wine if you haven't done so already. (I hope you have done so already.)

Serve on a plate with salad and the lemon. The salad is nice to moosh around in the thickened cream of the casserole. I like it that way, but you'll have your own ideas.

As long as your ideas include maximum enjoyment of company and food, we're good.

We were good that night.

So it was a very nice night.

KENTUCKY CURRY OR TALKING FOOD OVER WITH FRIENDS

One of my favorite games is the "what's in your refrigerator?" game. What I like to do (in fact, I get so enthusiastic in this game that I end up tripping all over myself in my eagerness to play) is get on the phone with a friend or two, find out what they've got in their kitchen, talk about what they feel like eating, and then construct a menu out of those elements.

It's especially fun, I have to admit, when the person whose kitchen is at issue insists there is NOTHING in that kitchen with which to make a meal. I once came up with six different possibilities for dinner in such a kitchen, but of course, Jennifer and Jeff, the couple who owned the kitchen, had totally forgotten all that late autumn chard they still had in their garden, and the bowl of purple potatoes on the sideboard. Not to mention the eggs.

Recently, I played this with my friends Margaret and Marie, who, I must admit, are no slouches in the kitchen-stocking/cooking department. I mean, when they told me what they had in their refrigerator, and the cupboards surrounding that refrigerator, I was overwhelmed by an embarrassment of riches, as it were. And they knew it, too. In fact, I realized that they were just being kind, letting me play with their kitchen like that. Being friendly. They didn't need me at all. Still, it was fun to play.

And their kitchen, in the South, was filled with typically American 21st-Century ingredients, as well as all the bounty one expects from a southern household that keeps a garden. So, I mean, this was such a no-brainer, I had to make it more difficult for myself. I cudgeled my brain as to how to do this as Margaret chanted, "And then there are the vegetables we froze from the garden, there's green beans, and okra, oh, and tomatoes, I almost forgot that, and…"

"Wait, wait, wait!" I wailed. "Isn't there something you have in there that you don't know what to do with? Something I can really (figuratively) sink my teeth into?"

There was a moment's silence.

"Well," Marie said. "There's that coconut milk."

"I don't know what she was thinking, buying that coconut milk," said Margaret.

"It is just sitting there," Marie admitted.

"Hah!" I said. "HAH! Eureka!" Then I said cautiously, "Wait a minute, in all that list you gave me, you never mentioned garlic or onions."

"Oh," Margaret scoffed, "Of course we have THOSE."

"We ALWAYS have those," Marie said.

True cooks. That is their mark. So for two true cooks, who let me play with their kitchen that day, I made the recipe below, from ingredients they found in their refrigerator:

Kentucky Curry (atop Tabouli Salad)

For two you need:

◊ A chopped or sliced onion
◊ A bit of minced fresh chile pepper or a pod of dried
◊ Frozen vegetables from the garden: green beans, okra, tomatoes
◊ Whole peeled garlic cloves
◊ Coconut milk
◊ A bit of olive oil
◊ A bit of minced fresh ginger
◊ Curry powder
◊ Salt
◊ Chopped fresh mint from the Southern winter garden

and

◊ Tabouli
◊ Kale/parsley/romaine salad
◊ Lemon juice

In a big skillet, fry the chopped onion in a bit of oil till soft. Add a bit of minced fresh chile pepper or a crushed dried chile pod. Add the minced ginger and about a teaspoon of curry powder. Salt. Taste to see if you want more curry powder, and if you do, then add a little more. Fry till it all smells wonderfully of curry and ginger. Then add as many frozen green beans and okra as you think both of you can eat, with a few extra for lunch leftovers the next day. Coat well in the curry oil, then add the whole garlic cloves and one or two or three frozen tomatoes, chopped. Cook it all till the veggies are defrosted and the tomato has started to disintegrate. Then add enough coconut milk to make a nice sauce, as much as you like. Cook till the whole begins to amalgamate in a deliriously aromatic way.

In the meantime, prepare the tabouli. Mix with as much chopped kale/parsley/romaine salad as you like. Squirt it with lemon juice to taste.

To serve: Spoon the Kentucky Curry atop the tabouli, sprinkle with chopped fresh mint from the garden.

I suspect Margaret and Marie were humoring me with this—in fact, I know it, because I found out later what they had for dinner later that night was reheated pot roast with corn bread and salad and a nice Beaujolais. But I still maintain Kentucky Curry is a cheerful dish to cook in the depths of any winter, and I know for sure that the recipe has already given me a lot of satisfaction: as so often happens in cookery, much of the pleasure in any dish comes from the plotting of it and the thought of it and the enjoyment of the discussion together.

Thanks for that, Margaret and Marie!

TORTILLA ESPAÑOLA

Do you know Tortilla Española? Spanish omelet? Otherwise known as Potato and Garlic Frittata? No matter what its name (and it's confusing to realize it's an egg dish, not a corn one from Latin America), it's delicious. Always good for a party. And it's one of those things I love to take to a party because it's made with ingredients I almost always have about me. It's flexible. Inexpensive. Delicious. And can be, with a few judicious additions, exotic— leading friends and family to gaze at the cook admiringly as they eat. Which is never a bad thing.

The one thing about Tortilla Española which is a bit daunting (actually, there are two, but I'll get to the other one in a bit), as with all frittatas or flat omelets, is that you're expected to flip the damn thing over after it's cooked on the bottom side. Now I don't know about you, but this flipping thing is just beyond me. I can't even bring myself to attempt it, not after that last unfortunate time anyway. I know this reveals me for the culinary coward I am, but we're being honest here, aren't we? (Because if we aren't, we might as well pack up and go home.)

What I always do, when making a frittata, is try to make the lovely eggy little thing in a nonstick pan that can go under the broiler for the last browning of the top. This means no plastic handle. (It also means, these days, no Teflon, since Teflon makes me nervous, along with a lot of other technological innovations that came out of twentieth-century military research…I include nuclear energy and Tang in this general condemnation.)

But then, I was invited to come have a glass of wine with a new friend, a lawyer and a librarian and a fascinating talker, and she said she had an evening board meeting afterward, "So that means 'heavy appetizers,' if you can figure THAT out!" Moved by sympathy at the idea of her long workday, as well as a sneaking desire to impress a new friend, I decided I should bring something to go with the excellent wine she always poured, that her husband, in fact, blended. The best thing I could think of was an order of

Tortilla Española. Comforting. Excellent at room temperature. Cut into squares, easily handled while we sat at the little corner table in her office, with the view of the Rocky Mountains at sunset. Impressive in its own casual sort of way. And, as I said, good for a party—even a party of two. So that seemed about perfect.

One problem. At the house we had moved into in Colorado, I completely lacked a nonstick skillet that could go under the broiler. Buying kitchen gear mostly, as I do, at thrift stores, means you don't buy nonstick pans there—it's like buying running shoes, a used pair is practically useless for the purpose intended or it wouldn't have been given away in the first place. What I had were two ceramic-lined skillets of varying sizes with plastic handles, an inexpensive experiment bought on impulse at the local hardware store.

I contemplated this situation. I could try that flipping thing, I mused, then shuddered at the memory of the last time I so attempted. I could do what I'd done before in similar circumstances, and what recipes generally advise to the faint of heart, which is slide a big flat pan lid on top of the skillet and flip the omelet onto that, sliding it back, uncooked side down, into the pan. Well, that works. But what I dislike about that method, and what they never mention when they recommend this strategy, is that all that uncooked egg ends up on the pan lid. And I don't want the uncooked egg on the pan lid, I want it on top of the rest of the egg, where it belongs.

Then I had a brain wave. Now, I'm sure others have had this brain wave before me—there are no original brain waves in cooking, no matter what those big fancy chefs tell you, and who wants to turn perfectly good food into foam anyway?—but it still gave me that frisson of pleasure that always comes when I make some kind of mild personal breakthrough, especially in the kitchen. It was those two ceramic-lined skillets I was looking at. Why not? I thought. Why not cook the flat omelet in the smaller of the pans, and then flip it into the larger and cook the other side? Sure, it would mean two pans to clean instead of one, but these are ceramic-lined, for pity's sake, they practically need no more cleansing than a quick paper-toweling before putting them back in the cupboard.

Would it work? It worked! And we had a lovely Tortilla for dinner that cocktail hour, and my friend very generously gave me the proper amount of friendly admiring looks. It went spectacularly with her husband's red wine. In fact, so spectacularly that I have no idea how she got through that board meeting later. Well, the "heavy appetizers" might have helped.

Here's what I did.

For two people for dinner or, theoretically, four people as appetizers. I say theoretically, since on the evening in question, we ate the whole thing:

◊ Two medium to large russet potatoes
◊ A clove or two of crushed garlic (preferably two)
◊ Six eggs
◊ 1 teaspoon smoked paprika
◊ Salt
◊ Olive oil alone, or mixed with goose or duck fat if you have some—enough when melted to cover the bottom of the skillet

Peel and slice the potatoes thinly. I use the slicing side of a box grater, but it doesn't matter if you slice them more thickly; they just take longer to cook that way.

Crush the garlic (or slice it if you like it that way).

Heat the fat in a skillet. (I used a mixture of goose fat and olive oil, since I had some of the former stashed in the fridge. A good fruity olive oil is key to the Spanish taste, but a little goose or duck fat can never hurt.)

When it sizzles, add the potatoes and garlic. Salt. Turn the heat to medium-low, and sauté—stew, really—till the potatoes easily break when you poke them. You can stand there and flip, or you can turn the heat down even lower, clap a lid on the skillet, and walk away for ten minutes, coming back to flip until they are done. The main point is they shouldn't brown. This isn't hash browns (though nothing against hash browns, nothing at all), it's Tortilla Española. This is why most recipes call for about two cups of olive oil for the potatoes to stew in on low heat, and then, in those recipes (authentically Spanish), you drain the oil off the potatoes when they're done, save it and use for another day. This is that second point about Tortilla Española that I find daunting, but I solve it by using less oil, just watching the potatoes more closely…and then, if there is any extra oil left at the end, I use it to oil the pan in which to cook the actual frittata. So there.

(By the way, if the potatoes DO brown, don't worry…they'll still taste terrific. Just different. Terrific and different is not a bad combination to work with.)

Now, here's MY frisson for Tortilla Española. While the potatoes cook, add a teaspoon of smoked paprika. Yum. You'll be glad you did.

Once they are done, turn off the heat. Let the pan sit till it cools.

Meanwhile, crack six eggs into a bowl, and stir them until blended, or whip them, or do whatever it is you like to do to eggs in this condition.

When the potatoes and garlic are cool enough, dump into the eggs. Stir.

Wipe out the pan with a paper towel. Have another, slightly larger, pan on standby.

Heat the smaller pan until a flick of water sizzles and skitters on it. Add olive oil, about a tablespoon or so. When that sizzles, add the egg/potato mixture, lifting it up and letting runny bits run down the way you always do when making an omelet. Feel smug as you think about how you don't need to be as anxious as usual about that flipping thing at this moment.

Heat the larger pan on another burner. Apply high heat till a bit of water skitters on it, then turn it down to medium.

When the omelet is firm and browned on one side in the smaller pan, turn it over onto the uncooked side into the larger pan.

Turn off that first burner! Now concentrate on browning the uncooked side, which probably won't take all that long.

You want a Tortilla Española to cook all the way through, not to be runny like a folded omelet, but sturdy like a frittata.

When it's done, slide it onto a platter. It's good hot, cold, or at room temperature. I prefer room temperature myself, which makes it ideal for a casual dinner.

Serve in wedges if it's the main course. Or, if you want it for an appetizer, as I did that evening, cut it into little squares and, if you're feeling fancy, serve on toothpicks, or, if you're not, just let people pick it up with their fingers. That's what we did.

Good with garlic mayonnaise, if you have any on hand. (I didn't, but don't let that stop you.)

If there's any leftover (hah!), it's great as a sandwich, slapped between bread slices slathered with the aforementioned garlic mayonnaise.

There are a lot of exotic and domestic twists you can do to this basic recipe. Add sliced onions to the potatoes. Add more garlic. Add some cooked crumbled sausage. Add chopped parsley. Harissa spice instead of the smoked paprika. Crumbled red pepper instead of either of those. Chopped cooked chard. Go crazy. But not too crazy. The basic potato, garlic, olive oil goodness is good enough for kings and queens and it certainly was for my friend and me. And if you use that two-skillet flipping trick, you won't feel a moment's anxiety as you cook your way into your friends' hearts. Not that you're not there already. But this way, you'll be there AND they'll be well-fed.

And speaking of well-fed, what about the dogs? You knew I wouldn't forget about the dogs, didn't you? I mean, when speaking about food for friends…

LIVER DOG TREATS

It's nice living in a community. Actually, it's more than nice—it's necessary for happiness, at least it is for mine, and I suspect I am not alone in this. It's knowing where you belong, and that the people alongside you (even the ones you don't like much, and there are certainly a few of those) belong there, too. The neighborhood gossip, the neighborhood joys, and the neighborhood sorrows are part and parcel of what I think of as the Good Life. And then there are the stories of the lives of your neighbors, which are always so gripping. For example, my neighbor Cindy, of Cindy and Drew, came over the other day allegedly to give me some electrician's advice. We forgot all about that. Instead, we sat down, had a couple of glasses of wine, and she told me about how she and Drew had driven their cows home from the pasture the day before. It was a three-mile drive, she told me, in 100-degree heat, and they did it on horseback with two heeler dogs ("Doc was useless, but Dinah's pretty good at it"). Fifteen cows, one bull, and two calves. They did it in an hour.

Not bad.

Aside from always having some fascinating story to tell, Cindy is a particularly good neighbor. The Beloved Vegetarian Husband and I came home last winter to find three feet of snow had fallen overnight, and she, welcoming us, had dug a path from the driveway to the front door through the snow. And then she hung on the front door a bag that held the following:

◊ A jar of honey from her bees
◊ A jar of almonds
◊ A dozen of the eggs from her hens
◊ And a bag of dried liver dog treats

This last was made from the liver of one of her cows. The dogs go absolutely mad for these. I mean, they will do anything to get some. Gray, our male, is given to going on walkabout at the full moon, and you just don't want to know what he can do to a neighbor's garbage can, even when that can is thoroughly bear-proofed. (Or maybe you do—he has been seen leveraging the stepladder laid across the can till he gets it off, knocking the lid back in the process. And they say dogs don't know how to use tools. They do if there's chocolate cake in the offing, is my experience.) But if I see him sneaking off (and it is sneaking, never let it be said that dogs don't think about what they're doing), I call him back by saying, "Gray! Liver treat!" He contemplates his options, thinks the better of that seductive chocolate cake or leftover pizza or hambone he smells from across the road, the eating of which will inevitably make him sick, and me more than a little annoyed, and he turns around and trots right back to me, virtuous, a balloon coming out over his head saying, "Me? Eat the neighbor's garbage? Wouldn't think of it." In the end, he reckons a good, healthy pleasure is better than the hangover that's going to come from partying down, and I figure that's all to the good, and I've conquered his desire for gluttonous excess one more full moon.

So while we were talking about the cattle drive, I remembered those liver treats, which presumably came from those cows. "Oh yeah," she said. "Every so often we have to slaughter one for one reason or another. And you wouldn't believe how cow livers go to waste. Nobody wants them. Even the dogs won't eat a lot of fresh liver unless you cook it." Cindy and I have this in common: we both hate waste. So that was how she began making liver treats.

I asked Cindy how she did it, and this is how:

"You take a whole liver, which from a mature cow weighs about eight pounds. (Note: obviously, you can do this with as much or as little of store-bought liver as you like as well.)

Then you slice it into slabs about ¾ inch thick.

Grill to well-done on gas or charcoal.

Slice the barbequed liver into strips ¾ inch x ¾ inch.

Put them on racks over sheet pans in a low oven—about 200°—or in a dehydrator until they're dry.

These last indefinitely!"

You can do the same thing with beef heart, she told me. And then she said:

"Technically, of course you don't have to barbeque. But this way you can be more flexible about the cooking times—once the slabs are well done, I can just stick them in the refrigerator for days before I have to dry them out. And you know, I think the dogs like the grilled flavor. At least, I'm sure my dogs do."

I'm sure my dogs do, too.

And so would yours. I promise. Not that they need these to be your best friend. But it certainly can't hurt.

Food for Feasts

BEST SPRING DINNER FOR TWO

Toasted cheese sandwiches with fried eggs. And a salad on the side. With a glass of wine. And a glass of water.

This does not sound like much, does it? Sounds too simple. Too everyday. Too…dull.

But on the spring night that we had that dinner, it was one of the most perfect meals we've ever shared, one of the most thoroughly enjoyable. One of the most memorable.

Why was that, now? I have to think.

It was different all right, from the picture the words conjure up.

The difference, I have a feeling, is in the recipe.

So here is a recipe for: Best Spring Dinner for Two.

Take one cool spring evening, at the end of a long, cool spring. Light a madrone fire in the hearth. Sit with the newspaper and a glass of rosé and your husband and the dogs. (These ingredients can be changed to suit what you have in your pantry. For example: Take a warm summer evening, or a nippy autumn evening, or a cold winter evening. Play Mozart low rather than light a fire. Or Brian Eno. Sit with reading material of your choice, or sewing, or knitting, or…or…or… For company, choose from a wide variety of possibilities. You get the general idea, I'm sure.)

Then…

For two…

Cut four good slices of sourdough bread from a loaf made by a friend, preferably a friend who is the best cook you know and who runs your favorite restaurant. It helps if the bread was delivered to the store by your friend's brother, and it's even better if your friend's brother lets you pick the best loaf out of the basket he's delivering to the shelves, while you exchange words about how nice it is that the weather has finally warmed up.

Butter two of the slices. Unsalted is best. Unsalted and made within 100 miles is even better. Dijon mustard on two of the slices. It is nice if you live in Dijon and the mustard comes from someone you know, but if that's not possible, you can spare a moment to fantasize about going to Dijon some day and eating all that Burgundian food without gaining any weight.

Slice some extra-sharp cheddar and some Monterey Jack cheese thinly, enough for two sandwiches. Best if you know where the cheese comes from. If you have passed the cows who give the milk for the cheese on one of your holidays, and speculated aloud on exactly what kind of cow IS black and white, anyway?, that's tastier still.

Divide the cheese onto the two slices of mustard-covered bread. Cover with the buttered bread.

Turn heat on low under a cast-iron skillet just big enough to hold two sandwiches. Add a dollop of unsalted butter. When it's melted, add the sandwiches, and continue to cook slowly on low while you—

Go into the garden and snip off with scissors the smallest and widest variety of salad leaves you can find, preferably into a wide and beautiful bowl. Arugula. Mizuna. Tatsoi. Red Leaf. Add small leaves from herb plants as you pass—thyme, oregano, mint, lemon verbena, marjoram, chervil. Use the scissors to snip bits of chive on top. Don't stint on the quantities here. As many leaves as you think you can eat plus a bit extra is good.

Back to the stove. Check the sandwiches. If they're golden and the cheese is beginning to melt, slide some more butter down the side into the pan, let it melt, and turn the sandwiches over.

Take out another skillet, one just big enough for four fried eggs to fit in a neighborly way together without crowding.

Take out four eggs. These should be eggs from someone like Dawn the Egg Lady, who coddles her chickens in a warm shed built against her house, and feeds them table scraps. Preferably they should have been collected earlier that day by Doug, who is married to Dawn the Egg Lady, after you drove up their drive and he suddenly remembered he'd forgotten to get them earlier. You can talk to Dawn while he grabs them out from under the hens, preferably chatting with her about the madrone stacked in their driveway that Doug is now cutting into lengths for you to burn next winter. Discuss delivery of the wood until Doug runs back lightly holding six eggs (how does he do that?), which he adds to an old egg-carton already holding another six, meanwhile avoiding being knocked over by one of their three enthusiastic Labrador dogs.

For some reason those eggs taste best. Don't ask me why.

Melt some butter in the skillet at medium-high heat. When the butter sizzles, crack four eggs, one by one, first into a cup to make sure the yolk doesn't break, then slide each egg into the skillet. Salt and pepper. Whatever kind you like. For example, Maldon salt is tasty if you had a nice conversation at US Customs when you brought back four boxes of it from the UK about how hard it is to find in Oregon. Even tastier if the woman at Customs tells you what HER favorite salt is. (People in San Francisco Airport love to talk about food.)

Clap a lid on the pan, turn off the heat. Set the timer for seven minutes.

Set the table. Light the candles. Pour out glasses of water. If the water comes from a spring you share with your neighbor, and your husband has just that day unplugged a lot of leaves from the lines so it's running particularly clear, that's even better.

Check the eggs. The whites should be set, but the yolks should still be deep gold and runny. No hard yolks for this dish.

Check the sandwiches. Are they gold on both sides? Yes? Good.

Announce dinner is imminent so your company can pour themselves glasses of whatever else they think will go well with this dinner. Dark beer is nice. Rosé is my personal favorite.

Toss the salad leaves with a tiny bit of salt and some grinds of pepper. Then add a capful or two of walnut oil. No lemon, no vinegar—not on this particular salad. Toss again, and pile lightly, divided between two wide, white Wedgwood plates. Leave room for the sandwiches, though they're nice nestled on top of the salad, too.

Cut the sandwiches in half. Arrange two halves each on each plate.

Top each half with a fried egg.

Sit down at a table that looks out onto a peaceful scene. A forest. A garden. A neighborhood street. Even a desert. Whatever spot you pick, for maximum tastiness, it should be a well-loved place.

If the light is just starting to turn dark blue-green, that's even better.

Toast your loved one with your glass. Spear the yolk of one egg so it runs all over your sandwich half. Eat a bite of salad. Savor. Pick up the yolk-soaked sandwich half and eat with your hands.

Laugh. Repeat.

Have another sip of rosé.

And think about how very lucky you are, and hope fervently that as many people as can be are, that night, lucky, each in her or his own way, too.

SPONTANEOUS PICNIC

The Beloved Vegetarian Husband and I do rather get into a routine when we're at home in the woods in Oregon, back from our urban encampment in Colorado. We so love it there that we tend to stay put, working at our respective projects, me in my study and him in his hut in the meadow, with both of us hardly stirring to go elsewhere except for supplies…and the occasional swim in Indigo Ray's pond after picking her strawberries.

But then, it being summer and all, there are some days when the heat just gets too much—even in the mountains. And on such days, inevitably, one of us will say to the other: "Let's go crayfish hunting."

Now this is a bit of a marital in-joke, dating from the time when we did, seriously, plan on catching some crayfish with a bucket, a line, and a half-open can of cat food. I'd read some article in the local paper about how this was supposed to be a breeze at a river not too far south from us.

Needless to say, we didn't catch any crayfish that day. Oh, we saw the little bastards scuttling all over the riverbed right at the bar where we fished for them, but none of them seemed to fancy Fancy Feast.

Eventually, we named that spot "Birthday Bar," in honor of the next year's foray for crayfish, armed as we were then with an actual crayfish trap sent as a present by my brother John (thanks, John!). We were no more successful that year than the year before, and we saw even MORE crayfish scuttling around; really we should have just picked them up with our hands. But I suppose that wasn't the point. The point was to get out of the heat and into the river, and out of the routine, and into a more lazy way of being (although as I recall, that second year, I spent the afternoon by the river editing a manuscript for the press).

The next hot day, we explored even farther down the river and settled at a particularly beautiful, isolated little cove. When I tell you that place is now called, chez us, "No Crayfish Bar," you'll have almost the whole picture.

Almost.

You probably know what's coming next. Going crayfish hunting is just shorthand in our house for "let's put the two camp chairs and the ice chest and the dogs in the car, grab the swimsuits and some reading material and go hang out in the river today, because it's just too damn hot." Now this means a spontaneous picnic. And in this particular case, this particular year, it meant putting together a picnic feast out of items that we had on hand, and that didn't need to be cooked—since the kitchen was, this particular day, still totally out of commission.

But...no fear. There are two dishes that, in summer, I nearly always have the ingredients for on hand. Mainly because the first is so flexible, and the second so simple. Pan Bagnat and Iced Tomato Soup.

Pan Bagnat is just the fancy name for a sloppy, utterly transportable, utterly delectable sandwich as they make it, so they say, in the south of France.

For each sandwich, it involves a couple of slices of sturdy bread, filled with your choice of veggies (always tomatoes, but after that, onions, garlic, peppers, arugula, mushrooms, grated carrots...anything you fancy), olives, capers, tuna and lots of olive oil. Bread is then pressed down on the filling, sandwich is thoroughly wrapped, and the whole can be squished under the weight of your choice, whether books going to the picnic or six packs of beer. You can even just sit on them (with a towel between you and the sandwich, of course). The idea is that the filling soaks the bread and mushes the sandwich together, turning the sum of its parts into a transcendent whole.

This is what I had for fixings that day:

A loaf of sourdough bread, slightly stale. I cut four thick slices and toasted them, rubbing them with a cut garlic half. (I always toast slightly stale bread for sandwiches.)

Laying one piece for each sandwich on a plate, I dribbled olive oil. Then layered sliced tomato. A layer of arugula, Some canned, drained tuna. A few capers. Some thinly sliced white onion. (I didn't have any olives at the time, so had to leave them out, though they're very good in a Pan Bagnat.) Finished layering, I salted and peppered, and dribbled some more olive oil on top. I was a bit wistful at not having any fresh basil, which really makes this sandwich sing, when I remembered I'd bought a jar of store pesto in case of just this kind of emergency. So I slathered the pesto on the remaining slices of bread, clapped them down on the sandwiches, wrapped them tightly, and stored them under a six-pack of beer, a bottle of rosé wine, and ice cubes poured into a plastic bag to keep them from melting all over the place. This went in the ice chest while I made the Iced Tomato Soup.

Iced Tomato Soup is a brilliant idea originating, I believe, with James Beard. Particularly brilliant if you, like me, often have a hankering for Campbell's Tomato Soup as a comfort food from your childhood, and keep a few cans in the cupboard for emergencies. Of course, for this dish you must also, like me, always have a carton of plain yoghurt in the fridge, full-fat Greek for choice, or even (oh, riches! oh, calories!) a carton of sour cream.

You also need a blender or something to mix it all up. I use a food processor.

Like this:

◊ A bit of some kind of onion
◊ A can of condensed (yes, condensed!) tomato soup
◊ A can's worth of plain yoghurt, sour cream, or a mixture of the two
◊ Two or three ice cubes
◊ Some basil or pesto if you have some handy

First either mince by hand, or in the processor/blender, some version of onion—shallot, red onion, scallion, chives. I used scallions that day because it was what I had, having already used white onion in the sandwich (also the green flecks look nice in the finished soup).

Then add to the minced onions a can of tomato soup. A can's worth of plain yoghurt or sour cream. And two or three ice cubes.

Whirr till the ice cubes are chopped into the soup, and the soup is nice and chilled. If too thick, add another ice cube or two and whirl again.

Decant into a thermos, stopper, and carry to serve with your picnic. A couple of mugs are nice to serve it in.

Delicious. I often add basil when I have it, so this day I just spooned in another swirl from that jar of pesto and stirred it around.

So now you have my secret for a spontaneous picnic meal. You can eat it anywhere, as long as you are cool and languidly happy, and in not any kind of a hurry to get anywhere on time. It tastes great that way. With or without crayfish.

MORE ABOUT PICNIC FOOD

There's nothing like losing the use of your kitchen for the summer months to make a gal think about picnic food. Stuff you can make and shove into the refrigerator that's sitting in what presently remains of your living room, and then dish out at a later happy hour.

Picnic food is perfect for that. The kind of picnic food that can be made in larger quantities than needed for one meal, and still come out refreshing and delicious at later meals…especially those later meals where you are just too hot and tired to actually cook.

Such a dish is a marinated salad. Of any variety. The basics of which are: vegetables (raw or cooked), herbs of your choice, a carbo if you'd like it to be heartier, and a meat or cooked fish of some kind if you'd like it heartier still.

Cubed cheese can always be added if you want to go for maximum hearty. I mean, cubed cheese can always be added to just about anything in my opinion.

Such a dish is the kale salad I pushed and pulled and turned into a kale/potato/anchovy/tuna salad (see recipe p.25). That's one. Then there are rice salads. Add any of the above (oh, and wait—quartered hardboiled eggs, you can always add them). And the pasta salads—same basic template.

But there was one day that was so hot and so filled with other activity, that I wanted something light and sharp-tasting, something to tease my taste buds and not overwhelm them when I went back to my desk afterwards.

Luckily, I had such a dish in my refrigerator from dinner the night before.

Tomato Salad with Thyme, Garlic, and Walla Walla Onions.

Like this:

◊ Tomatoes
◊ Juicy summer garlic
◊ Fresh thyme sprigs
◊ A Walla Walla onion
◊ A lemon or a lime
◊ Olive oil
◊ Coarse salt
◊ Pepper

Take some ripe tomatoes, preferably those character-actor-type Heritage

Tomatoes you see so jauntily appearing in summer markets. As many as you like and can pile, sliced, on your nicest picnic platter. Slice thinly. Layer on said platter.

Now, if you like (and of course you know I like), mince some juicy summer garlic and scatter over the tomatoes. Take a couple of sprigs of fresh thyme and strip the leaves off the stems, scattering half of them on the tomatoes, leaving the next half for the next phase.

Scatter some coarse salt and grind some pepper atop.

Now...take a Walla Walla onion. Thinly slice as much of it as you want (don't go overboard, but don't be stingy here either—this onion is a variety that's meant to be tasty raw). Layer the rings on top of the tomatoes.

Scatter the other half of the thyme leaves on top of the onion layer. A little more coarse salt. A good hefty grinding of pepper.

Stand back and admire your work.

Now, take a half a lemon or lime and squeeze over the whole construction. More if you like it. Then take your trusty bottle of olive oil and thread it atop as well.

If you're going to eat it later that day, just let it sit out on a counter (I usually stick my plate in a plastic bag to protect it from insects and overly curious dogs). If you're going to eat it tomorrow, or even the day after that, put it in the refrigerator, and then take it out about fifteen minutes before serving to take the chill off it.

When you think of it, tilt the platter and spoon up the juice that said platter acquires, bathing the salad with the juice anew. Don't worry if you don't think of it, though. Everything will still be well.

Eat at will. I had it plain one night, and then the next day for lunch put it on top of clover sprouts, and scattered some grated Parmesan to gild the lily for good measure.

It was great both ways. It would have been great, also, on top of shredded lettuce of any kind. And if I had had some basil instead of the thyme, it would have been sublime.

But even unsublime tomato and Walla Walla onion salad is worth having. Any summer's day, picnic or no.

(And by the way, if you don't want to bother with a platter—if all you have is a very nice bowl—don't worry. Just dice the tomatoes and chop the onions and mix them all together with the other ingredients, and all, as I continually say, will be well. All will be very well indeed.)

CASSOULET, OR FEASTING WITH WHAT YOU HAVE

At first glance, you would think that title was almost demonically contradictory. All these years I've been looking at those cassoulet recipes… you know the ones, you who read cookbooks: recipes discussing the authentic dish of Carcassonne, or Toulouse. Recipes arguing about whether it's a true cassoulet if you don't include duck confit, or shoulder of mutton. Recipes that call for about half a ton of goose fat, which when you look for sources on the internet, costs roughly about as much as half a ton of semi-precious stones. All these years I've been reading those recipes, and thinking ha! Well, maybe when hell freezes over.

I mean, you read these recipes and you think: forget cassoulet. At least, that's what I thought, given the way I cook, which is based on a) what I feel like at that moment and b) what I have easily available at the moment and c) what fits in, cooking-wise, with my schedule at the moment.

So imagine my surprise, even my sly delight, when a little light went off the other night, and I realized that ALL THREE of those requirements were met by, of all things, cassoulet.

1) I was home alone for a week, which meant I could eat meat, since the Beloved Vegetarian Husband was safely at work in another state. 2) I felt like having something hearty, something that would qualify as a feast but that could cook undisturbed while I worked through a largish pile on my desk, and that would smell wonderful while I did. 3) I actually had all the ingredients, just hanging about...if not for the Perfect Cassoulet, or even for an Authentic Toulouse Cassoulet, or even for Just Any Old Recipe for Cassoulet, at least I had all the stuff you would need if you were a peasant wife in the south of France in the nineteenth century trying to figure out what she was going to do that week for the family's meals.

All those years of reading those cassoulet recipes, and those articles in food magazines about cassoulet. They suddenly converged into one absolutely clear, outstanding fact: cassoulet is baked beans. Baked beans and miscellaneous meats and herbs cooked a really, really, really long time.

Now I had about three-quarters of a pound of white beans lying around from the last time the organic ones were on sale at the Co-op. And I had a bunch of herbs drying, left over from a late autumn foray into Indigo Ray's garden. I had canned tomatoes. I had ends of bread in the freezer waiting to be made into bread crumbs (cassoulets have a crumbly topping, just perfect with the unction underneath). Most importantly, I had all these little bits and pieces of meat in the freezer that I'd bought when I found something cheap and interesting at the market. Lamb neck. Lamb riblets. A pork hock. When I see stuff like this, I bring it home and hoard it, figuring I'll do something with it later, when I'm alone, and the Beloved Vegetarian Husband is elsewhere.

I had thought I'd make a tiny stew from the lamb neck. I'd thought I'd bake the riblets. The pork hock had been mainly destined to bake with some sauerkraut. But somehow none of these things had occurred, and there they were, cluttering up my freezer en masse.

More important, though, was the small container of melted duck fat left over from the last time I roasted a duck. One of the rules of my life is that I always save the duck fat, since it's just about the most delicious part of the duck. It's great used for sautéing potatoes. For cooking onions and garlic before you mash in the cooked pinto beans. As the fat base for sauerkraut.

And then—ta da!—there was that pork skin I found in a market that caters to our local Latin American and Southeast Asian cooks. I'd looked at it longingly, in its huge five-pound packages, every time I'd gone by, remembering what smooth silkiness it used to add to my pot roasts, in the days when I cooked a lot of pot roasts. But what on earth would I do with five pounds of pork skin?

Then the last time I was in that market, as I stood there looking longingly once again, a butcher appeared with a tray of meat. I said, almost before I knew what I was doing, "I don't suppose you could let me have just a half a pound of that pork skin, could you?" And she gave me a look like I was nuts, not for wanting the pork skin, but for thinking for even a moment that she wouldn't be delighted to cut some up for me. (This market, by the way, is called Food For Less, and it looks like an industrial warehouse, and it stocks more local stuff and has more happy employees than just about any market I've ever been in. And its butchers, who mainly deal in locally raised animals, are second to none. I mean, you know where that liver came from.) I went away clutching my half-pound of pork skin in triumph, and cut it into little rolls and froze them when I got home.

So I had pork skin, the main ingredient that adds the oommpphhh to your average cassoulet. (You can use olive oil, but it won't be the same. And, honest to God, stop worrying so much about eating fat. As my wonderful sister-in-law Cindy says, "Just don't eat so damn much!")

Here's what I did, a leisurely and pleasant three nights' cooking, very little time spent at the stove. The first night I covered the beans with an inch of water and brought them to a boil, then let them sit, covered, for an hour. (While this was going on, I made myself a very simple dinner of a lamb chop cooked on the griddle, with a carrot salad on the side—took about ten minutes, start to finish, and boy, was it good.) Then I drained them, put them back in the pot, covered them with more water, added a couple of branches of dried thyme, a stem of parsley, a pinch of dried oregano, a bay leaf, a chopped carrot, a chopped half onion, eight crushed cloves of garlic, the pork hock, and about a quarter pound of pork skin cut into small pieces and tied in a piece of cheesecloth.

(Now about that pork skin. You can add a whole piece and fish it out later. You can add the little squares cut up without tying them in the cheesecloth, and eat them with the beans later. Or you can do the cheesecloth routine. I cut the pieces up to get that extra unction, then tied them up because I didn't really want to eat them, and I figured—correctly—that they would, after they'd done their bit for me, make the dogs go wild with joy.)

I let this cook (on top of the woodstove, which was going anyway) for an hour or so, till the beans were tender but not overcooked. Then I carried it over to the counter and let it cool overnight. Next day, I fished out the cheesecloth, what was left of the stems of the herbs, and the pork hock. Cut the skin off the pork hock and tossed it in a dish with the pork skin bits decanted from the cheesecloth—that was for the dogs, later. Then I chopped the meat off the bones, and put the meat back in with the beans—that was for me. Put the beans in the fridge.

While I made a small dinner for myself the second night (again a lamb chop, I'd liked it so much the night before, this time with an avocado and mesclun salad, and a small piece of whole-meal toast with peanut butter and cherry jam for dessert), I cooked the other meats. Melted a little duck fat in a big skillet, browned the lamb neck pieces. Added the lamb riblets and browned them. Added a chopped carrot, a chopped half onion, and about eight crushed garlic cloves. Another piece of thyme, another bay leaf, another pinch of dried oregano. After it had all browned a little, about ten minutes, I added a cup of canned tomatoes and half a cup of white wine (needless to say, you don't need to be fussy about these measurements, you're just adding liquid to what's essentially a little meat stew). Cooked that down a bit. Added about a cup of duck broth I'd had lying around in the freezer from the last time I roasted that duck and made a broth from its bones. I let the whole thing cook on low while I turned the ends of bread from the freezer into breadcrumbs in the Cuisinart, then I ate dinner (oh, it took about an hour), then I added the stew to the pot of beans. Covered the top with a satisfying blanket of breadcrumbs and dribbled some melted duck fat on top.

Now it was all ready for its final cooking, to take place, effortlessly, on a day I had specially chosen since I would be very distracted by work, and in need of a little solace after. A little feast. On THAT day, I popped it into a 300° oven, uncovered, three hours before I wanted to eat it.

Oh my, the smells that started wafting through the house about an hour later. And then two hours later. It was a good thing I had so much work to do, or I wouldn't have been able to keep from wading into it early. After about three hours, I looked in, and there it was, bubbling away in a friendly and inviting sort of way. I turned the oven up to 500°, to brown the crumbs for a last five minutes, tossed myself a heap of mesclun leaves with a tiny bit of walnut oil and lemon juice, and then, as M.F.K. Fisher says, served it forth with a big honking glass of hearty red wine. That first night I had one of the chunks of lamb neck and all of the riblets. It was absolutely, soul-searingly, happiness-inducingly delicious.

And you know what? It wasn't a hassle. Not because it wasn't a lot of work and a lot of ingredients, but because the work and the ingredients fit exactly with my life at exactly that moment in time. That's the important thing, I've discovered: is it the right thing at the right time? Does it work with what's around you? And does it fit who you are, not what someone else has told you, but you, what you know about you? Does it do all those things? Because if it does, then even making a cassoulet is a breeze, even if I had to wait about thirty years till I hit that exact moment in time. But once I did hit it, it was a feast.

159

TURKEY SOUP, OR FEASTING WITH FAMILY

There's something really satisfying about just tossing what otherwise might be thought of as holiday detritus into a pot and, while you're sprawling on the sofa in the vicinity of your loved ones, sharing an evening of post-festivity digestion, knowing that lunch for the next day is cooking up with hardly a finger lifted on your part. Which is just as well, because after making the holiday meal, lifting said finger is just more effort than you're willing to, at that moment, sign on for.

Turkey Soup. The inevitable and lovely luncheon for the day after Thanksgiving. When, next day, everyone comes trooping in from the cold, from the walk they all felt they had to take in the woods, after the ingestion the night before of the heritage brined turkey (fabulous, and cooked in half the time expected, because, we decided as we ate, it wasn't bung-full of God Knows What injected in the Torture Farm where the usual butterball is raised), potatoes mashed with cream and butter and cheddar and green onions, carrots cooked in cream…and a wild variety of homemade cookies… among other things…when everyone sits down at the lunch table, needing nourishment, but feeling just the tiniest bit jaded in the taste buds, that is when Turkey Soup really comes into its own.

Of course, the traditional Turkey Soup is even easier than the one I essayed this particular year, being made up of, literally, leftovers: mashed potatoes, carrots, peas, stuffing, all mingled with a broth. But I didn't make any stuffing that year, and there weren't any potatoes or carrots left, thanks to some very interested teenagers. And, also, I had my own cravings. The cook is allowed to have these. The artist cannot be denied her inspiration. It's part of the deal.

However, I do know my family of origin. Hard-core traditionalists. Suspicious, even, of garlic mayonnaise if it's served on any Anglo holiday.

So I cannily had some minestrone in the freezer, which I brought out and warmed up in case there might be an initial difficulty luring said traditionalists outside of their comfort zone. And then I merrily put the terrifically rich turkey broth I'd made the night before together with some sliced celery and mushrooms, a lot of garlic, a little soy sauce, some cooked brown rice, what was left of the minimal wine gravy I'd made to go with the bird (pan drippings deglazed with red wine, then a little butter swished in off the heat; irresistible even with brined pan drippings—or maybe because of them, come to think of it). At the last minute, a bag of frozen spinach, and a lot of chopped green onions.

Sure enough, everyone but me went for the minestrone first. Everyone but me and my canny eighteen-year-old nephew who had already won major points by declining an all-day hike in favor of the meal ("What? Miss one of Aunt Tod's lunches? No way!"). He just looked at me when he got to the two faintly bubbling pots on the stove, and all it took was a slight nudge of my head toward the Turkey Soup to send him, happily, in the same direction, announcing as he filled his bowl that he was going to have the minestrone AFTER.

The sight and smell of that Turkey Soup at his place and at mine had all the minestrone eaters pausing in midbite. They sniffed the air. I noticed one of my brothers covertly watching my nephew to see his reaction. At the look of pure bliss that swept over my nephew's face, my brother finished his own bowl with a contemplative air and then got up to go back to the stove. Came back with a steaming golden bowl of that Strange Turkey Soup. Sipped it and said, without even a grudging hint to his voice, "Okay. This is the best Turkey Soup I ever had. I wouldn't've believed it when I heard that stuff about mushrooms and brown rice, but I gotta…" His voice trailed off and he went back to eating with a faint smile.

One by one, the other minestrone eaters got up and got new helpings, too. And there were faint smiles all around the table.

Even on my Vegetarian Husband's face. He, of course, stuck to the minestrone. But he was the only one who ate it topped with garlic mayonnaise. It's impossible for him to eat garlic mayonnaise without a smile.

161

But for the Turkey Soup, here's how:

◊ Turkey broth
◊ Sliced mushrooms
◊ Sliced celery
◊ Soy sauce
◊ Drippings from the turkey
◊ A little red wine
◊ Salt and pepper
◊ Some kind of cooked starch: noodles, or rice, or diced potatoes, or cooked beans
◊ Spinach, fresh or frozen
◊ Leftover turkey, chopped or shredded
◊ Chopped scallions (aka green onions)

First make your Turkey Broth. I've seen recipes that say a brined turkey doesn't make a good broth, and I can't figure out what they mean. That brined turkey made a particularly rich, gelatinous, delicious broth in our house. But on reflection, it's possible that this is because the original turkey was one of Dawn the Egg Lady's turkeys, one of the ones that used to run about her front yard, dodging the new puppy, and heading for the family compost heap for the stray squash seeds there. I mean, these were well-exercised, happy turkeys (insofar as a turkey can be said to be happy), and the one I got was no different. So maybe this recipe should start: "Take the carcass of a happy bird."

So. Take the carcass of a happy bird. Just toss the cleaned bones from the plates returning empty to the kitchen after dinner into a large stock pot that already holds the turkey neck, giblets, and cleaned trimmings from the vegetables you served with the main meal (in this case, celeriac peelings, carrot peelings and ends, celery ends and tops), a few cloves of unpeeled garlic (I tossed in a whole head), a few peppercorns, and a bay leaf. If you feel up to it, take whatever meat is left from the turkey carcass, store separately, chop the bones up and toss them in, too. Simmer until it smells terrific and tastes unctuous—about an hour, but I never keep track, and it doesn't hurt it to go longer. This last simmer can happen that night, or the next morning. If your house is normally heated—if you're not one of those people who keeps it like a hothouse year round—you can even just leave the pot out on the stove and bring it to a boil first thing in the morning, before turning it down to the simmer.

About an hour before lunch, drain the finished broth into another pot through a colander; throw out the detritus left (or save it, minus the bones, to feed your dogs like I do). For the soup, use as much broth as you think you'll need for the family (take out the rest and freeze for later dishes). Add to this about a cup of sliced mushrooms, as much sliced celery as you have left in the fridge (say, about half a bunch), a couple of tablespoons of soy sauce, and some of the drippings from the turkey. A little red wine, if you have some left from the night before, doesn't come amiss, but isn't at all necessary.

Cook this about fifteen minutes, half an hour. Add salt and freshly ground pepper to taste. Correct the seasoning—you might want to add a little more soy sauce. You can turn off the heat now, and let it wait a half hour or so before the final touch, if you like. Right before you call everyone to fill their bowl, bring the soup back to a boil, turn it down to a simmer, add as much chopped or shredded turkey meat as you like, a handful or two of whatever cooked starch you have in the fridge (I had a choice of cooked white beans, cooked whole wheat fusilli, or cooked brown rice, and went for the last on the theory that it was the only starch not already found in the minestrone), and a bag, if you have it, of frozen spinach. Heat through. Serve with a bowl of chopped green onions to sprinkle on top at will. Anything left over in the green onion department can be added to the leftover soup to serve as the cook's lunch the day after THAT.

Happy lunch. And afterwards, if you're at all like my family, you'll find your thoughts and conversation turning to Christmas dinner....

GREEN MOLD

Do you remember the festivals your family had when you were a child, and what was most important about them for you? We celebrated all of ours with my Aunt Celia and Uncle John and their raucously good-humored family, my cousins. This aunt and uncle were a touchstone for the children in my own family, being warm-hearted, affectionate, and down-to-earth: three qualities children of all kinds respond to and never forget. I think I've mentioned that Aunt Celia and Uncle John were also my godparents, which made for tremendous envy among my younger siblings, and gave me tremendous pride. As far as I was concerned, there was literally nothing either of them could do that would tarnish the glow that came from my thoughts about them. Not that either of them ever acted in any way other than admirably—and I was watching them. Oh, how sharply a child watches adults for signs of moral faltering! They never did falter, neither one of them. And every festival, every feast, with them was as golden in the celebrating as it is in the memory. Of how many events can that be truly said?

I was a terrible snob as a child, and worse, a terrible food snob. Just the kind of little brat who would have refused to eat spaghetti unless it was called pasta. And who drove the entire family mad by insisting on serving leg of lamb bloody rare just because I'd read it was supposed to be that way in some issue of *Gourmet*. (I'll never forget the look of amused patience on Aunt Celia's face as I struggled with that lamb—it was very similar to her look when, at age five, I had served her milk mixed with dried coconut in my plastic tea service for afternoon tea.) But there were things my Aunt Celia cooked that were to my mind beyond criticism of any kind, beyond caviling, and I would have fought even the most elevated of food editors to the ground in defense of those dishes. Not just because she cooked them, not just because they were part of our feasting ritual together, but because they tasted absolutely great.

For example: French onion soup dip served with ruffled potato chips.

I'm unsure exactly who invented this classic of an American Sixties childhood, although I suspect a PR consultant, but it goes like this: Mix a package of Lipton's dried onion soup mix with an 8-ounce carton of sour cream. Serve chilled with ridged potato chips for dipping.

Divine. Salty as all hell. Filled with preservatives, doubtless. But it just wasn't a party unless we had Aunt Celia's dip.

That, and what she called, with characteristic flair, "Green Mold."

These Jell-O/cottage cheese/mayonnaise molds have gone out of fashion (and how!), and probably there is much to be said for keeping them out of the forefront of our national cuisine these days. But I will say that this particular dish is a legend in my family of origin. A part of the legend is how our own mother kept trying to change the recipe to something that sounded a little less fattening, and a little more upmarket. But every change just seemed to diminish, mysteriously, the magic of the dish.

And where did that magic come from? From the festivals we all shared as a family. And from my Aunt Celia.

Of course, it didn't hurt that it tasted great, too.

Here is her recipe, as she wrote it out for all of us, with characteristic loving thoughtfulness, on the eve of her death.

Green Mold

Combine: 1 pkg lemon jello
            1 pkg lime jello
            2 cups hot water
Add: 20 oz can of crushed pineapple (drained)

Chill until slightly thickened. Then add the following to above.
            1 large can evaporated milk
            1 pt cottage cheese
            ½ cup chopped walnuts
            ½ cup mayonnaise

Mix well and chill. This makes a large mold or two small ones. Usually when I make one small mold, I use the lime jello, and divide all the other ingredients.

Cecilia F. Torres

EGGS À LA TOD

It's not just the feasting dishes from your childhood that are important—though it's great to have sustaining memories like that, and traditions to carry on (and perhaps tweak as the years go by; that's important too, let's remember). It's also important to establish your own signs of Festivity. We have a few of those around here, of course. Certain glasses we drink out of on holidays. Certain drinks we drink. A certain silver-plated tray engraved with my grandmother's name that is brought out every year, just before Christmas, and covered with dimpled deep-orange tangerines with their glossy green leaves still firmly attached.

Then there are the dishes that mean Feast Day.

Sometimes these are more complicated than a normal day's recipe, with more luxurious ingredients than everyday, like my paella, for example (see recipe below, p. 241). But often it's just a dish that somehow is associated in both our minds with a difference in the day, just a small festive difference—an occasion when the usual rules and scheduling don't apply. The days where we might pour out two flutes (in the festive crystal glasses) of champagne and take them out for a walk in the meadow before dusk, just because that seems like a festive thing to do. Or there might be a bath at midday followed by a nap. Something different, something simple, but something fun. Just because that is what a feast day is for. To be reminded of the importance of the daily round by a change, a heightening, of the daily round.

Anyway, such a dish for us is baked eggs. Baked eggs that have evolved in a certain way, so that the Beloved Vegetarian Husband refers to them as "Eggs à la Tod." As in, "It's my birthday tomorrow. Are we going to have Eggs à la

Tod for breakfast, I hope?" And of course we are.

Very simple. But somehow very satisfying. These started out being eggs cracked into melted butter in two small white ovenproof dishes, then feta cheese crumbled over the whites, peppered (the feta provided all the salt), and carefully baked in the toaster oven until the cheese was all puffy and browned, the whites cooked, and the yolks still deliciously liquid. Wonderfully savory. We would eat these with buttered toast.

Over the years, they evolved, as most things do, or should, anyway. The eggs got better, for one thing. I started sourcing them from neighbors who fed their chickens the kinds of bits and pieces from the kitchen that turned their egg yolks a deep sunflower gold. Then the feta cheese I had used, mainly because I'd found a good, inexpensive supply at a local market, suddenly disappeared from that market's shelves, and replacement feta elsewhere just seemed too expensive.

('Too expensive,' translated, means 'not worth it.' There's a kind of algorithm that goes on in my head when I make choices at the market: is this particular buy going to bring twice as much pleasure as the cost in time to make the money to buy it?)

The feta got replaced with finely grated Parmesan, which also puffed up and browned in a very satisfying way in the time it took the eggs to cook to perfection. But I missed that tang you get with feta. My solution: add a scattering of capers before grating on the cheese. That did it. That brought the smile of feast-day happiness at breakfast to the Beloved Vegetarian Husband's face. And to mine. Which was what I am in it for, after all.

Like this:

Eggs à la Tod (for two people)

◊ Eggs

◊ Butter

◊ Grated Parmesan cheese
◊ Capers
◊ Pepper, freshly ground

Take four of the best eggs you can find. Break them into four little cups, just to make sure you don't have a broken yolk. If you do, just put that egg aside for another use, and break another one into another cup.

Preheat an oven to 325°. (A toaster oven is great for this.)

Take two baking dishes, each of a size to hold two eggs in comfort. (We once used rectangular white dishes gotten from who knows what thrift shop, until one broke, and they were replaced with two more graceful white oval porcelain dishes my mother gave me when she cleaned out her closets that year.)

Put a nubbin of butter in each, and place in the preheating oven until the butter melts.

Slide the eggs gently onto the melted butter, two to a dish. Don't break those yolks. The fresher the eggs, the easier this will be.

Scatter two teaspoons of whole capers into the whites of the eggs, one teaspoon a dish (don't fuss about the amount, this is just a general idea, not a military command).

Grate Parmesan cheese finely over each dish, covering as much as you like of the eggs (I used to just cover the whites, but with the Parmesan, the whole dish gets a golden blanket).

Bake for eight to ten minutes, until the whites are set, and the cheese melted.

Keep the yolks beautifully fluid, unless you like them so you can (as a young woman I knew once used to order them in restaurants) "throw 'em at the wall."

Serve at once, with buttered toast and hot sauce for those who like it.

We now eat ours with buttered New Sammy's Cowboy sourdough, thin slices as long as a plate, and a jar of whatever homemade jam there is in the pantry—that, or the wonderful cherry preserves given me by my friend Bob, who found them in a Turkish market near his house. These have pits still in them, which makes for depth of flavor, but which is not for the faint of heart.

The Beloved Vegetarian Husband always has apple juice with this. I like freshly squeezed pink grapefruit juice.

And it is, indeed, a good way to start any day. But particularly good and gentle for a day of festival.

OATMEAL AND WHISKEY

And just to make a change, on very cold mornings, and feast-day mornings in particular, sometimes we like to have warmed bowls full of oatmeal, which we each dress to taste with butter, cream, honey, jam, and a little bit of Irish whiskey.

Butter, cream, honey, and whiskey for me.

Butter, jam, and whiskey for the Dear Husband.

We got the idea for this one year when we stayed in Edinburgh, and the hotel served a 'typical' Scottish breakfast, including an inviting little bottle of Glenlivet next to the oatmeal pot.

My friend Margaret, fellow food lover, marvelous cook, and loyal Scotswoman, almost fell over laughing when I described adding the scotch to my bowl of porridge.

"Never heard of such a thing!" she said. "Scots breakfast indeed!"

Well, it may have just been a gimmick for tourists, but who cares? It was delicious. And I've kept a bottle on hand of Irish whiskey for our own feast-day gimmicks ever since.

So if eggs aren't what you fancy, try making the oatmeal of your choice, decanting it into a warmed, wide bowl, melting atop it a pat of sweet unsalted butter, perhaps pouring a thread of full cream atop, and a spoonful of honey. Then fill a capful of whiskey from the whiskey bottle and anoint.

Eat slowly. Enjoy. And don't worry: it might not be authentic, but it sure does taste good.

Food for Oneself

ON BEING THE SOLITARY DINER

I'd like to speak up now for the pleasures of dining alone. And by "dining alone," I don't mean, here, Dining Alone at Home, though that has its own great pleasures, not the least of which is the possibility of eating, say, popcorn with melted butter, garlic salt, and Parmesan, while drinking a nice red wine, and reading a romantic novel—all of it in one's bathrobe.

No, I want to talk about the great satisfactions that can come to you through Dining Alone in a Restaurant.

Yes, that's right. The Solitary Diner. You. In a restaurant. All Alone.

"I hate eating in restaurants alone," I can hear you say. In fact, I heard a friend say that just yesterday, when she was describing to me how she carries her own food with her on business trips so she can eat in her hotel room alone.

Now, I have nothing against eating in a hotel room alone. Especially for breakfast. In fact, for breakfast, before a long, bleary-eyed day of business, I highly recommend it.

But you can't spend your life in a hotel room, can you? Or even that part of your life spent traveling alone for one reason or another. I mean, you can, but in my opinion you are wasting valuable time in which you could be experiencing another part of life. Even another part of what it means to be you.

What it means to be me, you say? I know what it means to be me. But do you? Do you really? Do you know for sure that you'd rather have an arugula salad on the side of your blackened snapper rather than a baked potato? Do you know whether or not you might like a few oysters to start? Do you know what kind of wine or beer or even just water you might like to drink tonight?

Do you know whether or not you might prefer to eat breakfast at nine p.m., maybe a nice Eggs Benedict with a dry white wine?

I never know, personally, until I'm sitting there dining with myself.

Well, it's true. I really, really, really like to dine alone in restaurants—it's one of my favorite things about traveling for business (there being few other ones, since I'd almost always rather be home). I love picking out the perfect table, one with enough elbow room, preferably by a window or in a corner, or sitting at the sushi bar in a Japanese restaurant. I love taking my time over the menu, thinking about just exactly what I feel like eating and drinking, amending it a little in my head, talking with the waitperson to see if I can trade the potatoes for the above-mentioned arugula salad…that kind of thing. I like dining with myself. Who am I closer to than that? Who should I want to treat with respect more than that self that works so hard for me and my goals?

I like to talk to the wait-staff, too. I think everyone should be a waiter at some point in their life…just as I think all young people should be strapped for cash, and all old people comfortably well off. I was one of those young people strapped for cash, and what it did for me was plunge me into a permanent meditation about what was truly important to me. What was I willing to work to get? (Time.) What would I be happy to give up? (Shopping, television, anything labeled "fun for the entire family," which Jerry Seinfeld rightly pointed out is impossible.)

One of the things I found was that I wasn't willing to give up good food. And so I had to figure out how to get it. This wasn't difficult in the city of my birth, since San Francisco when I was a young woman was a veritable cornucopia of wonderful, affordable food. But then I moved to Los Angeles—which NOW is a veritable cornucopia etc., but then was absolutely the direst restaurant scene you could imagine, except for expensive places that served $20 chopped salads, and breakfast at the late lamented Lafayette Café on Venice Beach. So I learned to cook. Well, I had to. It was either that or starve. Either that, or starve, or live on ramen, I should say.

But then, as I got older, I made a little more money, enough to get me out of the ramen-for-dinner-every-night class, and I started experimenting wherever I was with restaurants. It was quite an education, going to restaurants by myself. It was an education in how to be unselfconscious in public, for one thing. And how to tip the wait-staff without embarrassment. How to read a wine list and be unafraid to ask for advice. How to ask advice—that was a very important one, how to phrase the questions so I could actually get the information I wanted. ("I like a wine that stands up to you and almost knocks you down—what would you recommend?")

Most of all I got an education in what kinds of food I liked, and when and where. And what I learned early on was I liked to eat alone in restaurants. I like to do it because I'm alone with myself and I learn more about myself by relaxing alone with myself. It's a kind of recharge for me, after which I can cheerfully, even enthusiastically, plunge into the maelstrom of Other People.

I don't regard wait-staff as Other People. The right wait-staff (and I very rarely run up against the wrong kind) I regard as guardian angels of my solitude.

The impression I get from the women I know who dislike eating alone— for example, my hotel-room-eating friend of yesterday— is that they feel exposed, unwanted in some way, as if to dine alone is a confession of failure— "she couldn't get a date."

Of course there are the women who love walking into a place and making a part of it their own for a brief hour. Those women have always been my role models. In studying their behavior, I noted that the one thing they had in common was a firm belief that they mattered. That their desires mattered. That they had the right—even the obligation—to treat themselves well.

Now, mind you, I do not under any circumstances mean 'spoil themselves.' I have a sort of generalized disdain for those ghastly advertisements that urge "Spoil yourself!" "You deserve it!" etc. No one deserves anything, in my opinion, but we all have our wants, and if we ignore those wants and don't deal with them, working out what's best for ourselves and others among them, we run the risk of turning into unhappy, enslaved, sour individuals who make ourselves and everyone around us miserable.

If you're going to treat others well, as I learned from watching those who treated me well, you have to start with yourself. But that treatment then should spread to others. If it stops with you, you've missed the point of the exercise.

But back to eating alone. I've had a lot of wonderful meals that way—just last week, in fact, one in Salt Lake City airport (corner table, lovely waiter, extra blue cheese dressing on my Cobb salad), and one in Denver airport two days later (window table, even lovelier waiter—about ninety years old, and called me 'madam' every third word—excellent smoked salmon)—but the one I want to talk about is the one where I realized that while I had been dining alone before, it had always been a rather furtive activity, rather like saving the good towels for when you have guests rather than enjoying them yourself. Up till that evening I had always gotten the least expensive thing on the menu, eaten it quickly, giving no thought to drink, just to nourishing myself enough to have the energy to move on to the next important engagement… 'important' being defined as being with other people.

Then I found myself in London alone at the dinner hour. Why was this? I can't remember, it was so long ago. But there is a certain nostalgic sadness around the memory, so I'm hazarding the guess of a lovers' quarrel or something; that seems right. In this memory, I am drifting around Soho at a loss for what to do with myself, when I realize I am hungry. I realize I am actually very hungry. And I realize one of my favorite restaurants in London is just around the corner.

It's gone now—Manzi's fish restaurant, right behind Leicester Square. A lovely square box of a room, manned by Italian waiters who all had that 'madam' thing down pat. I'd always been treated wonderfully at Manzi's, but of course I had always been there with someone else, and so, even though I remembered wistfully a few Irish oysters I had thoroughly enjoyed on my last visit, I was filled with trepidation at the idea of walking in myself.

What would they think? Would they put me at a 'bad' table? Would I know how to order some wine? Would I know how to tip? Would I embarrass myself? And I didn't have a book with me. What on earth would I do while waiting for the food to arrive?

I don't know how it was, but somehow I steeled myself and walked right in. I think I'd already settled the wine problem ("Just order a glass of the house white, you damned fool!"), and the tip problem ("You can do math, I presume? You can figure out fifteen per cent, yes?"—oh, I was haughty with myself in those days, a fault I hope I've corrected). And at this point in my life, I had realized that if you wanted to really get something out of an experience, you had to be willing to take a pratfall or two. So I took in a deep breath, and headed inside.

It was such a lovely dinner. They gave me the table I asked for, just against the far wall so I could see everyone else in the restaurant, which solved the problem of what I was to look at while I waited for my food. My waiter treated me like a long-lost niece. He gave me the three oysters I wanted to start (no more, no less), and looked on encouragingly while I looked dubiously at the mignonette sauce and dabbed a little, to my satisfaction a moment later, on the first. He gave me a glass of house white wine, and then, when I had gotten my confidence back, a second with my order of (I can still remember) a dish called Trout Cleopatra. It was one of the least expensive on the menu (I hadn't gotten the black belt in ordering just what I want as of yet, that was still deliciously to come), but it was also something I had always wanted to try: a whole trout sautéed, with a white wine, capers and lemon sauce.

How I enjoyed that trout, and that white wine, and how wonderfully sated and cared for I felt as I paid the reasonable bill and made my way out into the Soho night. I still remember. But what I remember most of all was how self-confident the meal had made me feel, how well-fed and capable, and I seem to recall taking immediate, resourceful steps to mend whatever had been torn in the earlier lovers' quarrel, which was far far easier then, after I had seen that I could enjoy myself so thoroughly alone. Somehow, love is always easier once you know you can enjoy yourself alone. It sounds like a paradox, and perhaps it is, like so much else about love. But there you are.

THE BEST FOOD I EVER ATE

It was raining. It was raining and my front meadow was awash in mud, and yet my front meadow was what was between the RV we had rented to live in while our flooded-out house was made fit again for human habitation, and said house, where much of our stuff (including our refrigerator, at that time parked in the living room) resided. So the days were an exercise in "on one side of the river you have a sheep, a hen, and a coyote. You have a canoe that only lets you take one across at a time. You can't leave the coyote alone with either the sheep or the hen. How do you manage?" I sometimes feel—and I know there are a lot of you out there who must often feel the same—that my life is an exercise in this kind of puzzle. Modern life, that's it. Modern life IS logistics.

Rainy logistics that day. I'd given up on maintaining a mud-free floor in the RV, so that's kind of letting the coyote eat the hen, and figuring the answer is just go buy another one later.

There are worse things. Nevertheless, this was one of those days where the many mundane decisions pile up so high, like a huge seagull-infested garbage dump, that you just slump down at the bottom, suddenly paralyzed, your mind simply refusing to move. You know what kind of day I'm talking about.

This was one of those days. Now, we all have these days. So I will now put in writing what I tell myself when they occur: there's no avoiding them. The best thing to do is to try to avoid excess frustration. Just give in to the idea that you're not going to get much done. Don't try to paper the dullness over with some kind of unhealthy stimulant (well, not too much anyway). Don't try to quarrel with a loved one in order to pass the time (almost impossible to avoid, but my heartfelt and earnest advice to myself is TRY). Just give in. Either assign yourself a dull, mindless task (since I'm dull and mindless anyway, might as well tick off a job that needs to be done). Or daydream about a thing I particularly like. If I choose this last option, my advice to myself is: choose a dry and safe and warm spot. Sit in a comfortable chair. Attach a pleasant beverage to your arm. Sip. Think. Imagine.

Take yourself off to a kinder, gentler time.

That was my strategy that day. Safe, warm, quiet. Small glass of red wine at my elbow. And I sat dreaming about the best meals I have eaten. As it is even more fun to reminisce about said meals with friends, and as the printed word is more or less a captive audience, my choice is to use the strategy here, in this space.

For example:

When I was nineteen years old, in San Francisco, and just learning the delight of solitary meals in restaurants (and they are delightful, you know I think they're delightful), I would inevitably find myself at dinner time up the street at a tiny Chinese restaurant that sold plate rice for under two dollars a plate. And I always, always had roast pork/tofu plate rice with scallions. It was a dollar and sixty-five cents, and nothing that cost the same has ever given me anywhere near the same pleasure (except for perhaps those dinners of ramen boiled, drained, mixed with the flavor packet and eaten from a pretty blue bowl with chopsticks and extra lashings of soy and hot sauce…circa the same time). Sitting at a little rickety table near the front window where the huge round aluminum steamers of pork buns sent out deliriously exciting fumes, I would shovel that plate rice into a happy young inexperienced mouth. I've never forgotten that meal, those meals. Those early meals where you begin to know what you like are exciting in another way that never comes again. The first wild mushrooms collected and sautéed for me by my first love. The first time I ate Moroccan chicken with my knees folded at a table two feet high. The first time I had potstickers and jumped with delight at how juicy they were when I bit through the wrapping. My first bite of tuna sashimi. The bowl of raw chocolate-chip cookie dough I ate by myself in bed watching Saturday night TV—the *Mary Tyler Moore Show*. My favorite. (Especially the "Death of Chuckles the Clown" episode.)

The huevos rancheros with salsa verde at the late lamented Lafayette restaurant on the Venice, California beach. (Come to think of it, they only cost $1.49, and I enjoyed them almost as much as the plate rice in San Francisco.)

I feel sorry for people who are rich when they are young. As A. J. Liebling says, they never learn what they really like, since they can have what they think they like any time, and never branch out. I do agree with him there. It bears repeating too: everyone should be poor when they're young. And everyone should be rich when they're old. That would be the whole of my economic theory. When you're poor, you have to think, really think, about what to do next, and that thinking often turns up the most delicious surprises along the way.

I never got rich. But then I'm not entirely old, not yet. But I did manage to have quite a few meals along the way that were out of the reach of my younger, hungrier, more omnivorous self. Such as…

The wild teal at St. John Restaurant, in London. I still remember that as one of the best meals ever. I love duck, and this was beyond duck—wild duck, cooked rare and tasting of the sky. Served with some (just enough) sautéed kale, as I recall. And a wonderful, inspiring glass of recommended red wine to go with it. Still in a dream of its perfection, after dinner I made my way to the washroom, and in the corridors, ran into a guy in chef whites. Overcome, I shared my enthusiasm for what I'd just eaten, and his face lit up. "I'm so glad," he said simply. "It was me who cooked that for you." Which made it, in retrospect, all the more perfect a meal.

The chicken livers in red wine sauce at a long-gone dining counter that was the original Little Joe's in San Francisco. My best friend and I used to go and stand in the line and wait specially for that, and when we finally got our seats at the counter, never tired of watching the cooks make it up, tossing the morsels in olive oil in blackened iron skillets, over a blazing-hot gas fire. They tasted even better if it had been raining while we waited in line. Raining just a little, mind you, just enough so we could shake the water off our coats before we sat on them and set to eat.

The black and pink double paella rice in that restaurant in Madrid some nice film producer took me to with the Beloved Vegetarian Husband, in company with some visiting cinema dignitary. One side pink rice, flavored with what tasted like a thousand shells of particularly toothsomely shelled crustaceans, and the other side black, flavored with the ink of squids fed exclusively on garlic. Heaven.

The green garlic custard with fresh morel sauce made by Charlene Rollins at my favorite restaurant in the world, New Sammy's Cowboy Bistro. Ah, and while I'm at it: her grilled quail, served at room temperature atop her baby kale, garlic, and thick-cut bacon warm salad.

The pot au feu I ate in a Montmartre restaurant, deliriously happy to be in Paris, in love, and with a plate in front of me served with a little bowl of coarse salt and a little bowl of mustard so that I could play with my food to my heart's content.

The grilled calamari at the Spanish beach restaurant where we knew the owners, who teased us all the way through the meal, because somehow we'd lost the keys to our rental car in the Mediterranean. We didn't worry too much about that. And I can still taste the bright blue of the sea out the window as I ate.

The salt cod patties at the restaurant in Oporto, served by the most professional waiter I have ever met—he took one look at our bleary, hungover, sated-with-festivity selves, and brought just one order, divided onto two plates: the perfect amount of food for just then, and how did he know? And how did they get salt cod to taste like that, like the kind of food I imagine was served in Regency London, at midnight at a grand ball in honor of a sister of the Tsar?

The Dungeness crab bisque, with which I drank a glass of fizzy French wine, at my second-favorite restaurant in the world, the Alloro Wine Bar, in Bandon, on the Oregon coast.

And speaking of the Oregon coast, the razor clams and poached eggs at that restaurant with the gift shop that looks like the food should taste like it usually does at a restaurant with a gift shop, but which turns out to have been a sly way of hiding a perhaps threatening enthusiasm for gourmandise from people who it might abash, but who, in that atmosphere, were tucking in with all the gusto at their command. Us, too.

The tripitas tacos at a taco truck now long gone. Deep-fried chopped beef intestines with cilantro and chopped white onion on perfect corn tortillas, and if you haven't ever tasted such a thing, don't be thinking you wouldn't find it as celestial as I did and do.

A salad made from the first-grown spring leaves of the Dear Husband's garden, mixed lightly with nothing but Maldon salt and a little walnut oil— the only salad I've ever had that seemed to levitate on the plate.

My own brown rice paella, made differently every time, for any celebration we feel might need it. No matter what I put in it (octopus? sausage? green peas? shrimp, clams, mussels, salt cod?), or how we eat it (chopped cilantro scattered on top? lemon halves to squeeze? an overly garlicky aioli?), it seems, every time, like the best meal ever. (See recipe p. 241.)

There, I feel better now. Thank you for letting me share.

I wish I could hear about what were your favorite meals. If you think of it, and you have a dull day, too, maybe you could write the memories of them down and send them on to me?* Then I can read them the next time this kind of dull day hits. That would be very nice, I think. Very nice indeed.

*tod@exterminatingangel.com

SMOKED TURKEY BREAST AND EGGS

I was tired and only a little hungry, but I wanted to make something nice, different, and not too heavy for myself for dinner, before I settled down to a pile of neglected reading materials. My mind was really only half on what I was doing, the other half still back in the unfinished chores of the day. This is not a good situation, I scolded myself. Your mind should be wholly on what you're doing at the time. And at this time, what I was doing was making myself a solitary dinner.

That was when I saw it. I'd totally forgotten I'd bought a piece of smoked turkey breast from a local butcher. Local turkey, they'd smoked it themselves. Normally I'm not crazy about turkey—kind of dry and too tame, is my usual impression, probably from a lifetime of having eaten mostly factory-farmed Thanksgiving birds—but, as usual, I was entranced at the fact that this was made in-house, by people I actually have met and talked with.

So there it was. And, serendipitously, its package was leaning right up against the carton of eggs Cindy had just dropped by when she came to have a glass of wine.

Eggs. A favorite comfort food at the end of a long workday, especially when I'm not feeling up to very much, gourmandise-wise.

And why not? Eggs and smoked turkey breast. I wasn't very hungry, so I didn't even consider any toast or potatoes. But there was a beautifully ripe heritage tomato scored off my favorite farm stand, and, in a flower vase, that huge bouquet of herbs from Cindy's garden: parsley, dill, and basil.

So I sliced the tomato, sprinkled it with a little coarse salt, tore a plethora of basil leaves atop, anointed it with olive oil, and squeezed a lemon quarter over it all. I let it sit while I had a tomato juice with Tabasco and Worcestershire sauce in my chair on the deck, as the late summer sun went down behind the trees.

Then I went inside. Got out a skillet big enough for a couple of pieces of thinly sliced turkey breast and two eggs. And made Smoked Turkey Breast and Eggs. The turkey breast seared in a little oil and butter, so it was brown and crusty, and the eggs just cooked so the whites were set, and the dark gold yolks still runny and ready to explode on my plate in a very satisfying way.

And man, it was delicious. A helping of tomatoes on a white plate, with the turkey breast nestled beside it, and the eggs carefully laid on top. A beautiful plate to look at, and, once the yolks were speared, a beautiful plate to eat.

In fact, it was so delicious, I woke up this morning craving it, and made it all over again. Although, because this was breakfast, I only made one slice of turkey and one egg. And instead of the glass of white wine I had with dinner, there was a satisfyingly tart glass of pomegranate juice.

I'll remember that recipe. It's good to cook, and it's good to eat.

This is how:

◊ Smoked turkey breast
◊ Eggs
◊ Oil and butter
◊ Salt and pepper

Take a smoked turkey breast, and slice thinly as much as you want for as many people as you are going to feed. At least one slice per egg.

Take as many free-range eggs as you want to serve.

Break each egg in a little cup, to make sure the yolk doesn't break.

Heat a skillet big enough to lay all the turkey slices in flat.

Add a little oil and butter, heat till they foam.

Put the turkey slices in, brown on one side, then the other.

When they're browned, push them over to one side of skillet—you can even move this side a little off the burner, so they all stay warm, but stop cooking too much.

Carefully slide the eggs from their cups into the pan on the side of the skillet that's over the heat. Salt and pepper.

Let them cook just a moment, then clap a lid on the pan and turn off the heat.

Give them about three or four minutes. Check. Are the whites cooked through, but the yolks still liquid? If not, clap the lid on again for another two minutes and check again.

When the eggs are perfect, carefully lift out the turkey breast onto plates, and lift the eggs and put them on top.

Serve them forth.

And if you're like me, give a huge sigh of perfect contentment as you spear the yolks and watch the gold liquid spill out over the browned turkey.
Eat with pleasure, knowing you've been fed.

THE WONDERS OF ROASTED TRI TIP, INTERNET STYLE

I do love following my neighbor Cindy to her deep freeze, in anticipation of what's going to be yanked out of its mysterious depths for my delectation. In fact, one of the proudest moments of my life was the time she rustled around amid the white butcher-paper-wrapped packages, pulled out one triumphantly and said, "Elk neck. No one else knows how to cook this, but I know you will." Did I know how to cook elk neck? No, I can't say I did. But I went ahead and tried my best (the usual carrots/onions/garlic/red wine fest), and the result had my carnivorous friend Teri saying, "You're the only person I know who makes great food out of weird things."

Another proud moment.

But part of the secret of my cuisine, I have to confess here, is that my best cooking derives from the challenge of weird things. I don't know why. It's my karma somehow. What this means is that the more regular ingredients, the more regular cuts of meat, the pieces that everyone seems to know how to deal with, sometimes are just beyond me. Or, if not beyond me, require me to screw my courage to the sticking place in dealing with them.

Tripe? Neck? Sweetbreads? No problem. Hand them over. I'll be perfectly cavalier about those. But when Cindy held out a package marked: "Tri Tip: 1.5 pounds," I had a moment's hesitation.

Let me analyze this. Could it be a Fear of Failure? Yes, I have to reluctantly admit. It is definitely that bugaboo of all cooks: Fear of Not Living Up to Other People's Cooking.

I mean, if I fail at tripe, neck, sweetbreads, where exactly is my comparison? True, they are less expensive than other more popular pieces of meat, and they seem to accept cavalier treatment with more graciousness. But that wasn't it. I knew what it was. There's not quite as much competition in that arena as in, for example, the steak/prime rib/leg of lamb contest.

And here I thought I never worried about competition. Okay, I ask myself, if that's true, you big fat liar, why are you worried about cooking that Tri Tip?

Erm. Um. Umph.

But I couldn't resist taking that Tri Tip. I was all alone at home, for the Beloved Vegetarian Husband wasn't due back for three days (there was a pot of split pea soup simmering on the woodstove, awaiting him—see recipe p. 39), and I had all my culinary attention available to give to it. And I felt like eating beef. Boy, did I feel like eating beef. Especially beef that had been kindly and cunningly raised eating grass provided for it in the meadows of my neighbors. I particularly felt like eating that kind of beef.

So I brought it home. I unwrapped it. And stared at it as if by sheer willpower and eye contact I could force it to reveal its secrets. How did it best want to be cooked? Cindy said she always just barbequed hers, but it was snowing outside, and besides, I don't have a barbeque in Oregon.

Did it want to be pot-roasted? Well, it was going to have to forget it if it did; I wanted the beef that night, and pot-roasting, proper pot-roasting, takes a calm, unhurried attitude that can afford delayed gratification.

I did not want delayed gratification. I wanted steak.

And yet, I felt as I communed with that Tri Tip, to just cook it the way I normally cook my steak—broil over high heat in a cast-iron pan, either in duck fat or a little olive oil mixed with butter—was going to be to lose some kind of advantage I could only just tantalizingly feel the corner of.

Something was nagging at the back of my mind about that cut. Something I had once heard, once read about, once thought of. I couldn't quite catch hold of it, though.

So I did what I always do in cases like this. I poured myself a glass of red wine and went browsing through my cookbook collection.

Now, there is a dearth of carnivorously oriented cookbooks in my collection. Well, not a dearth…but it is not as complete an archive as it might be, given more than twenty years of cooking for a mixed marriage with a Beloved Vegetarian Husband. I have all the basic cookbooks that describe the basic cuts. And I have one wonderful one by Fergus Henderson, of the miraculous St. John Restaurant in London, involving all sorts of wonderful and simple ways to cook various kinds of meats. But not only was that one back in Colorado, but I knew for sure there was nothing in it about Tri Tip, which does seem to be an American cut. More than an American cut: a California cut. More than a California cut…a…a…a…

That was when I remembered it. Santa Maria. A town in California's Central Valley. Famous for its barbeque. Famous for its…Tri Tip Barbeque.

I'd always wistfully looked at the signs for Santa Maria Barbeque as we drove past on our way, the Beloved Vegetarian Husband's and my way, to or from Los Angeles. But, you know, when your husband is both beloved and vegetarian, you don't really like to suggest a lunch detour involving charred cow.

I had been curious, though. I had looked it up to see what it was. And I'd found it was Tri Tip rubbed with a special spice mix, and then, of course, barbequed. That memory stayed in some corner of my mind and now was trying to make its way fully into the light.

This is when the internet comes into its own. This is when googling for a recipe cannot be beat. The perfect time.

For a moment, let me make a slight detour, and mention why I am a collector of cookbooks, nay, more than a collector, a veritable cookbook-collecting fiend, and why I do not rely, generally, on recipes from the internet. This is why: a cookbook is more than just a vehicle to convey the bare abstract facts of a recipe. It is, to the food lover, as an evening with a friend compares to an email exchange. A cookbook involves personality, physical heft, design elements to delight the eye…and more than that, personal experience (Where did I find it? What else was happening at the time? What did I cook out of it? What is that stain on p. 137, where the book seems to open magically by itself, oh yes, I remember that dinner party…). It is an actual experience rather than a virtual one. I regard each and every cookbook that I own as a friend. (And if you could see my bookshelves you would say, "Man. That's a lot of friends.")

Mind you, I'm not knocking virtual. I think virtual is a boon and a treasure, in its rightful place. It's just that, generally speaking, I am more of an enjoyer of the actual. Generally speaking.

But at this moment, when I remembered Santa Maria Tri Tip, virtual was the boon and the treasure it can be. I hastened to the computer. I googled. And I found.

Santa Maria Tri Tip is the cut rubbed with Santa Maria spice rub, and then barbequed, broiled, or roasted at high heat to rare or medium rare done.

I mentally high fived myself. Yes! This was sounding exactly like something I wanted to eat THAT NIGHT.

Now my confidence came flooding back. Looking at the various recipes for differing spice rubs, I itched to make my own with what I had in the cupboard. Almost all of the recipes included celery salt, and I have no celery salt. I never have celery salt. I believe I never have had celery salt. However I did have a quarter inch left of organic garlic salt in the organic garlic salt jar I generally used for skirt steak (see skirt steak recipe, p. 45). So I opened up the top of that jar and considered what else I could add to that quarter inch to make a decent Tri Tip rub. Ground aji chile, once given me as a gift, turned out to be perfect for this purpose. Ground Aleppo pepper, also given me as a gift. Poured a bit of each of those in. Thought about it, poured more of both. Spanish hot paprika, but the unsmoked kind this time, since that was what I felt like just then. Freshly ground black pepper.

I added all of those to the jar with the remains of the garlic salt, shook it around to blend, and then rubbed it all over that Tri Tip. Let the meat sit for an hour while I made a green bean/shallot/roasted tomato/pesto salad to go with it (see recipe p. 77). Then I roasted it in a really hot oven for hardly any time at all (although "hardly any time at all" turned out to be a little too long for me, who likes her meat a lot rarer than the virtual recipes I took the timing from—but it was still tender and tasty, so I'm not complaining; I'll just know better next time). Then I covered it with foil and let it sit so it could, as beef likes to do, reabsorb its juices and plump up before serving. And it was… well. It was a heavenly bit of meat. I sliced it against the grain in differing thicknesses just to see which I liked best. What won out was a slightly thick slice of about a half an inch. But if you'd been looking, you wouldn't have seen me shunning the slices either thinner or thicker than that. And there was more than enough for lunch the next day, too. (Truth to tell, there should have been enough for three meals, but that just goes to show you how very good it was.)

Here's how good it was:

Tri Tip, Santa Maria Internet Style

◊ A 1½ pound Tri Tip
◊ Spice rub of your own choice (might I suggest a mix of garlic salt, pepper, aji chile powder, ground Aleppo pepper, and unsmoked hot paprika?)

Rub the spices all over the meat, and let the meat sit for anywhere from one to 24 hours.

Preheat the oven to 425°.

Put the meat on a rack in a shallow roasting pan, or, do what I did—preheat a ridged cast-iron pan in the oven, and when it is heated, put the meat atop the hot ridges.

Cook the meat for about fifteen minutes for rare, about twenty minutes for medium rare. You can cook it longer, but why?

Temperature on a meat thermometer for rare is 125°, for medium rare 135°. It'll keep cooking after you've taken it out, while it rests, and you don't want it to cook too much. It's a thinnish cut, but don't worry: it will be beautifully browned on the outside in that time. And if it isn't on the top, just turn it over—it will be on that side for sure.

When done to your liking, take it out, put it on a carving board and cover with a tent of aluminum foil. Let it sit for ten to fifteen minutes. Carve against the grain in slices the thickness of your choice.

Enjoy. Seriously. Enjoy.

And here is how the triumphs of the solitary diner can turn into a really good idea for food for friends…

EASY AS DUCK SOUP

My idea of a triumph is finding something at the grocery store that is priced cheap because no one else really gets what a great deal it is. So you can imagine my delight, the day I went, awestruck, into the Pacific Ocean Market, the Asian market near me in Colorado. It's the size and variety of Chinatown inside, I swear, and I wandered the aisles in a kind of trance. Frozen dim sum. A real fish market with real fish (live crab! fish with heads on! fish I'd never heard of!). Seventy kinds of seaweed. Rice, rice, rice. Roast duck, real Chinese roast duck.

Duck wings. Yes. Duck wings. Packed together. Ninety-nine cents a pound. DUCK WINGS. NINETY-NINE CENTS A POUND.

The Hallelujah Chorus played loud in my head as I tenderly ushered two pounds into my shopping cart. Did I mention they had duck wings? For ninety-nine cents a pound? Yes, I thought I did.

Duck is my favorite meat. Duck broth is my favorite broth. And the bony bits of anything edible are my favorite bits of edibles.

So I chucked them in the freezer against the inevitable day when the Beloved Husband would fly off to a film festival, or drive off to a camping trip. And when that inevitable day arrived, here is what I did:

Turned the oven on to 400°. Peeled and quartered about five carrots (peels and ends into the dog stodge bag in the fridge, where I keep the veggies I add to the dog's food—aka dog stodge [find that recipe in the original Jam

191

Today] for when I make said stodge later in the week). Peeled about a head of garlic (aside from duck, what I really love is garlic…I assume this does not surprise you by now).

Pulled out a large Pyrex baking dish. Tossed the duck wings, the carrots, and the garlic with a little salt and spread them around the dish. No oil. Duck has enough fat even in the wings, bless it. And very tasty fat it is, too.

Then I shoved the whole lot into the preheated oven. Poured myself a big glass of red wine (aside from duck and garlic, what I really love is red wine), and settled down to watch a day-old Stephen Colbert show on the internet. Got up whenever there was one of those stupid internet commercials on, and stirred the whole wonderful-smelling mess around. The house filled with the smell of duck and garlic. The wine-glass levels dropped, and were replenished before dropping again.

Watched *The Daily Show* on the internet. Continued my evasion of commercials by stirring duck wings and adding just a smidgen more red wine to the glass.

After about an hour, or an hour and a half of this (at some point, I also started reading a P.D. James novel), I noticed the carrots were caramelizing, and the duck wings were nice and brown. I did think I was going to have some of this for lunch the next day, but it didn't work out that way.

I piled half of the wonderful smelling pile on a plate, poured out a little more wine, and had at it with my fingers.

Gave a happy sigh. Got up, scraped the bones into a soup pot. Gazed at the remaining roasted duck wings and carrots and garlic. Shrugged, gave in to fate, and decanted the rest onto my plate.

When it was all over, dumped the rest of the bones in the soup pot. Added a couple of unpeeled garlic cloves, a scrubbed broken-up carrot, a washed piece of celery, a couple of sprigs of parsley, and a bay leaf. Turned the heat on high underneath, and let it come to a boil while I did the dishes. Turned it down to low, turned it off before I went to bed, turned it back on when I got up. Cooked a couple of hours more, strained it and then…

Duck soup.

Now I did turn that duck soup into onion soup, because I had found a whole bunch of ninety-nine-cents-a-pound organic onions at the local market the other day.

But here's another really good idea, just in case you have some duck broth in your freezer, and you just happen to have a bunch of mushrooms hanging out in the veggie drawer.

Mushroom Duck Soup

Even better: CREAM of Mushroom Duck Soup.

Like this:

◊ Duck broth
◊ White wine
◊ Butter
◊ Flour
◊ Finely chopped mushrooms
◊ Finely chopped onions
◊ Cream

Melt a little bit of butter in a soup pot. Whisk in the same amount of flour (I use Wondra, but plain is fine); cook for five minutes or so. Stir in a half-cup or so of white wine. Then add about 3 cups of duck broth, and a little dried thyme. Bring to a boil, reduce the heat, simmer for about ten minutes. Salt and pepper as desired.

Now—and this is the clever part—you're going to add RAW mushrooms and onion and cook them just lightly. I got this idea from Michael Roberts' *Parisian Home Cooking*, and it's a corker. He purees about a pound of mushrooms and half an onion in the food processor, but I find if I just chop them fine (and don't worry too much about the quantities, either, having done this with half a pound of mushrooms and a whole onion with great success) that not only works, but also gives the soup a nice texture.

The lightly cooked mushrooms and onions give the whole soup a really lovely flavor. Add them raw to the simmering broth, add a little cream to taste, and simmer just till cooked through, about five minutes.

Serve hot, and feel happy. As I hope is always true for you and yours at the end of every meal.

LAMB SHOULDER CHOPS AND INSPIRATION

Another time a solitary meal really inspired a feast was the evening I contemplated a lone lamb shoulder chop, bought, as is my wont, from some market's marked-down bin. I love those marked-down bins. For everything but fish, I love those marked-down bins. (I still remember with perfect clarity my agony at watching a supermarket employee THROW AWAY a beautiful wedge of Roquefort cheese because it was past the due date. I begged him to give it to me. I reminded him that people were able to eat Roquefort cheeses found in French caverns where they had lain for decades. But he, American and hygienic, refused, and backed away from me cautiously, as if I was a crazy person. A crazy cheese-obsessed person.)

Anyway, on this particular night, I was remembering with some nostalgia the lamb shoulder chops of my childhood. This is the cheapest of the lamb chops, so the only one a large and hungry family could really afford, even if only once in a while. You need to braise, rather than grill them, since they're a little tougher than the loin chops. But like all meat that is a little tougher, they tend to have more flavor if you coax it out correctly. (There's a metaphor in here, which I like to explore in quieter moments.) I believe my mother used to braise them in margarine, and they were utterly divine to a hungry child.

So now I was a hungry adult. A hungry adult alone for dinner. I knew I should braise the chop, but there were things in the refrigerator I felt should get used up. This sometimes happens, I confess guiltily, since I really do not believe in using myself as a garbage disposal...but it works within reason, as it did this particular evening. Even though I felt braising the chop in butter would be delicious, I did happen to have a handful of mushrooms that might not last another few days in the refrigerator. I had a bounty of onions. And a little bit of fast-wilting parsley.

I remembered a recipe I'd read and considered once long ago in James Beard's *American Cookery* that combined all those ingredients. So I hauled it out, and considered what it said. I thought about how to adapt a recipe for six down to a recipe for one. And I had at it.

This is what I did:

Braised Shoulder Lamb Chop with Mushrooms and Onions (for one)

◊   1 shoulder chop, about ½ inch thick
◊   1 clove of garlic, minced
◊   1 onion, sliced thinly
◊   A handful of mushrooms, sliced
◊   Salt
◊   A handful of parsley, chopped

I rubbed a heavy skillet with the lamb's fat. Browned the chop on both sides, and added the garlic, onions and mushrooms. Cooked it briskly until the mixture started to give up its moisture, then covered it, reduced the heat, and braised it all in its own liquid for about 20 minutes. The mixture was beautifully moist, so I never bothered with any butter. I salted to taste (I rarely add pepper while cooking, preferring to grind it over the finished dish once it's off the heat—my feeling is that tastes better), added the parsley, cooked a bit longer while I made a salad, and served it forth.

It was fantastic. The braising liquid conjured by the mix of mushrooms, onions, and lamb fat was just the right medium to lift that chop right into the toothsome category. Success, I thought, feeling, at the end of that solitary meal, particularly well fed. Thank you, James Beard.

About a month later, I was on a visit to my mother's house, where I had offered to cook dinner for her and some other members of my family. I always want to cook dinner for my mother, I think to make it up to her for all those years she was chained to a stove by the needs of my brothers and myself. But she very rarely lets me. This time she agreed, and we went shopping together for the proposed feast.

She wanted osso buco, I suspect because osso buco was something we could never afford in the long-lost days of an enormous family of permanently hungry children, but there was no osso buco to be had in the market that day. I pointed at the lamb shoulder chops in the case, but she shied off from that, remembering, I suspect, the lamb shoulder chops of the past, which memory probably had a much different meaning for her than for me.

We compromised on a relatively inexpensive rolled "leg of lamb," "on special." "You can make it into a stew!" she pointed out enthusiastically. And of course, when we got home and unwrapped it from its rather silly hairnet-like thing holding it together, it proved to be bits and bobs trimmed off other lamb cuts, all held together as a faux roast. Perfect, as she had surmised, to be cut into large pieces and turned into a stew of some sort.

Well, why not? I thought, remembering the wonderful savor of that lone shoulder chop I'd made for myself. Why not just turn that recipe into a stew? We had plenty of mushrooms and garlic and onions. No parsley, but we could do without that this once.

So I made a stew. I cut that lamb 'roast' up into nice big uneven-looking pieces, and browned them their own fat—no flour. Salted them, and, even though I usually don't pepper things before I cook, I peppered these. Why? I think, looking back, because my mother always peppered meat at this point, and I, cooking at her stove, somehow was channeling her techniques as well. I piled the browned meat into a big stew pot, sautéed sliced onions and sliced mushrooms and chopped garlic in the remaining lamb fat eked out with a little butter, and then poured all of that on top. Gave it a lovely enthusiastic stir to mix it all together, clapped a lid on it, and stuck it in the oven at 350°, along with a pot of grated carrots mixed with cream, and some Retro Green Beans (see recipe p. 99). It was my cunning plan to get everything together in the oven and just let it cook on its own, so that instead of the usual last-minute mother-finishing-up-cooking brouhaha, we could all sit down and enjoy a comfortable family catch-up. Especially my mother. I wanted her to sit down at an hour she had always spent standing. I wanted to set her free from being chained to the family stove, I suppose. Must have been a wish in childhood.

After a while, though, Mother jumped up, peered in the oven, muttered something about that gravy needing more to mop it up than the baby potatoes I was going to boil at the last minute. So while the rest of us sat there, and in spite of our protests, she stood at the stove and made some rice. She was right that the stew needed it, of course. The lamb and mushrooms and onions and garlic made a huge unexpected amount of deeply savory sauce, and one of my brothers is not really a potato person at heart. Then, just for good measure, my mother whipped up her cucumber salad (see recipe p. 209) while she stood there waiting for the rice to be done. And I realized it was just possible she liked being 'chained' to that stove as much as I do.

After all, I must have gotten it from somewhere.

It was a lovely feast. As we ate it, I realized something about myself: I like to eat alone. I like to eat à deux with the Beloved Vegetarian Husband. I like to eat quietly with a few close friends. And my deep enjoyment of these pleasures springs from this: that I have the luxury of knowing I have always had a family to feast with whenever I like.

We Are How We Eat

THE REVOLUTION WILL NOT BE CATERED

Really, it was like lunch with the Marx Brothers.

We had stopped in a little northern California coastal town to grab some lunch at a cafe we remembered fondly from a few years ago. What you might call a hippie cafe. You had to bring your own mugs (we had those). Everything was fair trade. The coffee had been terrific, the tea had been perfect, the food had shown signs of being lovingly prepared.

We were hungry and we were tired, and we were looking forward to it. It had been a four-hour drive to get there, and we still had another four to go.

I should have known, though. When we drove past to park on the town's cliffs, there wasn't anyone sitting outside. Lunch time, too. And the parking lot at the 'normal' place across the street ("Best Clam Chowder on the Coast!") was full. I put that down to prejudice.

Should have known.

Always check those parking lots. It's not an infallible sign (vivid memories flood in from a certain lunch at a Mexican restaurant in Susanville), but generally, the locals know. Of course they do.

They knew this time.

It was kind of hysterical, really. Alex sat outside with the dogs, and told me what he wanted. I went in and ordered. Oh, the girl behind the counter told me, we don't have any tuna. I went back outside and came back with another idea. Oh, she said, I forgot to tell you before you went out that we don't have any bread.

One o'clock, mind you. Lunchtime. They have a whole list of sandwiches, and there's no one in the place.

But you have that garlic bagel I just ordered for myself, right? Oh yes, she said, beaming, we have that. He can have his sandwich on that if he wants.

I went back outside. Came back in with the okay.

Then I said, "About my order—can I add something to it?"

"We've already started it."

"Oh, okay, don't worry about it."

Went outside. Waited. Went back inside.

The girl working the kitchen said she'd burned Alex's garlic bagel, "And it was the last one!", but fortunately, "We have lots of Multicultural Bagels!"

So I said, sure, make it with a multicultural bagel.

Went back outside. More time passed.

The girl from behind the counter came out and proudly presented Alex's order. We looked at it. I looked at her.

"Didn't you finish my order?"

"Wasn't this all you ordered?"

"Don't you remember the bagel you told me you'd already started?"

She looked at me blankly. Alex suggested I share his bagel. He could already tell what was likely to happen if we got into it anymore.

We shared. It was fine. We had a good laugh.

Then I took our mugs in to get some coffee and tea to go. I poured the Fair Trade Mexican coffee into Alex's mug. The girl behind the counter put a tea bag in my mug and filled it up with water.

I thanked her, paid, and then I felt the side of my mug.

Lukewarm water.

"Honey," I said as patiently as I could—though the fact that I was addressing her as 'honey' showed both of us I was losing what I had—, "I actually need the water to be hotter in order for the tea to steep."

The other girl came over and silently poured some of my water out and refilled it with hotter.

It was terrible tea.

As we walked away, Alex sipped his coffee, then laughed and laughed. He laughed so hard he cried.

"Doesn't even taste like coffee," he said, wiping his eyes.

We threw the stuff away and I said, "That whole time they were making our lunch? They were talking about a hydroelectric plant in Brazil, and how horrible that is, and how they were going to protest it."

And we laughed some more. Mind you, we were sympathetic. We have had our own lifetimes of thinking that what we felt about hydroelectric plants in Brazil was more important than paying attention to what was in front of us.

But there you go. Horrible lunch. Horrible tea and coffee. Little things, sure. But they had been in the control of those young women who had spent their time instead thinking about how they were going to make the world a better place.

And there we had been—waiting for them to help us make our world a better place.

The Revolution will not be catered, you know. In fact, we hope that when the Revolution comes, no one will be off the hook for being kind and alert and making sure that they do the job that's right in front of them.

Because that is the only way to make a better world.

In the meantime, at least (if we pay attention) we can make a better cup of tea.

A Good Cup of Tea:

◊ A cup
◊ Some loose tea
◊ Water
◊ Sweetener and milk (opt.)

Put the kettle on to boil. Warm the cup with a little hot water. Dump out that hot water. Pick a good tea, and put it in a linen bag, or a strainer, or a tea ball of some kind. Put the tea in the cup. Pour water from the kettle at the very moment it boils over the tea.

Let it steep for three to five minutes. Take out the tea.

Add the sweeteners and milks of your choice. Honey is nice. A little dash of cream is superb.

Sit down somewhere pleasant and sip.

Then get back on your own path to making the world a better place for yourself, your loved ones, and everyone else your path can reach.

If that path makes it to Brazil, that's great. No matter what, though, don't forget to pay attention when you're making that cup of tea.

FISH WITH MUSTARD, CREAM AND SWISS CHEESE

There are those periods where the Beloved Vegetarian Husband and I spend a lot of time on the road. This can have dire consequences, at least foodwise, and I was going to tell the truly horrifying story of the Worst Meal Either of Us Has Ever Had Without Being Actively Poisoned (the WMEoUHEH With Being Poisoned having taken place in Hull, in England, and involved an ancient piece of skate and a truly bizarre avocado salad), but as the memory fades thankfully into grayness, pushed out of consciousness by a series of subsequently smashing meals, I can't feel the same vengeful urge I originally did. Suffice to say this dinner involved the Worst Food, the Worst Service, the Dirtiest Cutlery and Glasses, and, to top it off, a whining owner who came to the table to ask us, stunned as we were, "how it all was," and then launched into a pathetic tale about how he was supposed to be building a "biofuels factory in Peru! for the environment!" but because he couldn't find decent help, was chained to the restaurant.

As I said, several soothingly lovely meals after that have dimmed the trauma. But really, you know, there is no place like home for the eating of lovely meals that make you forget there are actually people out there running restaurants who a) hate food, b) hate themselves, and c) hate customers generally.

I cannot emphasize that enough. There. Is. No. Place. Like. Home.

There have been so many opportunities to erase the infamy of that Horrible Meal on the Road, I almost couldn't think of which one to give the recipe for. There was the turnip/potato/garlic/cream gratin, made from an enormous turnip somehow overlooked in the first scouring of The Indigo Ray's garden. (She gave it to me to give the dogs, but on my peeling and slicing it, the turnip was revealed to be first-rate human-consumption-type food...particularly with cream.) There were the filets of sole baked with breadcrumbs, garlic, tarragon, and butter. There was the Hubbard squash that, when melded with fried sage leaves and sweet garlic, formed the most exquisite of soups.

But really, best of all, and easiest, too, was one of our favorite home-cooked dinners: cod filets baked with mustard and cream and Swiss cheese, served with tiny baked potatoes, a salad dressed with a mustard vinaigrette, and little dishes of cumin-spiced pickled beets on the side. That was one of those dinners that looks absolutely beautiful on the plate, and where all the elements interact with each other in ways as joyful as the dancers in a Balanchine ballet.

I can't imagine why I hadn't tried that recipe before, the one for Grey Sea Mullet with Gruyere and Mustard in Darina Allen's *Simply Delicious Suppers* (she got the recipe from Jane Grigson, and we all know who SHE was), unless it was because my mind couldn't wrap itself around the fact that it is perfectly easy to make with the kind of fish one can usually find in the market. But somehow, when I found these lovely Alaskan cod filets at the Co-op one day, it finally clicked. I didn't have any Gruyere, and—it being as expensive as it is—probably wouldn't have used it this way if I had, but I did have some nice raw Swiss cheese. I had cream. And of course I had Dijon mustard, of which, at any one time, there are at least two backup jars hidden away in the back of some shelf.

Very simple recipe:

Cod. Swiss cheese. Cream. Dijon mustard. You just grate some cheese, mix it with cream and mustard, spread it on top of the filets in a buttered baking dish, pop into a preheated 350° oven for twenty minutes till browned. Serve.

I fiddled with this a bit, of course. For one thing, I mistrusted that twenty minutes in the oven thing, given that the filets I had were fairly thin, not the nice thick chunks of cod I remember from England, where this recipe originated.

So this is what I did:

For two people:

Preheated the oven to 350° (meanwhile, the tiny potatoes were baking in the toaster oven at 400°).

Buttered a baking dish large enough to hold the filets.

Then I laid one filet out, and spread it with half of this mixture:

◊ ¼ lb. grated Swiss cheese
◊ 1 teaspoon Dijon mustard
◊ 4 or 5 teaspoons cream

I topped that with the second filet, and spread it with the second half of the cheese/mustard/cream.

I cut this long, double decker filet in half, and put both halves into the dish.

Popped the dish into the oven. Set the timer for twenty minutes. Checked the fish a couple of times in there to make sure it wasn't cooking too fast. (Made the salad, dished out the beets.)

At the end of twenty minutes, when the cod looked done but not TOO done, if you know what I mean, I put the dish under the broiler till it bubbled and turned brown.

Put the portions on each plate with the crackling little baked potatoes and a lavish line of mustardy salad greens. Put the plates on the candlelit table beside individual dishes of cold vinegary, oniony pickled beets. Called the Beloved Vegetarian Husband to the table.

And had at it.

Not only was it a lovely meal, not only was it served and eaten with love, but we didn't have to endure any bullshit self-exculpatory babble at the end of it from an incompetent restaurateur. That may have been the best thing of all.

Well. Except for that fish. That was maybe truly the best.

There really is no place like home, after all...

HYBRID SOUP OF THE EVENING, BEAUTIFUL SOUP!

One of my favorite comfort foods is seaweed and cucumber salad, which probably will alert a future sociologist or historian that I am writing in the western states of America in the period of the Blossoming of the Hybrid Cuisines. Yes, indeed, I grew up in San Francisco, where the cuisine is so damned hybrid now it constitutes a separate tradition. This tradition is, I assert, thoroughly American. My own genealogy is similarly thoroughly American: Portuguese, Chinese, English, Irish, Polish, Austrian, French. My mother had a theory that the more nationalities went into a child, the stronger the child was going to be, and I cannot say after watching my contemporaries and the children of my contemporaries grow that she was at all wrong.

This kind of biological exuberance that burst out in all directions in the city of my childhood, and then the nation of my adulthood, shows itself in the way we all eat nowadays. It sometimes seems to me that there is no mall in America lacking a pho restaurant. Or a sushi bar (although this may not be a good thing, given the state of our oceans nowadays—but that is another subject entirely). And home cooking has changed.

The Beloved Vegetarian Husband, who often finds much to depress himself with in the daily news, likes to say, "It's like we're living in the Fifties all over again. Except," he continues thoughtfully, "the food is much better. That's the one thing that has improved since World War II. We have much better food."

I'm happy to say he usually says this kind of thing during dinner.

Anyway, my Macanese (which means a Chinese and Portuguese blend) mother grew up in Japan, and so I learned that Japanese food was, luckily, part of my heritage (and what a heritage!). I've always loved nori, the seaweed that we use to wrap nigiri sushi. I love those seaweed-wrapped rice triangles you can buy in corner markets in Tokyo as a snack. And I love seaweed salad. I especially love seaweed and cucumber salad.

For that salad you make a dressing, of rice vinegar, soy sauce, and a little sugar. Elizabeth Andoh, in *At Home with Japanese Cooking*, gives the proportions as 4 tablespoons rice vinegar, 3 tablespoons soy sauce, 2 teaspoons sugar. I do stick to those proportions, generally, though it doesn't hurt in the slightest if you fiddle with them to taste. I like this with red wine vinegar, since that's the way my mother used to make a cucumber salad I adored as a child (and still do, come to think of it). Her cucumber salad was a Japanese/Macanese/*Joy of Cooking* hybrid, where she mixed a little white sugar with some cold water till it dissolved (Andoh suggests boiling the ingredients till the sugar dissolves, but this, while nice, isn't always necessary in my experience... as long as the sugar dissolves, it doesn't matter how you get there). Then my mother added red wine vinegar and soy sauce to taste, and marinated thinly sliced, peeled cucumbers that had been salted and squeezed. I make that salad from time to time, too. And the seaweed/cucumber salad is an obvious change rung on the same tune. You still salt the cucumber, though in this case, you peel or not peel, depending on the waxiness or nonwaxiness of the veggie, and cut lengthwise in half, scooping out and discarding the seeds. Then slice both halves into little half-moons. Salt and let stand for ten minutes or so, and squeeze the water out.

Meanwhile, you should be soaking your seaweed. This takes far less time than it used to for some reason (are they processing seaweed differently these days?). So follow the directions on the package. I think wakame, the traditional seaweed for this salad, is traditional for a reason: it's the best. When it's doubled in size and pliable, drain it and squeeze it to get the excess water out.

Mix the cucumber, seaweed, and dressing. Chill.

This is the most refreshing summer salad imaginable. No matter how sultry the day, this salad perks you right up. And then, when the weather changes suddenly—

That's what it did recently. It got cold overnight, in that lovely way that tentatively announces the stop-and-go arrival of fall. And I, to celebrate, had made first a boiled short rib meal (see p. 114), which left me with a beautiful broth that I used a portion of for my monumental oxtail stew (see p. 116). But one dinner, one chilly night, I didn't feel like eating a big, or even a biggish, meal. I was by myself, and tired, and wanted a little encouragement. When I want a little encouragement, I find what I often want is soup.

There was this big bowlful of beautiful soup of the evening, beautiful soup—beef broth, flavored with garlic and thyme, just sitting there.

And there in the refrigerator was a bowl of seaweed and cucumber salad. There in the kitchen I had a brainwave prompted by my own desires: **Seaweed and Cucumber Soup**! Soup of the evening, beautiful soup!

I brought the broth to a roiling boil. I put as much seaweed and cucumber salad as I wanted (a lot) in a deep ceramic Japanese bowl I keep for these kinds of meals. And then I poured the broth over it. Sat down at the counter and ate it, with Sriracha sauce squirted on top, with contentment as deep as the bowl. A beautiful inspiration, seaweed salad soup. I'll have it again, too.

This is how:

◊ Seaweed
◊ Cucumber
◊ Salt
◊ Soy sauce
◊ Rice vinegar or red wine vinegar
◊ Sugar
◊ Broth
◊ Sriracha sauce

Make a seaweed/cucumber salad.

Have some broth on hand: chicken, beef, vegetable, whatever you fancy. Canned is fine, though homemade from bones of former meals you've frozen for just this purpose is by far the nicest.

Heat the broth to boiling.

Put seaweed salad in bowls that can withstand heat.

Pour the boiling broth atop.

Don't worry about salt, since the salad already is salted.

Serve with Sriracha sauce at once.

Hybrid soup of the evening, beautiful hybrid soup!

And speaking of seaweed (we were speaking of seaweed, weren't we? or anyway, we should have been, the amount of vitamins and trace minerals even the most commonly available form contains), there is one dish I love to make that mixes it with carrots. This comes, as do so many other terrific ideas, from Deborah Madison's *Vegetarian Cooking for Everyone*, and the basic idea is that you stir-fry ginger and shredded carrot in a little sesame oil till the carrots start to look done, then add plumped-up seaweed of your choice (she uses hijiki, which is great, and I use arame, which is usually easier to find around here), and continue to stir-fry, adding soy sauce to taste.

I love this dish. It perks my body right up when said body is feeling down; it revives me when I've overindulged in any manner of less healthful dishes. And it's so forgiving. I can grate as many carrots as I feel like, and soak as much seaweed as I want, and throw them all together in a wok or a skillet over some high heat, adding a bit of the seaweed's soaking water as needed, to keep it all moist and prevent it from sticking to the pan.

There are lots of things you can do with it too, and, trust me, I do all of them. Eat it as is in a bowl, topped with Sriracha sauce. Wrap it in a whole-wheat tortilla that's been smeared with hoisin sauce on which rest a couple of shredded green onions. Or, if I happen to have some cooked noodles in the fridge (and it's not a bad idea to have a bowl of these there, from time to time), I decant the cooked carrots and seaweed into a bowl, scour out the wok with a paper towel, reheat it, add some more oil (sunflower or peanut, for choice), a little salt, and fry the noodles up, adding the carrots and seaweed at the last minute. A noodle stir-fry!

So this is how you make **Carrots and Seaweed**:

◊ Hijiki or arame
◊ Grated carrots
◊ Ginger
◊ Sesame oil
◊ Soy sauce
◊ Salt

Soak as much seaweed, hijiki or arame, as you'd like, according to the package directions, knowing it will double in size. Reserve the soaking water.

Grate as many carrots as you like. I'd say about three or four per person.

Shred or mince a quarter's size of ginger.

Heat a glug of sesame oil in a wok or large skillet.

Add salt.

When the oil sizzles at a drop of water flicked its way, add the ginger.

Stir till fragrant.

Add the grated carrots. Stir till they start to look cooked, even browned.

Add the seaweed. Stir till heated through. If the mixture looks dry, add a bit of the reserved seaweed soaking water.

Turn the heat down to medium. Add soy sauce to taste.

Serve, as above, as you will.

This is what you might call a gateway recipe to a lifetime seaweed habit. And a very good habit it is to have, too. When you consider what it gives in exchange for a little care.

NEVER THE SAME WAY TWICE FETTUCCINE WITH BROCCOLI

So I was having a chat with the head librarian at Cannon Beach Library. The librarians there had very kindly invited me to come talk about food (three of my favorite things, food, libraries, and the Oregon coast, in one), and he said he only had one problem with the way I cook.

"What if you just want something to come out exactly the same way as the way you had it somewhere else?" he asked me.

I turned that one over in my mind. For a bit, in fact. And in that moment, I had a flash of understanding: I am a person who is constitutionally incapable of wanting one moment to turn out exactly like another moment. I like them all to be different.

"Well," I said. "You might as well give up on that one. Because you can't."

"You CAN'T?"

"You can't." I said this flatly and firmly, because you really can't.

"WHY can't you?"

"Because," I said, "you'll never be in the same place, with the same ingredients, with the same equipment, with the same atmosphere, with the same audience, in the same mood, more than just one time."

He laughed.

"I'm serious. You can look at Audrey Hepburn wearing a little black dress in Paris and say, 'I want to look just like that.' But you're not going to."

He laughed again.

Look. Let's not even get into the question of why you would want a recipe to taste exactly the same as the way someone else does it. No, wait a minute. Let's get into that question. Why do you want to? I don't mean you shouldn't want the food that results to give you and the people who eat it as much happiness and satisfaction as the original recipe—that's a given. I mean, why do you want it to taste the same?

I guess what I'm saying is: you have a chance, every time you cook, to figure out who you are and what your world is like. These are the two questions that interest me mainly, and food is just a way of getting more answers for me, not an end in itself. Which is why it is endlessly fascinating. And not just that—endlessly productive. I don't mean endlessly productive of meals (though there certainly is that benefit!), but, rather, endlessly productive of insight. Insight that leads me to a firmer understanding of my likes and dislikes, and, through that, to building my own autonomy. Autonomy, I truly believe, is what each person owes the world—because only an autonomous adult, who knows who she/he is, and knows what her/his duties and rights are, can participate in making our world better for everyone.

And what else am I in it for? I mean, I ask you. Most of all, I ask myself.

So if that's my goal, why on earth would I want to cook something just like Martha Stewart? Although I must say, I'm interested in what the way Martha Stewart cooks says about her.

Here's what I cooked the other night. And I guarantee you won't be able to replicate it in your own home. I guarantee I'll never be able to replicate it in my own home…not again, anyway. Well, just look at the list of ingredients.

Fettuccine with broccoli, shallots, roast tomatoes, blue cheese, and Parmesan (for 2).

◊ ½ package dried fettuccine, which turns out to be lighter weight than it says on the package, so about 7 ounces rather than my usual 8

◊ 1 head of broccoli, peeled, chopped, and steamed

◊ 1 shallot minced and let to sit in a tablespoon of lemon juice to sweeten

◊ 3½ roasted tomatoes, diced

◊ a nubbin of blue cheese, squished between your fingers

◊ a nubbin of Parmesan, grated

◊ a couple of minced garlic cloves

◊ a squish of anchovy paste

◊ the olive oil that was left in the bottle, rounded out by some walnut oil

◊ a dab of butter

Cook the fettuccine. While it's boiling, warm the minced garlic cloves and anchovy paste in the oil. When the pasta is done to your liking, drain it and put it back on the stove in the still-warm pot. Add the hot oil and garlic/anchovy, and the shallot. Toss. Toss with the blue cheese and Parmesan. Taste for salt. Toss with the broccoli and roast tomatoes. Taste again. If you think you need it, add a dab of butter and toss again.

Serve up with a lemon wedge and salad. Or be lazy like I was, and serve by itself with tangerines and dried fruit to follow.

If you like, wear that little black dress you saw on Audrey Hepburn. You won't look like her. But you might look better. You'll look different, anyway, and more like yourself, which sounds to me like more fun in the end.

(WARNING: The above does not apply to baking. That was another question the nice librarian asked me, what am I crap at cooking? The answer will come as no surprise: anything that requires precise measurements. Baking requires precise measurements unless you want to end up with something somewhere between soup and a hockey puck when what you're aiming for is a cake. Baking is a precision activity. Even I highly recommend you try to get the same results time after time with baking.)

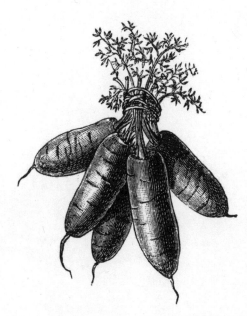

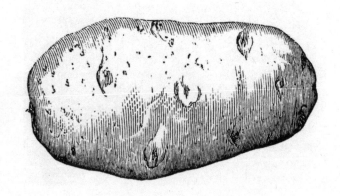

Food for Thought

FEMINISM AND THE BAKED POTATO

So there was a good article by Michael Pollan in the *New York Times* about the rise in fascination with watching others cook (i.e., professional chefs), and the decline in home cooking (also, just as a riveting aside, mentioning research that shows the rise in obesity as linked to the decline of the home meal). And there was tweeting about it—one can almost imagine this as being practically knee-jerk, a no-brainer—about how Michael Pollan wants us women back in the kitchen. Which made me immediately yelp, "You GUYS, you're missing the point!"

Because it's exactly at this point that feminism has gotten into a cul de sac, even a slightly resentful, surly cul de sac. I mean, you can see why the feminism of the late Fifties through the Seventies emphasized that girls aren't allowed to do what boys do. And, I'm afraid to say, you can also see why they were encouraged by the mass media and the corporations to emphasize and campaign about this.

Look. In a patriarchal society, what the boys do automatically becomes more important than what the girls do. This means, for example, that being an investment banker becomes more important than being a nursery school teacher. Okay, we all know that one. We all bemoan that one. But do we look at the roots of it and what it really means? It means, of course, that being someone whose default setting is to beat the hell out of the other guy and be the dominant one gets more prestige and more resources than someone whose default setting is to care for and nurture others.

I daresay just about anyone out there can see where THAT got us.

So feminism, I have to say, has got to go back to work on this one. It can't just be about doing what the boys do. It has to be about upholding the importance of what the girls do. Because it's more important to eat and to feed your loved ones than it is to make money. Well, it is. It IS.

In other words, all you women who were forced to give up cooking for yourself and your family (and all you men, too, as a matter of fact) because you have no time anymore, do not hide out in the faux virtue of thinking that means you've taken a step forward out of the kitchen. Unh-uh. What you've done is walk into a rabbit trap with your eyes wide shut. You've given up something of basic importance to the achievement of your own autonomy for the convenience of a world that regards you as just something to be milked. Work long hours. Spend money from working long hours. Work longer hours to have more money to spend. Get less and less gratification in the process. Get madder and madder, and so get sold more and more crap that promises you a reward for how mad you are.

This is not feminism. This is being conned in a big, big way.

Okay, you really don't like to cook? Don't cook then. It's like sex, though. There are probably some people who authentically don't like sex, but my guess is they're a very small group of people. On the other hand, if you're forced to have sex, you're going to hate it worse than cleaning out the attic on a hot day.

You get my point? There has to be freedom from constraint, there has to be leisure enough to contemplate, there has to be calm before you can know who you are and what you want. And once you do know that, my own feeling is that you're going to love sex, you're going to love nature, and you're going to love FOOD. I mean, if you're a human being. How can you help it? I mean, unless you're so drugged up by pharmaceuticals, recreationals, audiovisuals, and terror that you can't even feel your own self.

If that is true, stop it right now. I'm not kidding. You're not just making your own life worse, but the lives of those around you, and the world, too.

And one way to stop that is to recast Feminism as support for those virtues of nurturing, compassion, partnership, and just all-round pleasure that have always been denigrated in our culture as 'girly stuff.' I personally

220

adore girly stuff. Girly stuff needs to be reclaimed as a ruling power in our culture…before it's too late.

So let's start reclaiming it. Start with something easy. Let's start with a Baked Potato.

For everyone who says cooking at home is too difficult, too time-consuming, a Baked Potato is the ideal riposte. Of course, you do have to have an hour before you eat it. At least before you eat it the first time (you should bake a lot of Baked Potatoes at once, save energy, use the leftovers for all manner of easily thrown-together meals). But with a little planning, this can be managed.

First buy your potato. This should be an organic one, not treated with sprouticide, which is a particularly hard to get rid of pesticide. This should also be one that has a nice dusky, papery skin, no sprouts, no green stuff (that green stuff means incorrect storage, and makes you a little nauseous if you eat it; just cut the green part off…but you want the skin with a baked potato so try to get one absolutely ungreen to start with). Scrub until clinging dirt unclings. Stick a knife into it in a few places so it doesn't explode when you cook it. Put it in the oven (a toaster oven is ideal for this) at 400° for about forty-five minutes to an hour, depending on its size and how done you like it. Squeeze it gently or poke with a fork to test doneness. It won't hurt to leave it in the oven for longer (just makes the skin even crispier), or turn off the oven and leave it warm till you want to eat it. Then EAT IT. Split it in half, mash with a fork, top with topping of your choice: unsalted butter, sour cream, hot sauce, garlic mayonnaise. You make the call.

With a salad and a piece of corn, this makes a pretty darn good meal. It probably cost you twenty cents for the potato. All you had to do was wash it, pierce it, stick it in the oven, and pull it out again. This is probably less trouble than it takes to unwrap a hamburger from Wendy's and then throw the detritus away.

As for those extra baked potatoes you made? Many choices available to you. Dice 'em and fry 'em later with onions for hash browns. Scoop out the pulp and mash it with cheese and butter and milk, bake it later. The skins can be cut with scissors into lengths, basted with butter and hot sauce, and baked till they taste like high-class versions of potato chips.

And so on.

If you do this feeling that you're degraded by being in the kitchen, consider this: who is actually cooking the meals you are actually consuming? Is it right that someone so much lower on the economic food chain, so dissed and overworked, is the person who provides you with something essential to your well-being? Is this the kind of culture we want? Is this the kind of culture Feminism is meant to help deliver?

I think not.

Back to the Baked Potato. We had ours for lunch. And for dinner, they'll be hashed, served with a frittata and a tomato and chive salad.

Now, THAT'S a Feminist meal, for sure.

MEN IN THE KITCHEN

And while we're on the subject of people being enslaved by cultural expectations that benefit someone other than themselves, we need to talk about how men get trapped good and proper by the same. What I'm thinking of specifically is that default setting insidiously underlying so much of our cultural activity that says someone's always got to be on the top and someone's always got to be on the bottom. That says the only way to move our culture forward is through constant competition to see who is going to be on the top, and who is going to be etc.

Take the way a Man in the Kitchen gets portrayed, so frequently, in the mass media. There seem to be only a few kinds held up for our viewing. There's the Complete Culinary Genius, hard drinkin', hard druggin', and a complete asshole to the people who work with…no, excuse me, who work *for* him. And then there's the Complete Culinary Fumbler, who doesn't have a clue how to boil water. In between there's what we might call the Complete

Gourmet Fusspot who has to have a designer kitchen and three kinds of truffle oil before creating his masterworks to loud domestic applause.

All three of these images have one thing in common: they are a portrait of a completely self-centered individualist who thinks only about himself and his goals, and nothing about others and theirs.

This leaves no room for what I think of as your good, normal, healthy, food- and family-loving male, a man who not only thinks about others, but who understands that thinking about them…feeling about them…is what makes his life worthwhile. Who just wants to have a good time with his friends and loved ones and who thinks food is one of the ways to do it. You know. The kind of person I actually like to have as a friend and/or loved one. There are a lot of them around. In fact, I suspect (and I hope, too) that they are the majority out there. We rarely get to hear about them somehow. The guys who think of cooking less as a competitive blood sport, and more as a way of enjoying themselves and helping others around them to enjoy themselves too. Who know cooking is another way of expressing how they feel about themselves and their world, and another way of showing their curiosity about and involvement in that world. Of sharing all of that, too.

The first real boyfriend I ever had was like that. I was just fifteen, and he was just seventeen, and he loved food. He loved cooking and eating and sharing both experiences, and he taught me a lot of what I still know about the pleasures of enjoying the table together. He taught me how to forage for wild mushrooms, and then how to cook them with butter and a touch of garlic. He taught me that chuck blade steak was great served with a little Worcestershire sauce. He taught me that the only way to serve beef liver was seared rare and heaped with plenty of sautéed onions. And he taught me that men love to cook and are as excellent at it and at nurturing others as women are.

I have never forgotten any of those lessons. Even after all these years.

The main objection I have to the culinary clichés about men in the kitchen is that they deny men the right to be as nurturing, as caring, and as loving as women are allowed to be. There are a whole lot of men out there who are claiming that right. And lucky for us, too. Not just lucky for their friends and family (not to mention their co-workers), but for the culture as a whole. Because all anyone has to do is just look around to see that what we need now is not more individualism, not more genius, not more applause-seeking, but a little more nurturing, a little more sharing, and a little more mutual joy.

And speaking of mutual joy. My family of origin experienced it regularly, but never more so than over a billowing golden mass of my father's Yorkshire Pudding, which he cooked with a prime rib roast on the most special of family holidays. I personally have never been able to get my Yorkshire Pudding to billow anywhere near his heights, but my brother Peter seems to have inherited the knack, which his family now reaps the benefits of.

I asked him for his secret, and he sent me this recipe:

Perfect Yorkshire Pudding

◊ 1 cup milk
◊ 1 cup flour
◊ 2 eggs
◊ ½ tsp salt

Beat eggs, milk, salt & flour till smooth.

Melt 2 tbls butter or suet in baking dish.

Bake at 400 deg 35 to 45 min till puff and brown.

Yeah, well okay, but that recipe doesn't explain anything. What about that billowing? So I went back to him, and he added, "The key ingredient I forgot to mention in the recipe is a nice big prime rib toast. Take care not to trim any fat from it before roasting. And I forgot to mention that it's important to cook the Yorkshire in the drip pan used to cook the roast beast."

Something still nagged at me, though. There was still something missing. The secret ingredient. Which was revealed at Christmas, when he called to wish the Beloved Vegetarian Husband and me compliments of the season, and I could hear my family in the background making those contented noises my family does at the end of a feast.

And Peter said, "Oh yeah. I forgot to tell you. About the Yorkshire Pudding. I only just realized I make it different every time. And every time it comes out great. I have no idea why that is. But it does."

I know why. When Peter makes that Yorkshire Pudding it always comes out great because he makes it with love. Which gives me a very warm feeling about the way it's possible to partner with our food and the way we feed our loved ones. Especially when we want our loved ones to feast. Men and women both, we love—or we should—to watch our loved ones feast.

MY CALMING AND SOOTHING PASTA SALAD

There are those hot summer days when it tries the calmest, most patient, most down-to-earth soul to keep her temper as she reads the news—especially if she doesn't particularly do well in weather that reaches the triple digits. So you can imagine what those days do to someone like me, who is not the calmest, most patient, most down-to-earth soul, and who definitely doesn't do well in weather etc. In theory, and on cooler afternoons, I feel it is good to be tolerant of people who hold what seem to me to be demented, even injurious opinions, but in practice, especially when there is no air-conditioning and somehow the one fan in the attic has mysteriously disappeared...well. As I said, I'm not the calmest, most patient, etc.

So what do I do?

Here is my most recent solution, not the end of all solutions, but the one I find works for me, at least until I find a better one. I grit my teeth. I concentrate on being courteous to those around me. And I get on with it.

In other words, I concentrate on my work here and now, do the best I can, and keep going.

And in aid of that goal (especially in hot weather), I find cooking to be just about the perfect kind of meditation. I think about what I want to eat. I think about what I have. I think about what my Beloved Vegetarian Husband would like to eat. And, in hot weather, I think about how hot it is. Then I start meditatively chopping and slicing and dicing, and if, in my fantasies, this chopping and slicing and dicing is helpful to my mood, well, that's my right to be amused as I get on with it, don't you think?

Here is an idea for a chopping, slicing and dicing meal:

A Calming and Nourishing Pasta Salad

First off, what do I have in my larder? This is what I should have:

◊ Some kind of onion (scallion, shallot, yellow, red, or white).
◊ Some kind of green fresh herb (parsley or basil or even cilantro).
◊ At least two kinds of vegetables (celery, tomatoes, carrots, mushrooms, even frozen peas work well here).
◊ Fixings for any favorite salad dressing. (In my case, generally a garlicky vinaigrette.)
◊ Some dried pasta, any shape, in the amount of my choice. Half a pound for two main dishes or four side dishes is what I usually reckon. Unless I have lots of veggies, in which case just a handful of the stuff will suffice.

I cook the veggies that need it. Cool.

I make a salad dressing. As I said, for myself, it's usually a good strong vinaigrette. For half a pound of pasta and a load of veggies, 1½ tablespoons of a good wine vinegar, or 1 tablespoon sherry vinegar, followed by 3 tablespoons of olive oil (with the wine vinegar) or walnut oil (good with the sherry vinegar). I mash a garlic clove into it. Salt and pepper.

I marinate the chopped, diced, or sliced onion in the dressing while I make the rest of it.

I cook the pasta (anywhere from a handful, as I said, if I have lots and lots of veggies, to half a pound if I don't).

I chop the raw veggies. Or, in the case of the carrot, grate it. I mix all the raw veggies with the salad dressing, with the exception of the diced tomato (I hold that back for a bit). Leave them to marinate while the rest of the dish happens.

I let the pasta cool off. I just dump it in a colander, run some cold water on it, tossing it about with my fingers, and then leaving it to drain. As it cools, so, mysteriously, do I…

When drained and cool (both me and the noodles), I toss the pasta with the marinated veggies and the dressing. Now I add the diced tomatoes. Then I chop up as much fresh green herb as I like, and add it and toss again. I taste. Need more oil? More vinegar? More salt or pepper? I add judiciously at will.

Then I check my teeth. Ungritted? Yes, thankfully. So I have a glass of wine. Contemplate the possibilities of a different world. And the pleasures of this one.

Then I have a good evening. Turn off the news. Sit with my loved ones. And I'm happy. Because Living Well is not only the Best Revenge, it's the Best Example, too.

NO TIME TO COOK

There are those times where you just have to make decisions about what you've got time for. And I really hate giving up making meals for myself and the Beloved Vegetarian Husband just because I've got a work binge on. It's making those meals that's a lot of my entertainment in life (at least, as long as I'm not making them in an RV, see above). I love thinking about them and making them almost as much as I love eating them. Usually.

So there I was, with only a week between trips out, and with a huge amount of work to get through, too. Well, the obvious answer is to order in fast food, or eat out, or just starve, I guess, and since none of those options is an appealing one, I just had to think of some way round. Really, the only way round is to just get as efficient and creative as you can, and cut yourself some slack when you hit your own personal efficiency and creativity ceiling.

This was the attitude I took.

I hit my own ceiling when it came to shopping. My brain was just too full of other stuff to really focus on what I might need for a series of a) varied meals and b) meals that would create leftovers that I could leave for the Husband when I was away on the next trip. Now, I know a lot of you women out there are saying, "let the guy get his own meals, for God's sake!" and I agree, I totally agree, in fact, HE totally agrees, bless him. But the thing is, I LIKE leaving meals for him, just like (I assume) he likes getting in the wood for me every winter. I LIKE it. I could give it up, but I don't really want to if I don't have to. It adds something to my life.

Not to mention the fact that if I don't do this, he reverts to cheese and salsa sandwiches. Which I do not feel is a good nutritional foundation for the long run.

Well, so here were my parameters: Not much time. Just what I had in the cupboard and fridge already. An attenuated attention span.

(It helps when you're playing this kind of culinary game that you have loved ones who appreciate what you do, and are not given to finding little picky things to complain about to bring you down when you can't do as much as you usually do. Although, if you have the latter, I suggest seriously thinking about either retraining them, or keeping them well away when you have key work to do of your own.)

I was so involved in my own work that I didn't even notice what I cooked the night before. I mean, I could barely remember eating it. But I think it was good—and I know it provided some leftovers for the Husband to reheat (mashed potatoes with pesto spread in a baking dish, covered with grated Swiss cheese and baked till bubbly; carrots and parsley; salad with avocado and blue cheese).

The next day I had to finish a proofing job. Well, I am not crazy about proofing, so I take it one chapter at a time. One or two. Or three. I did this at the kitchen counter. And in between, I wandered over to the stove and the sink and made:

Vegetable soup for lunch. Chopped a couple of onions (I knew I was going to make a couple of other things, too, from those onions, so get it done all at once), put a bit of chopped onion in a pan with some melted butter and curry powder. Peeled and diced the lone potato left from last night's potato fest, added that to the pot. A little thyme. Covered with a couple of cups of water and brought to a simmer. When the veggies were tender, I added the leftover carrots from the night before and cooked to blend flavors. There was so much of it—flavor, I mean—that I added a little more water, with the idea of leaving one extra serving for Alex for a lunch when I was away. When that was done, shoved it to the back of the stove to wait for a final enrichment with a little butter, a sprinkling of parsley and toast for lunch.

Back to the proofing. Two more chapters. Even three.

Then back to the stove. Heated two separate skillets. In one, a dollop of sunflower oil as the base for enchilada sauce. In the other, olive oil as the base for a sauce for polenta and mushrooms. Split what was left of the chopped onion between the two and sautéed them till they were golden. Then opened a can of crushed tomatoes and puree and put half in one skillet, half in the other. Chopped garlic and added to each skillet (of course—who did you think you were dealing with, anyway?). Added three minced chipotle chilies and some of their sauce to the enchilada sauce. Added a sprig of rosemary to the polenta sauce. Salt to both. Then I needed to thin them. Leftover beer to thin the enchilada sauce. White wine to thin the polenta sauce.

Put them both onto simmer and went back to proofing. Three more chapters.

Back to the stove, gave them both a stir, turned off the heat and covered them.

That night, I dipped some corn tortillas in the enchilada sauce, rolled each one up around a little grated cheese and minced green onion, lined them all up in a baking dish, and covered them with more sauce, cheese, and onion. Baked till done, and the leftovers to be reheated at will by the Beloved Husband. We ate refried beans with this (I already had them in the fridge from another day), the beans spooned on top of lettuce, and an avocado and cilantro salad on the side.

Lunch the following day was reheated beans on top of grated carrot on a whole-wheat tortilla, the whole thing topped with more cilantro and avocado and grated cheese.

Then dinner was the polenta stuffed with sautéed mushrooms (just happened to have some lurking in the fridge), and topped with tomato/rosemary sauce and grated Parmesan. Plenty of leftovers, terrific reheated. We had it the first time with what was left of the lettuce in the fridge, mixed with grated carrot, as a salad.

I finished the proofing job right on time. Then on to packing for the next trip. But in the meantime, I thought, we've got to eat, and, as you know, my motto is: Anything you've got to do, you might as well have a good time doing.

And I'm serious about that, too.

230

PERSONAL AUTONOMY AND POTATOES ANNA

As always (and it really doesn't matter what I'm doing, this is what I'm constantly meditating on), I was thinking about how increasing one's personal autonomy is the only possible response to a world out of whack; if we don't know who we are, how can we know how to work with our world? And there I was getting ready to cook Christmas dinner, which was to be (if you're as interested as I am in what other people eat) green salad with celery and aioli/lemon dressing, roast duck, scalloped oysters, Potatoes Anna, and See's chocolates.

I scoured my cookbooks for a scalloped oyster recipe I remembered as being heavenly: all bread crumbs (no crackers), minced green onions, garlic, parsley, with cream on top. But I couldn't find it. Not in Julia Child. Not in James Beard. Not in James Vilas. Not anywhere. There were recipes with just breadcrumbs. There were recipes that used green onions. But none fit the bill precisely, and I knew for sure somewhere in that bookcase was a recipe that fit the bill precisely.

You probably know the end of that story. Yep. Finally I thought to look in my own cookbook, in *Jam Today*, and there it was, the best scalloped oyster recipe ever.

That made me laugh.

This also set me off on another train of thought, while I was throwing together my own version of Potatoes Anna. I thought about why I'd written *Jam Today* in the first place—not to write a cookbook, but to join together sides of life that get artificially separated: as if what you eat every day doesn't have to do with who you are and where you fit in your world. I really wrote it to support the idea that everyone should be looking at what they're doing (not at what everyone else is doing), and use that as a tool to understand more fully who they are and who they want to be. Because I really think that's the only way the individual can be effective in the world, in helping move the world out of its present dead end. It's the only way I can be effective. So that's what I want. And that's true of what I want from *Jam Today Too* as well.

So I know you're saying, what the hell does this have to do with Potatoes Anna? And of course you have a point. So I'll try get to that, I swear.

The way I made those oysters tells me a lot about myself. It tells me I don't particularly like to fuss, but I like to eat. It tells me I don't have crackers in the house, normally, and I don't like to buy ingredients just for one special dish. It tells me...oh, it tells me more stuff than that.

And my Potatoes Anna recipe, at least the one I slapped together for Christmas dinner, tells me pretty much the same thing.

Potatoes Anna, in case you missed hearing about her before, is this wonderful kind of potato cake, crusty on the outside, melting on the inside, cooked in the oven with so much butter you could have cardiac arrest just preparing it (although you pour most of the butter off later and use it again, which is the kind of thing I'm always attracted to).

Now, if you want the most perfect potato dish ever, I recommend you follow Julia Child's recipe in *Mastering the Art of French Cooking*. Like every one of her recipes I've tried, if you follow every step precisely, you'll have a most wonderful-tasting dish.

But me, I can usually only do that following-the-fiddly-recipe-precisely thing once. After that, it's a free-for-all. And my basic plan is: make something that fits with the rest of my life (not yanking it in another direction through its complexity), and that is going to taste really good. It doesn't have to taste haute. It just has to taste good. And like it was made with love.

So here is my Potatoes Anna recipe for two, which really did fit that bill.

◊ Two russet potatoes
◊ Clarified butter
◊ Salt and pepper

Take two russet potatoes (which is the kind of potato I usually already have in the house). Clarify a stick of butter (which means heat at low heat, skim off the solids on top, pour the clear butter away from the curds left at the bottom…voila!)—although you can skip this step and just use a melted stick of butter if you want; the result won't be as perfect, but so what?

Take a small cast-iron pan (mine is about six inches across and just the right size for a two-potato Potatoes Anna)…or a small heavy ovenproof/stovetop-proof skillet or dish…

Peel the first potato. Slice it thinly (I just sliced these on the side of a box grater). Heat a little clarified butter, in low heat, in the pan on top of the stove. Arrange the slices in a layer on the butter. (You're going to turn the cake over when it's done, so this is what will show.) Sprinkle more butter, salt and pepper, arrange another layer. Repeat until the potato is used up. Then peel the other potato and slice, and add to the skillet in the same way. Finish by pouring what's left of the butter on top, and press the whole thing down with a spatula to get it level. Shake the pan and run the spatula underneath to unstick any sticking taters. (It doesn't matter if it does stick, it'll still taste good. I don't fuss too much over how things look, as long as they work. I mean, you should see my car.)

Stick the pan in a 400° oven and bake for 30 to 45 minutes, till the bottom is all crusty and brown, and the interior potatoes all tender.

Take out of the oven. Pour the excess butter into another dish to use for something else (maybe another round of Potatoes Anna). Unmold the cake on a plate. Cut into wedges, or halves, and serve.

Aahh.

For more people, just use twice the amount of potatoes and butter, and use an 8-inch cast-iron pan.

This combines two qualities I find I admire when they're in close conjunction, in no matter what the arena: practicality and festivity. And if you can manage to be both practical and festive in your own arena, I'd have to say you're doing about the best of anyone around.

But what about dessert? Shouldn't we finish with dessert?

BAKED PEARS IN AUTUMN

By now, you've probably got the idea that I'm not big on sweets. It's true. I really don't think about them much—except, of course, to long for See's candy around the holidays (especially the dark chocolate-covered marzipan). I don't dream about cakes, or yearn to spend a Sunday baking cookies, and my mind's palate does not waste its time tasting phantom pies. Nope. Definitely not a dessert person. Oh sure, I'll have some ice cream now and then, and when there's company, I'll serve out a dish of it with a little capful of Grand Marnier spilled on top, just to dress it up a little, at not much extra hassle to the cook. And sometimes when I'm alone, what I really want after my meal is a big piece of toasted New Sammy's sourdough bread, slathered with butter and either honey or raspberry jam—although that probably hardly counts as a sweet to a true dessert person.

On the other contradictory hand, I have always been annoyed by recipes that say things like: "Of course, this dish is so rich, that you should serve nothing but fresh fruit to follow." Oh yeah, sure, I think to myself when I read that. Fresh fruit. Like they're serving that themselves.

But the truth is, I do like a little fresh fruit after a meal. In fact, a lot of lunches get finished off with an apple or a pear sliced up and put on the table between me and the Beloved Vegetarian Husband while we read our respective luncheon reading material. Or a handful of cherries. Or a bowl of just-washed grapes. Or (best) a few fresh ripe figs. I mean, if I look at it objectively, I really shouldn't get so annoyed when I read that recommendation about fresh fruit. I really shouldn't think of it as just Nazi calorie-policing.

I eat a lot of fruit, a lot of different ways. Although not for the health bit. It turns out I just like it that way.

It's true that unadorned fresh fruit is not my idea of an after-dinner treat. But, again when I think about it, almost all my favorite home desserts are adorned fruit—one way or another. It's decked-out fruit of one kind or another that gets passed around if I'm dining, as I often am, with loved ones and friends. Fruit that's been just a little bit fussed with, its tie straightened and its hair brushed for company. No matter what I think I like to eat, what I do proves that, in the end, what I like to eat is fruit.

Like so: Pieces of dried fruit (mango, papaya, fig, apricot, persimmon) scattered on a plate with a few chocolate chips or jagged pieces of broken-up dark chocolate. Slices of quince paste alternating with slices of full-fat Monterey Jack cheese, to be eaten together in one luscious, squishy bite. Fresh raspberries nestled in cream, crystal brown sugar scattered on top. Strawberries dipped in sour cream and the same brown sugar. Baked apples.

My favorite, though, is baked pears. The way Martha Rose Shulman taught me how to make them, in her divine book *Provençal Light*, which is an example of a cookbook meant to help you eat less fat (usually my most hated form of cookbook) that turns out to help you cook simply and deliciously no matter how many calories you think you should consume. She says she learned this method from Christine Picasso. Another bit of art we have to thank a Picasso for, in my opinion, and, much as I admire Cubism in theory, I have to say that in the end this recipe has done more to improve my quality of life.

Of course, I've fiddled with it, and tamed it to where I don't have to pay as much attention to it as perhaps Ms. Shulman or Ms. Picasso would like.

But it's to their credit entirely that no matter how lazy I get with it, it still always comes out right. And of course, it's the ideal dessert for one of my favorite cooking methods: pile everything in one oven, in different dishes at different times, and have them all come out at the same time.

The other night, once I'd got the hang of it with that dinosaur oxtail of Cindy's, I was braising an oxtail just for myself alone, in a basin of red wine and herbs, and of course we all know now how long an oxtail takes to submit to your will—i.e., a really long time. I couldn't bear to turn on the oven just for it alone; what a waste. So I grated some carrots, put them in some cream, and shoved them in after. Then a few potatoes to bake, on the theory that I could use them later for soup or whatever (I did, too, and the whatever was delicious).

I halved a couple of tomatoes, too, scattered some rosemary on them, and put them on the lowest shelf underneath everything else.

But there was still a little room in the oven.

Looking around the kitchen speculatively, my eye landed on my overflowing fruit bowl. It was autumn, and autumn means Indigo Ray is desperately trying to find a home for all of her apples and all of her pears, all of which seem to ripen at approximately the same time. So I had a big haul, just sitting there, piled. The pears were almost ripe but not quite. And that, as a matter of fact, is the best kind of pear to use for Baked Pears.

Like so:

◊ Pears, not too ripe
◊ Honey
◊ Cloves

Take as many pears as you like and will fit into whatever baking dish you choose. Wash them, and cut a little circle out of each one's bottom with a paring knife. As you do, fill the hole with a spoonful of honey, then quickly set the pear right side up in the baking dish. When they're all nestled neatly, each one next to its neighbor, comfortable but not spread out, pour about an inch of water into the bottom of the dish. Scatter a few whole cloves about. You can sprinkle a bit of sugar on top, but I never bother. Put into an oven at whatever temperature you've got everything else going at, and bake for a really long time until the pears are wizened and crackly-looking, and the water/honey mixture has thickened. This takes about 2 hours at 350°, or about an hour and a half at 400°. Or more or less, you know, as usual. Cook 'em till they look and smell done to you.

They're great hot on their own or with a little cream poured over, or next to a scoop of ice cream. They're great the next day for breakfast with some of the syrup spooned over them, and a little full-fat yoghurt on the side. They're a wonderful afterthought to the next night's dinner. And you can just keep them in their baking dish, covered, in the fridge, all week, and spoon them out, one by one, at will.

Well, if it's THAT kind of fruit. Well then. I definitely eat that kind of fruit for dessert, and when I do, I know I'm home.

Epilogue:
My Dear Paella Recipe

Everyone should have a recipe tucked away somewhere that means festivity, one that provides an atmosphere of feasting and plenty without the horrible anxiety that too often accompanies holidays. This means a recipe that is fairly easy in its parts (so that the cook, at the finish, is not a nervous wreck), interchangeable in its ingredients (so that the shopping for the dish does not become a Trail of Tears), requires very little last-minute fuss (so that the entire festivity can be enjoyed with the least amount of sturm und drang), and is extra specially delicious (reason obvious without further comment).

Such a recipe is my Dear Paella Recipe. Why do I refer to it as if it is an old friend? Well, because it is an old friend. I've been working on it for years, to get it streamlined to fulfill all of the above conditions, and at this point, I can make it in my sleep, or after a half bottle of champagne—the latter the more likely condition on a holiday. And it never fails to elicit the sighs of happy diners as everyone tucks in at table. It is the single most requested dish I make, and it has forgiven me many mistakes, always allowing me to somehow catch the disaster just as it's about to occur and turn it into another happy meal. In other words, it's nonjudgmental, supportive, fascinating, and special—all the things you expect from an old friend.

It's pretty easy if you break it down into its component parts. Which are: a sofrito (this is a mince of various vegetables sautéed as long as possible to deepen their flavor, with tomatoes and paprika added at the end); the rice (I use Lundberg's organic short-grain brown rice with spectacular results— white rice lovers, I urge you to try this JUST ONCE, okay?); the liquid (a mix of any kind of broth, water, and wine…I've even used spicy tomato juice); the trimmings (which can be vegetarian, fishetarian, carnivorous, or

239

a combination of two or all), something green and bright added at the end for color (frozen peas, for example…or chopped parsley, or even chopped cilantro).

The only immutable, absolutely without question unchangeable ingredients are salt…and SAFFRON. And then Paella (at least mine) can be full of anything you find appealing as long as it includes tomatoes, onion, garlic, rice, and saffron.

Now saffron is expensive, true. It comes in these little packets that cost a lot more than your average herb or spice, but there's a reason for this. It is the distilled stamens of about a thousand saffron flowers, and this is not an easy thing to obtain. But this is a feast dish, yes? I think we need one or two special ingredients for a feast dish. 'Special' is practically the synonym of feast. There's a reason we don't use feast ingredients every day. Think of the boredom of it. For a truly engaging life, we have to set out our own limitations and make a kind of poem of them. This is a struggle if you are very rich: you have no force pushing you to sculpt those lovely limitations into your own life. You have to work a little harder. Of course, being poor is much worse: you have those limitations forced on you, like a bad limerick, and little choice in the matter. On the other hand, there are those exquisite poets who do a wonderful job (perhaps more wonderful) with even those scanty ingredients. I bless and admire the hell out of them.

But if you are in the middle, and you have the same worries and joys as most of the rest of us, I think you can be happy that you must pick and choose what is special in your life and keep it for sharing on special days. Because there is something more than a little lovely in that. Something more than a little creative. We all need that. And the culture could use a lot more people being in a position to practice creativity, on feast days and every day.

So. We should all do everyone a favor, and make something delicious, be creative in that as in the rest of our lives, taking things lightheartedly when they go wrong, as surely they must—how can they not, if we're going to have any real life at all? You can, if you like, use my recipe here as a jumping-off place (and remember, this recipe is built out of much disaster, considered and then compensated for). Don't be intimidated by how long it is; it's an easy recipe once you get in the swing of it. Fiddle with it, play with it, make it your delicious own. Make yourself and your loved ones happy with it. Make it your friend. Make it with love. Because what demands more creativity from us than love?

Here's what I do:

(For four people with other dishes; for three hungry people with only a salad; for two people who also want enough for lunch, cold, the next day)

For the sofrito:

- ◊ Olive oil, or duck fat, or bacon fat, or a mixture of olive oil and duck or bacon fat
- ◊ Slices of sausage (Andouille, Polish sausage, or chorizo work well here)
- ◊ Squid or octopus cut into manageable pieces (optional)
- ◊ Chopped or minced onion
- ◊ Maybe a jalapeno or serrano chile, minced (with seeds if very spicy is wanted; without for a milder kick)
- ◊ As much chopped/minced garlic as you like
- ◊ Some chopped tomato pulp (roasted is good, canned is fine)
- ◊ 2 teaspoons smoked paprika aka Pimenton de la Vera (or regular paprika, but I highly recommend the smoked)
- ◊ Salt

So. Take a large pan that has a lid. Don't fuss too much about this. A big, wide, shallow paella pan is great (I have one that was a gift from a friend which works quite well), but a Dutch oven is just fine (I used a Le Creuset one for this for years, which led the nice friend to gift me with a proper pan…but both turn out delicious paellas).

Atop the stove, heat up some olive oil in the pan, or mix it with a little duck, goose, or bacon fat, if you like. If you're using sausages, slice them and brown the slices in the oil, removing and reserving when browned. Then sauté the optional squid/octopus in the oil, with a little garlic. Set aside. In the same oil (you may have to add a little more at this point), add the chopped onions, the optional chile pepper, and the garlic (you can also add a bit of chopped cilantro or parsley if you like the flavor). Cook on low heat for as long as you can get away with it—ten minutes is good, twenty is even better if you can caramelize everything without letting it get close to burning. I have even added finely chopped octopus or squid to the sofrito at this point, to deepen the flavor, and found that works very well (this is one of those recipes where mixing meat and seafood flavors only seems to up the delicious quotient…but a vegetarian version with neither is very satisfying too). When everything is soft and smells delicious, add two teaspoons of the paprika of your choice (once again, I urge the smoky Spanish paprika…it makes a real difference here). Give it a turn or two, watching closely so the paprika just toasts without burning, then add the tomato. This can be one tomato, chopped, if that's all you have. Two roasted tomatoes are even better. A few chopped canned tomatoes are fine. Or, if you and your family really like that tomatoey taste, go for as many as you like.

Sauté a little longer—ten or fifteen minutes—until the whole is a wonderful-smelling, gilded mass of sauce. Salt. You can keep this overnight if you like…it's just a highfalutin' version of tomato sauce. Refrigerate it, and the sautéed sausage and seafood, of course.

Now for the rice:

◊ 1½ cups of short-grain brown rice (you can use white rice here, preferably risotto or Spanish short-grain, only be aware the cooking time will be about half, and you won't need as much liquid)

◊ Enough liquid, a mix of any combination of veggie stock/meat stock/ fish stock/water/red or white wine…for the brown rice, 4 cups. One trick I like to use here is to save shrimp shells in the freezer from other shrimp dinners, and then simmer them in whatever liquid I'm planning on using for the paella. Strain and use at will.

◊ One or two pinches of saffron that has soaked for at least ten minutes in a little red or white wine

When you're ready to cook the rice (it will take about fifty-five minutes… after which, you need ten or fifteen minutes to cook the last-minute embellishments…and then allow ten or fifteen minutes to let it all settle—I use that time to serve a salad, usually), heat the sofrito gently to a sizzle and add the rice grains. Fry in the sauce until toasty. Add the stock/water/wine combination and bring to a boil. Turn down to a simmer, and add the saffron. Taste the broth, add a tiny bit of salt if it needs it.

Now here's where you make a decision about what's the easiest way to proceed. You can cook this on a burner atop the stove, or you can cook it in the oven for the same amount of time at 375°. Either way is fine. I usually cook the rice on top of the stove, on a very low burner, and then, when the seafood is arranged on top, finish in the oven. But you'll have your own way of doing it.

Whatever method you choose, the pan/pot should stay at a simmer for about 55 minutes. I just leave it on a burner, on low, and check it from time to time. You want the rice to cook without burning, of course, but you don't want to end up with soupy rice. This is easily dealt with. If the rice is done (a little bite in the middle, but not chalky or raw-tasting), but still too much liquid surrounds it, just turn up the heat and stir till the liquid gets soaked into the rice. Brown rice is comfortingly indestructible that way.

While the rice is cooking, prepare the items of your choice that will go in at the last minute.

The paella embellishments (use as many or as few as you have or desire):

◊ Shrimp, in the shell or unshelled, as you prefer, marinated in a little olive oil and minced garlic
◊ Scallops marinated in a little olive oil and minced garlic
◊ Clams in the shell, rinsed
◊ Mussels in the shell, debearded at the last minute and rinsed
◊ As many frozen peas as you like
◊ Minced parsley or cilantro if you like it (but not both, please)
◊ The reserved sausage and squid/octopus that you've already cooked

If you've cooked the rice atop the stove, but want to finish in the oven, now preheat the oven to 375°. You're going to have to be a little canny here, and pay attention to how your own stove behaves, since every one of them, in my experience, has its little quirks. When the rice is done but not overdone, add the embellishments: stir in the sausage, and squid or octopus, and the peas and herbs. Arrange the shrimp/scallops on top of the rice, and stick whatever clams and mussels you're using in the rice, hinge side down. You can, of course, continue cooking atop the stove, but I find that if I'm using shellfish, it's useful to give the whole thing a few moments at the end under the broiler to open up the stubborn, still-closed-at-the-last-minute clams or mussels.

Now cook for another ten to fifteen minutes till the shrimp glow pink and gold, and the scallops glow white and opaque, and all the shellfish open welcomingly.

Take off the heat, or out of the oven, and let the whole thing sit for ten minutes while you serve an hors d'oeuvre, or a salad, or another glass of wine. Then serve on plates with a generous wedge of lemon on each for personal squeezing. I like a bowl of aioli on the side, sometimes, just for extra unction and garlic punch. Sometimes I mix a little chopped cabbage with aioli and serve it on the side of the paella. Sometimes I... but you get the idea, yes? And I wonder what you would do with this very same recipe.

I always wonder about that. And I did serve this, one Easter dinner, to my dear friend Lanny. She's a vegetarian who eats fish, but both she and the Beloved Vegetarian Husband agreed that just that once, I could cook sausage with the sofrito, as long as they didn't have to eat any actual sausage slices with their paella. I believe I served it with a red wine, a salad to start, and baked pears for after. There was a long, satisfied, satiated sit over chamomile tea in front of the late spring fire, and then Lanny asked me for the recipe, of which I gave her a general description.

A few weeks later, she invited me over for dinner, and asked me again over the phone for another description of what I had cooked. She claimed she was going to make the same dish. But when I got there, and sat down to table, what was in front of me was a magnificent expression of something else altogether. I had three helpings, as I recall. And I asked her for the recipe. "But it's the same as yours!" she said. Of course it wasn't: it was hers. So I asked her to write it down for me, and this is what she said:

245

Tod,

I am so glad you asked me for my interpretation of your paella recipe as I love your approach to cooking—use what you can, buy some special items if and when you feel like it, etc. I am not good at specific amounts but think the ingredients and sequence are recorded correctly.

As I recall, you had impressed me with the absolute importance of saffron. Luckily I had bought some in Turkey a year and a half earlier and had kept it in its sealed pack. I wanted to add shrimp. So I bought enough for everyone to have 3 or 4, as they were rather big.

I put a pot to boil that was 2 to 2½ cups of water to one cup of risotto rice. I think I had about 2 cups of rice. I did not have any stock, but that wasn't a problem as I always keep a can or two of garbanzo beans for emergency vegetarian stock-use.

I threw the juice from the beans into the pot and while I normally then put the actual beans in a jar with olive oil, balsamic vinegar and garlic to add to salad later, in this instance the beans were put aside and added to the rice later.

In a liberal amount of olive oil (maybe 2 or more tablespoons), I sautéed some onions and lots of garlic. I certainly added a tomato, as sautéed and even slightly scorched tomatoes, along with chick peas, are a staple for vegetarian cooks—even ones who eat fish.

When everything was all soft and brown, it was added to the stock.

I then added the shrimp to the stock until just pink and curled, at which point they were immediately removed and thrown into a strainer in the sink filled with some ice to cool them down.

Then slowly, bit by bit, and stirring pretty much constantly, I added the stock to the rice. Taking a series of quick, intermittent breaks I managed to finely (very finely) chop a handful or a bit more of kale, then back to stirring and pouring.

Towards the end, when the rice bits began to get soft but still had a small crunch in their centers, I added:

—A pinch of Hungarian red pepper (chipotle pepper will also work, as it is the smoky taste I was after; simply use a lot less of the chipotle).

—A pinch of nutmeg, but no salt—yet.

—A liberal amount of any white wine available, about a cup or more for this recipe. It adds a nice sour taste and the paella should be tasted to make certain everything from texture to taste is going as planned.

—The handful of kale (could also be parsley, or any nice, somewhat bitter green, but not mustard greens which are also nice but not right for this).

Then when the stove was turned off, the shrimp was added; the paella was salted to taste and served with the option of Parmesan, if desired.

xoL

Well, there was one ingredient that was the same in her recipe as in mine. It was made (definitely) with love.

Happy cooking. Happy eating. And most of all, happy living.

Jam today!

On My Bookshelf

Cookbooks that I often dip into, mentioned in *Jam Today Too*:

Allen, Darina. *Simply Delicious Suppers*. Macmillan, 2001.

Beard, James. *American Cookery*. Little, Brown and Company, 1972.

——. *James Beard's Theory and Practice of Good Cooking*. Alfred A. Knopf, 1977.

Child, Julia, Louisette Bertholle and Simone Beck. *Mastering the Art of French Cooking. Volume One*. Alfred A. Knopf, 1961.

Child, Julia and Simone Beck. *Mastering the Art of French Cooking. Volume Two*. Alfred A. Knopf, 1970.

Cunningham, Marion. *The Fanny Farmer Baking Book*. Alfred A. Knopf, 1984.

David, Elizabeth. *French Provincial Cookery*. Penguin Classics, 1999.

Fisher, M.F.K. *With Bold Knife and Fork*. Putnam, 1969.

Gandia de Fernández, C. and Angeles de la Rosa. *Flavors of Mexico*. 101 Productions, 1979.

Henderson, Fergus. *The Whole Beast: Nose to Tail Eating*. Ecco, 2004.

Jaffrey, Madhur. *A Taste of the Far East*. Random House, 1997.

Madison, Deborah. *Vegetarian Cooking for Everyone*. Ten Speed Press, 2007.

Roberts, Michael. *Parisian Home Cooking*. William Morrow, 1999.

Rombauer, Irma S. *Joy of Cooking*. Bobbs-Merrill, 1975.

Shulman, Martha Rose. *Provençal Light*. Bantam, 1994.

Slater, Nigel. *Appetite*. Clarkson Potter, 2000.

Sunset Magazine. *Sunset Seafood Cookbook*. Lane Publishing Co.,1984.

Wolfert, Paula. *Mediterranean Grains and Greens*. HarperCollins, 1998.

Cookbook/memoirs that I love. Every one of them takes an individual and creative approach to food:

Beard, James. *Delights and Prejudices*. Running Press Book Publishers, 1992. *The Grand Poobah of American cooking on his life and food loves. And it all starts with an eccentric childhood in Oregon.*

Chamberlain, Samuel. *Clementine in the Kitchen*. David R. Godine, 1988. *The utterly charming classic of an American family discovering the pleasures of the table in pre–World War II France.*

Fisher, M.F.K. *The Art of Eating*. Macmillan, 1990. *A must-have for any serious reader/eater, by one of our best American authors, let alone one of our best food writers. "The Gastronomical Me" is more than the tale of an education through food, it's one of the most poignant love stories ever written.*

Gray, Patience. *Honey from a Weed*. Harper & Row, 1986. *An artist cooks and meditates on food and meaning. The subtitle says it all: "Fasting and Feasting in Tuscany, Catalonia, the Cyclades and Apulia."*

Lebo, Kate. *A Commonplace Book of Pie*. Chin Music Press, 2013. *A practical poet rhapsodizes about pie. She loves it, and she makes you love it, too.*

Lewis, Edna. *The Taste of Country Cooking*. Alfred A. Knopf, 1976. *The classic memoir of American country cooking. What could be more American than the cooking of a Virginia farming community settled by freed slaves?*

Lobrano, Alexander. *Hungry for Paris*. Random House, 2008. *More than just a guide to Paris restaurants, this is a love letter to the special places that have given pleasure to the author…and through him, to us, too. I can imagine rereading this long after the restaurants he describes have disappeared.*

Olney, Richard. *Lulu's Provençal Table*. Ten Speed Press, 2002.
Olney follows the legendary Lulu around her kitchen as she dips and dances and creates, by magic, ineradicable happiness with food.

Olney, Richard. *Ten Vineyard Lunches*. Interlink Books, 1988.
Such a pleasure to read menus and their recipes composed by a real artist.

Short, Kayann. *A Bushel's Worth: An Eco-Biography*. Torrey House Press, 2013.
This memoir of life on a postmodern farm brought tears to my eyes. Hope-filled and moving.

Strope, Nancy. *Cattle Country Cookbook*. Binfords & Mort, 1971.
An Eastern Oregon ranch wife writes with beautiful plainness about real ranch food. Not just a wonderful snapshot of a place and time, but absolutely chock full of practical recipes.

Toklas, Alice B. *The Alice B. Toklas Cookbook*. Doubleday, 1960.
Impossible to get more individual than this. I personally think Ms. Toklas was a greater artist than her partner—though a little quieter about it.

Villas, James. *Between Bites: Memoirs of a Hungry Hedonist*. John Wiley & Sons, 2002.
Hilariously truthful. If you've enjoyed his other writings as much as I have, you'll love finding out what REALLY happened during those fabulous meals—particularly his date with M.F.K. Fisher, where due to a bad case of food poisoning he couldn't swallow anything except a bit of milk toast. Recipe included.

Wechsberg, Joseph. *Blue Trout and Black Truffles*. Alfred A. Knopf, 1954.
Another must-have for the shelf of any serious food lover. Evocative and individual. Don't miss "The Sausage Millennium."

Also highly recommended is the TIME-LIFE "Foods of the World" series of books. Published in the late 1960s, these are not just physically beautiful in their design and photography, but endlessly fascinating in their descriptions of both the foods of the world and of post-war Western attitudes toward that world. Many of the greatest of the food writers of the time were enlisted in this series: M.F.K. Fisher to write the volume on provincial French cooking, Craig Claiborne on the Grand Cuisine of France, Waverly Root on Italian cooking, Joseph Wechsberg on the Austrian Empire of his youth…and great writers who loved food were also involved, most notably Laurens van der Post, who wrote, in his seventies, the volume *African Cooking*, in which he memorably says:

"Then I wondered, often in desperation, what in the world all the warring systems, countries, tribes and races still had indisputably in common. Oversimple and childlike as it may seem, one answer that popped up unbidden from my imagination was food. If I did what has never been done before—if I wrote about the food of Africa as a whole…—perhaps I could render some service and at least pay homage to my troubled continent… In a small way, too, I could recall for my readers the fact that all men are one in their needs and searchings, that whatever sets them apart is evil and whatever brings them peaceably together is good."

"All men are one in their needs and searchings." What could be a better quote with which to end a cookbook than that?

Temperatures, Weights, and some Measures

As in the first Jam Today, all of the measurements and temperatures in *Jam Today Too* are American ones, which means if you're cooking in the United Kingdom, and you want to use these as a guide, you have to make some adjustments. To give you an idea of what the equivalences are, more or less, I've listed a few here that I hope will be helpful—at least, they have been for me, who's spent some time cooking in both places.

Temperature

212 F = 100 C
225 F = 110 C
250 F = 130 C = Gas ½
275 F = 140 C = Gas 1
300 F = 150 C = Gas 2
325 F = 170 C = Gas 3
350 F = 180 C = Gas 4
375 F = 190 C = Gas 5
400 F = 200 C = Gas 6
425 F = 220 C = Gas 7
450 F = 230 C = Gas 8
475 F = 240 C = Gas 9

Weights

These are approximate. But in all the places I've used ounces, a little more or less in the gram area won't really matter…

½ oz. = 10 g.
1 oz. = 25 g.
2 oz. = 50 g.
3 oz. = 100 g.
5 oz. = 150 g.

Butter, Shortening, Cheese, and Other Fats

1 tbsp. = ⅛ stick = ½ oz. = 15 g.
2 tbsp. = ¼ stick = 1 oz. = 30 g.
4 tbsp. = ½ stick. = 2 oz. = 60 g. = ¼ cup
8 tbsp. = 1 stick = 4 oz. = 115 g. = ½ cup
16 tbsp. = 2 sticks = 8 oz. = 225 g. = 1 cup
32 tbsp. = 4 sticks = 16 oz. = 450 g. = 2 cups

Index

About the **Jam Today** series

We are what we eat. But even more, we are *how* we eat: how we discover our own desires and those of our loved ones, how we source the foods that fulfill those desires, how we prepare them, how we serve them. All of these seemingly small, daily decisions are the basis of everything we do, showing us who we truly are, what we need to change, what we need to aim for in the future. Food is the story we tell our bodies every day, and how our bodies and souls react to that story is the story of where we are going to go next. Food is important, thinking about it as well as consuming it—important and importantly fun, both at the same time. That's what the Jam Today series is all about—being creative in the kitchen as a step to bringing more creativity to the world around us.

Also from the Jam Today series

THANKS

The production of this book could not have happened without one of the best teams in independent publishing—and believe you me, a great team in independent publishing is like a great crew on a ship, if you don't have one, you sink in the middle of an unforgiving sea.

So thanks to a terrific crew:

Mike Madrid, EAP's creative director, who makes every EAP book, including this one, a small work of design art.

John Sutherland, whose conscientious and generous attitude toward typesetting keeps all our books on track.

Nate Dorward, the most elegant and precise of copyeditors.

Everyone at Consortium Book Sales & Distribution and all who sail in her, sales reps, staff and all.

And especially…

Molly Mikolowski of A Literary Light, whose title might read 'publicist,' but who is actually editor, business advisor, consigliere, and friend rolled into one.

Thank you all from the bottom of my heart. I owe you dinner!

TOD DAVIES is also the author of *Snotty Saves the Day* and *Lily the Silent*, both from The History of Arcadia series, and the cooking memoir *Jam Today: A Diary of Cooking With What You've Got*, the first book in the Jam Today series. Unsurprisingly, her attitude toward literature is the same as her attitude toward cooking, and, come to think of it, life in general: it's all about working with the best of what you have to find new ways of looking and new ways of being, and, in doing so, to rediscover the best of our humanity.

Davies lives with her husband, the filmmaker Alex Cox, and their two dogs Gray and Pearl, in the alpine valley of Colestin, Oregon, and at the foot of the Rocky Mountains, in Boulder, Colorado.